I Understand

I UNDERSTAND

A Handbook for Counseling In the Seventies

Edmund J. Elbert

SHEED AND WARD • NEW YORK

To

The Father of All

Library of Congress Catalog Card Number: 73-152320
Standard Book Number: 8362-1459-5
Manufactured in the United States of America

Contents

Preface

The word *vocation* is not an unusual one in the vocabulary of the clergyman regardless of his denomination. In fact, it frequently is misconstrued as relating only to a person who pursues the clerical profession as his life's work or calling.

The position of men who dedicate themselves to religion is always one of significance in a community. They can never really be judged simply as individuals. They are always accepted or rejected in terms of what they represent. Although this may have certain advantages, it also may be the cause of unfairness, especially when ignorance or suspicion or prejudice colors the impression. Even his most severe critics expect the clergyman to be essentially one who dedicates himself to service out of religious conviction.

In recent years, particularly in the United States, the image of the cleric has changed from "unreachable" to "totally involved." It is expected of him that he will be precisely the person from whose commitment the notion of community takes its true meaning. He is expected to be "all things to all" and to be actively engaged in the problems, individual and social, that militate against the realization of the ideal he proposes: human fulfillment as a preparation for divine reward.

As a consequence of this image, men feel that they should have constant and immediate access to the clergyman and that somehow, by some divine alchemy to which he as "God's man" has unlimited recourse, all problems will be solved or their solution at least begun. The front doors of parsonages and rectories are besieged by the troubled, lonely, guilty and frightened, and it is no small tribute to the call of the clergyman that it is from him that answers are expected.

Many times—perhaps more often than not—the answers come, the solutions are offered. Often, however, even better answers could be given, more meaningful solutions could be offered, if more complete insights were available. This is particularly true in the case of those who are emotionally disturbed and sometimes emotionally ill. To be willing to serve the troubled is reasonably to be expected of the cleric. That he offer his service with love is a natural corollary of his vocation. But to know how to serve and how to express that love is perhaps more than one should always expect from every clergyman everywhere.

This book is dedicated to enhancing the many efforts and services of the clergyman in behalf of the troubled and emotionally disturbed. It is not presumed to be a final or a brand new idea or approach to this dimension of the clergyman's service to men. It is simply an effort to help in the work of administering to those who are among the least of the brethren. Accordingly, it is divided into two main parts. The first concerns the more general concepts and principles that are essential to the understanding of this particular kind of human problem and are conducive of the best results on the part of those who are called upon to help. The second is more specific. It deals with the particular emotional problems and mental ills that the clergyman is most likely to encounter in his daily work, problems which definitely exist somewhere within his parochial confines.

It is the author's hope that this book may help to give direction to those who seek to direct—may help to engender sympathy, kindness, understanding and charity in those who seek to serve with love.

It would be impossible to mention here all those who helped in bringing this work to completion. It is only just, however, that I express my gratitude publicly to certain people whose special assistance I deeply appreciate. My gratitude goes to Pasquale A. Carone, M.D., whose encouragement and advice contributed to its inception; to Francis C. Bauer, M.D., and Joseph A. Manno, M.D., for their professional guidance in preparing the strictly psychiatric areas of the text; and to Paul A. Collins, PH. D., the Reverend Joseph P. Keane, M.A., and Josef McAvoy, M.A., for their assistance in the final editing of certain portions of the manuscript. Finally, I wish to thank Harry M. Firester for his support in defraying the various expenses incurred in preparing the manuscript and last but not least my sister, Rose, Martha Burke and Helen C. Hoesten, R.N., for their many hours of secretarial assistance.

PART ONE

1 Psychiatry and Religion

One of the most interesting, if somewhat unexpected, developments in relations among the disciplines in recent times is that between theology and psychiatry. In the case of the latter, which has really only developed within the last eighty years, there was much suspicion on the part of its proponents of any source of research that might claim that its proper object was the infinite. Conversely, theology took a rather dim view of this new branch of knowledge which claimed for itself the study of those aspects of man's existence that affect intimately his decisions and moral conduct.

The long period of distrust and suspicion between theology and psychiatry happily is coming to a conclusion. As among all branches of knowledge, there is an increasing awareness of interdependence. Theologians everywhere and of every shade of theological opinion are finally realizing that if man and the problem of his relationship to God is to be put in proper perspective, then those facets of man's personality that affect his growth, choices and values also must be understood. Many times these facets are not properly the object of theological investigation in the traditional sense. Consequently, theologians have had to yield to an area of competence that is not their own by either vocation or definition. They have recently realized that much can be learned about man and his natural struggle toward God if they are but willing to listen.

Simultaneously, or perhaps as an outgrowth, the scientists who deal with the minds of men have learned that they are deep in error when they insist on their traditional position that theology and those who engage in its study professionally are from another time and another place. They have come to know of the importance of the physician of the soul as a potential assistant in their work of releasing the human spirit from its imprisonment by fear. The modern psychiatrist who is worthy of his professional status is poignantly aware that more often than not the mentally ill patients who come to him can be restored to health only when life in its entirety is put in proper perspective. This can be accomplished by the professional who deals with the intricacies of the infinite—by the person who can offer to the sick the helpful hand of God's certitude, who can speak the consoling words of divine assurance.[1]

This is not to suggest that the interrelationship between the study of theology and the study of mental health is at this point properly proportioned and forever formulated. There is still much misunderstanding of terminology and objectives and much ignorance of respective techniques. There is still some suspicion of motives and jealousy concerning areas of competence. However, the gap is narrowing and thoughtful defenders of each position are attempting to understand what the other is trying to say and what it is attempting to accomplish. In this spirit of dedicated inquiry and honest respect, both psychiatrist and theologian—both practitioner and clergyman—cannot but advance the cause of mental health and ultimately succeed in offering to the mentally sick a hope for the future and a solution for the present.

Any attempt at an honest explanation of the prolonged period of mistrust between religion and psychiatry must acknowledge as a prominent cause the lack of understanding of the respective terminologies and the confusion of methods. For this proponents of both disciplines must be prepared to assume a major part of the blame. The clergyman has at times regarded the psychiatrist as an unwelcome intruder. The psychiatrist has at times regarded the clergyman as an incompetent quack. Both have been blinded by prejudice and misinformation and, as objectivity and truth make their still uncertain appearance, each now shares the responsibility of learning what the other has to contribute to the solution of a common problem.

The clergyman no longer can hold himself aloof from this pressing responsibility. He must learn to respect the findings of a recognized science and thoroughly familiarize himself with the efforts it is making to improve the lot of man and make easier his personal fulfillment and ultimate sanctification. His attitude must be objective if in a certain sense pragmatic. Natural science is telling us many things regarding man's nature and potentialities. Science also is telling us many things about forces completely outside man's nature that affect his judgments and responsibilities. If these are facts and influence the totality of one's humanity, then they must interest anyone whose vocation it is to give God to the world and the world back to God.

Unfortunately, many clergymen fail to see the picture of man as man. He becomes departmentalized as "spiritual man," "intellectual man," "volitional man," "economic man," "political man" and a host of other distinctions. This division of man can be quite useful for purposes of theoretical research. When, however, man is left divided in the order of reality he is no longer man and, coincidentally, the research project itself must suffer. If the science of men's minds has taught us anything it surely must be that man is a whole. He is integral, though complicated. He is united, despite any effort to dissect him for purposes of study or analysis. He is not therefore a soul *and* a body, as though one could exist without the other. He is not a being with an eternal destiny who does not have to work out that destiny in time and space. He does not possess a series of eminently free choices without having those choices constantly affected by emotions he must control and a personality his nature and nurture have developed.

The process of fragmenting man may have intrinsic value in terms of analysis but the process of integration must not be left to chance. The view of man as a whole is not only expected of the clergyman; it is required that he propagate this view in a world in which he enjoys some degree of influence. The responsibility of this influence cannot be ignored. The clergyman who hopes to fulfill his role as "God's man" must never permit himself to be passive in this regard. His role must be an active one and he must be the aggressor in ensuring man's position as an individual with an identity rather than as an uncertainty with a label. The recognition of this role in the drama of human existence—whose denouement is personal awareness—is thrust upon him by those who seek his help and expect him to offer a solution to the plot of their lives. It is estimated that nearly one-half of those afflicted with mental illness turn first to the resources of the clergyman—to resources human and proper to him as an individual and to those divine and proper to the position he represents. Although the explanation of this statistic may be argued without end or purpose, it is the experience of both the scientist of the mind and the healer of the soul.

This fact has serious implications for both the psychiatrist and the clergyman. It necessitates some mutual understanding of respective objectives and techniques and it requires that unworthy rivalry, immature suspicion and dishonest and unfounded disdain be put aside. It is the patient who is all-important and if both professionals are to be worthy of that term, they must be committed to the conviction that the individual who comes to them for help has paid them a high compliment and offered them a unique opportunity to render the service their professional status demands as its ultimate objective.

Our immediate concern here is with the clergyman and his need to understand his basic role in an area he is required to enter more and more frequently. If he is to fulfill the role he has before God as a "servant of his servants" he must be determined to acquire the knowledge and skills that will enable him to justify the confidence placed in him by those who seek his help.

The average traditional seminary training for the ministry has taken little if any account of the clergyman as the first source of contact for those who are mentally ill. Apart from having received perfunctory lectures on mental illness related to moral imputability or obsession with spiritual inadequacy, most graduates of accredited theologates are totally unprepared to deal with the practical problems presented by the mentally ill. How many, for example, are aware of the technical language involved in this highly sophisticated branch of medicine? How many recognize the symptoms that could be the key to the solution of relatively minor problems or perhaps could indicate that immediate highly professional skill is required? How many know when the patient must be left at least one of his symptoms if he is to be able to function? Do many clergymen realize that symptoms are defenses enabling the person to preserve his or her integrity? How many know, for example, when scruples should simply be made less uncomfortable, but not removed? Do they realize that such preoccupations may contain anxiety the root cause of which the person cannot face because of insufficient ego-strength? How many clergymen know when to seek out the "why" of a human problem and when to bypass that "why" and simply permit the person to ventilate or talk about his situation? On the other hand, does every clergyman realize that, at certain times, people should not talk about or be questioned about a sensitive personal problem?

These and related questions are no longer in the realm of academic speculation for the clergyman. He needs to know the answers to these practical problems which circumstances force him to face daily. Knowledge of this branch of pastoral medicine also is necessary as a protection against the assumption that he is technically trained to deal with every phase of mental illness. Such an assumption might have a devastating effect on the patient and could be more harmful than not dealing with the individual at all. It all comes down to a need on the part of the churchman to *know,* to be educated in the total meaning of the humans to whom he is sent. Every churchman and every physician of the mind must participate in the mutual effort to support and sustain the human person, who is the focal point of interest.

The clergyman should not be embarrassed by his practical inadequacy. This, after all, is not his field. Nonetheless, the world of the mentally ill does force upon him a task and with this task comes an opportunity to serve. The clergyman worthy of the name and the image he is to project to the world cannot but embrace the opportunity such service offers. Mental illness is the number one health problem in our country. With the number of people requiring help and crying out for some source of hope, it is essential that the clergyman immediately recognize his duty to acquire that knowledge and those skills that will enable him to fulfill the task that undeniably is his.[2] This requires that he realize his need for technical information as a tool in dealing with the mentally ill. To the credit of modern psychiatry, it has recognized the role of the clergyman and recently has offered many lectures, forums, seminars and simple old-fashioned discussions. In many communities individual psychiatrists have placed themselves at the disposal of clergymen for the purpose of individual consultation in the hope that they will be able to work together for the improvement of mental hygiene and the restoration of many to normal health. It now becomes the duty of the clergyman to take advantage of such opportunities and to inform himself so that he will be able to do the job that needs to be done.

The most recent thinking in the field of mental health makes it imperative that an illness that has its roots in the community ultimately must be solved within the framework of the community. The days of seeking the solution to mental illness behind the bars of an institution are fast coming to an end. More and more patients are to be found within the community. For that reason, more and more demands will he put upon those who by skill and vocation have the responsibility to find the problem's answer.[3]

A willing, dedicated helper is not all that the psychiatrist seeks in the clergyman. He also must be an informed observer and a knowledgeable technician. He must know when he can help and, equally clearly, when to refer his "patient" to more competent sources of help. In this area of men's minds—so sensitive, so delicate, so often completely unfathomable—there is room for the specialist who is concerned with mental health as such in this life, but there also is a necessity for the specialist who is concerned with spiritual development through mental health for the world to come.

This partnership has much to offer the man of today who has more than his share of confusion, more than his share of uncertainty. A healthy mind in a healthy body is not an aphorism. For the man of the atomic age it is the condition for survival.

For Further Reference

Braceland, Francis J., ed. *Faith, Reason and Modern Psychiatry.* New York: P. J. Kenedy & Sons, 1955.

Gemelli, Agostino. *Psychoanalysis Today.* New York: P. J. Kenedy & Sons, 1955.

Samson, Henri. *Spiritual Insights of a Practicing Psychiatrist.* New York: Alba House, 1966.

Stern, Karl. *The Third Revolution.* New York: Harcourt, Brace & Co., 1954.

White, Victor. *God and the Unconscious.* Chicago: Henry Regnery Co., 1953.

———. *Soul and Psyche.* New York: Harper & Brothers, 1960.

2 A Concept of Mental Illness

Mental illness constitutes the number one health problem in the United States. One out of ten Americans suffers from some sort of psychiatric problem; less than ten percent of those afflicted are receiving treatment. Two billion dollars of government money is being poured into a solution to the problem.[1] Despite these somewhat staggering statistics practically no one has come up with a satisfactory definition of the term *mental illness,* a term never more frequently used than in our present society.[2]

This lack of scientific accuracy is not surprising when we consider the vast scope of the term. Perhaps the best that can be achieved is a definition of what mental health is and therefore what mental illness is not. To many the terms are as individualistic as those to whom they are applied. As the Department of Health, Education and Welfare has stated: "Mental Health is a broad term and its activities are legion, involving the functions of the individual, masses of the population and professionals in many disciplines. Mental health activities therefore often have had a flavor of ethics and morals, a religious flavor and personal investment, unvalidated psychological concepts, value judgments, psychiatric theory, political science, welfare movement and cultism."[3]

The awareness on the part of those who use the expression *mental health* that they are expressing in fact many intangibles is in itself a certain safeguard against an oversimplified solution to a problem which is compounded by the intricacies of the society in which it exists. Despite this lack of clarity in terms and a lack of precision in definitions, those who pursue the study of mental illness and its cure see no overwhelming obstacle to their goal. They use the terms freely and invite others to do likewise. When pushed to the wall, they resort to descriptive definitions and then blithely categorize all their findings under the general headings of mental illness, mental health or mental hygiene. By some strange alchemy of intuition, everyone seems agreed that these terms are mutually understood. If we guard against the implication of a certain subjective standard in our discussion, we can proceed with our investigation.

What, then, is mental illness? Essentially it is a negation, a deviation from normal functioning or healthy behavior. As soon as we express this concept we are forced immediately to give expression to a norm for healthy behavior or normal functioning. Is the norm determined by custom? by habit? by the mores of a given milieu? If such were the case we would be forced to conclude that the same behavior pattern in two different societies would be both normal and abnormal, both healthy and sick. For example, self-inflicted death might be regarded as heroic to the point of sanctification in one society. In another, suicide would be considered abnormal and subject to legal restriction.

Even within the same society there is no sharp line of demarcation between normal and abnormal behavior. It seems generally accepted that the difference between the two is more of degree than of kind. If we push our analysis far enough we see that within the capacity or function of the same individual there is a variance that extends from perfectly acceptable behavior patterns to those completely out of harmony with the demands of normal response. Every mentally healthy person may, under numerous and persistent unfavorable stresses, display symptoms of abnormal behavior.

The mentally ill person, under elevating and favorable circumstances, may begin to behave in a manner that is at least more normal than he did in his previous condition. This criterion of normalcy becomes even more relative because it can vary from individual to individual. Each person makes the best adjustment he can in light of the experience only he has undergone. This adjustment will vary in accordance with his unique constitutional makeup and the environmental circumstances in which he currently must operate.

Some authors attempt to obviate the difficulty by equating the concept of "normalcy" with that of "average." Behavior is regarded as more or less normal if it follows the pattern that might be expected by the average person. Although this approach may have much to recommend it in terms of practical advantages, it suffers from the fundamental weakness that strictly speaking the concepts underlying the terms *normal* and *average* cannot be equated. Average is a statistical concept based upon a process of counting. Normal is qualitative in meaning and based more upon the nature under investigation, in this case man, who is unique, be he ill or well. For this reason, deviation from the average as a descriptive definition of a mentally ill person would violate the intensely personal and therefore unparalleled character of mental illness. We cannot, strictly speaking, discuss "average performance" when dealing with this problem. What might appear as average for a given number of fish or turnips would be meaningless when applied to the unique personality of man. Moreover, in a sick society the deviants from the majority would in fact be acting in a non-average but certainly normal manner. For example, the behavior patterns of a doctor or a nurse working in a clinic for the mentally retarded or severely brain-damaged would hardly conform to the standards of the majority of the patients. Yet, in spite of many jokes on the matter, it immediately would appear obvious even to the untrained eye who was treating whom.[4]

If we are to employ any criterion for the establishment of "normalcy" in human behavior, we must ask not merely what is done but the purpose for which it is done. The reasonable end of any human action ultimately may explain the act itself and put into proper focus an experience which, if taken without reference to an end or goal, may leave much to be desired in terms of its reasonableness. Thus the sailor waving semaphore signals would appear to the casual observer to be acting in a completely irrational way unless the purpose of his gestures was properly understood.

Accordingly, a normal person may be said to be one who is "free of symptoms, unhampered by mental conflict, able to maintain a satisfying working capacity and able to love someone other than himself."[5] If we add to this definition the following characteristics that have been suggested by J. R. Cavanagh and J. B. McGoldrick, we will have a reasonably well-rounded picture of the normal or healthy personality. The normal person may be said also to possess:

1. A well-balanced emotional life
2. An ability to adjust to environmental changes
3. An adequate regard or concern for future goals and needs
4. An ability to correct mistaken ideas and attitudes
5. An overall manner of behavior that conforms with the standards and expectations of the group
6. A reasonably happy disposition that stems from being alive and being this particular person[6]

We must, however, conclude that any understanding of the fact of normalcy and mental health or deviation and mental illness ultimately will depend upon two factors: descriptive observation and an analysis of the purpose of the action involved. "What?" and "Why?" are the two key questions whose answers will provide a meaningful definition for those who desire to be of some assistance to the nearly twenty million Americans who either are or will become mentally ill.

It would be a serious mistake to view the conduct of those who are mentally ill as though it were completely unrelated to the "real." Their actions and the thoughts that prompt those actions are, from the framework of their own reference, completely reasonable. It is precisely this understanding that is required of anyone who would attempt to appreciate the involved nature of this type of illness. Objectively, the conduct of the mentally ill may not make very good sense. Subjectively, in the distorted view of the patient, there invariably is some logical sequence involved. This is a basic consideration for understanding the patient and his problem. For the therapist it involves almost a "logic in reverse." The conduct itself or the purpose for which it is accomplished apparently is out of contact with the real situation. For the patient, however, there is some relationship between what he is doing and the "real" as he perceives it.

The "real as he perceives it" will hardly be understood unless the therapist has some knowledge of the history of the process by which a patient arrives at conduct that is in fact out of contact with objective reality. The mentally ill person does not ordinarily arrive at such a condition without some traceable evidence or indication that it ultimately will be his plight. He starts as we all do in a definite condition of tension born of basic needs to be satisfied and instincts to be fulfilled. In the personal effort at tension reduction, drives are sometimes readily abated by available and suitable objects and comfort ensues. More often, obstacles are met in the form of external interference which begets frustration or there is an internal clashing of incompatible motives which generates conflict. In either instance a rational appreciation of nonfulfillment dictates acceptance and healthy adjustment results. However, when needs are unfulfilled and we do not permit adjustment through acceptance or substitution, anxiety occurs and the first signs of trouble ahead become visible. When anxiety persists because of the frustration or conflict, our defenses ordinarily take over to distract us from the anxiety and the pain that accompanies it. This development is perfectly normal and desirable. The mentally ill, however, cannot permit the ordinary defenses to soothe the wounds of anxiety and so the patient extends his defenses in number, intensity and duration. Eventually, these collapse and the first symptoms of abnormal adjustment begin to appear.

An additional difficulty always present in this rather consistent pattern of deterioration is that frequently the patient is not aware of precisely what his need is or what the conflict or source of frustration might be. In the classic example of the alcoholic, his exaggerated defense of escapism as manifested in the abuse of drink will never tell him what it is he seeks to eliminate from the demands of conscious confrontation. There is surely some need that is not being satisfied. It in turn has given rise to some conflict or frustration, which in turn has introduced this overwhelming anxiety in his day-to-day existence. Subconsciously he believes that were he to accept the reality of the conflict and attempt to solve it the cure would be worse than the disease. Therefore, he must struggle on with his symptoms as the best compromise that can be made by him under these particular circumstances. It must be kept in mind constantly that the source of conflict or frustration frequently is unrecognized in the conscious mind of the subject. It is precisely because of this that he cannot make an adequate adjustment. His defenses and their extension into neurotic or even psychotic symptoms are the best protection he can develop against the realization of the basis of the anxiety he is experiencing. These defenses are necessary and at times the symptoms are the subject's only source of psychic survival.

One morning a youngster of twelve tripped coming down the stairs of his suburban home. His fall to the bottom of the staircase required medical attention and the first diagnosis was a fractured arm. Although X-rays indicated no broken bones a paralysis of the right arm ensued. There was no medical explanation for the immobility, but under no condition was it possible for the child to move his arm. Under hypnosis, it was moved in a perfectly normal manner. Psychotherapy revealed that the boy, a sixth grade student in a local parochial school, had a very poor relationship with the Sister who taught the class and a strong subconscious desire to strike her. The paralysis was eventually judged to be a symptom that protected the boy from striking the Sister, an act he could never consciously accept as suitable or acceptable behavior.

The therapist must understand this basic truth: The patient under strain should not be condemned for doing the best he can. For him, his conduct does not seem out of harmony with the demands of the situation in which he finds himself. His symptoms must be properly understood and should never be tampered with unless they are understood.[7] They are protective efforts he puts forth in order to maintain some semblance of integrity. With all his limitations, the patient must be accepted as someone who is trying desperately to survive in a contest with an adversary he frequently cannot even identify.

The natural tendency on the part of those who seek to help is to imagine that the first order of business is to determine the cause of the conflict and to eliminate the accompanying symptoms. Nothing could be further from the truth. The symptoms are protective and they ultimately may be the reason why the patient is able to survive at all. The symptoms may be recognized but they should be treated only by someone who can professionally assess the situation and determine to what extent the patient is capable of surviving without their protection. This recognition also must include the ability to realize the origins of mental illness in this particular patient.

The origins or causes of mental illness are as varied as they are frequently misunderstood. To assign as "cause" the factor of heredity or the socio-economic background of the patient is to oversimplify.[8] Nature and nurture are always involved, but more often than not they serve as predisposing factors. The true cause usually is deeply imbedded in the entire personality structure. With one individual it might be a lack of self-identity coupled with an impoverished self-image; with another, an unresolved Oedipal dependency; with another, a tyrannical superego; with still another, a generalized low frustration tolerance. In the context of such structural defects any specific stress situation or series of events may precipitate such anxiety that recourse to abnormal defensive behavior is demanded.

To suggest that mental ills are the result of sin as though they were some divine punishment for violation of a specific commandment may have had value in another age. Today it not only is regarded as poor science, it also is poor theology. There are probably many factors that contribute to the existence of mental illness in any specific individual. Heredity might be an important factor if the illness can be traced directly to poor physiological functioning. It might be more specifically attributable to accident or illness. Environment certainly plays an important role, for who can say what influence economic insecurity or social rejection may have on a person's ability to accept and adjust?

If we are to assign causes it seems logical to demand that the concept of "causality" be evaluated properly in this context and that the error of "many possible causes" be carefully avoided. In the experience of competent people in the field of mental health and welfare, there are no single factors in most instances of psychological maladjustment. The people we meet, the circumstances to which we are daily expected to adjust and the comments we hear are all stresses to which each person reacts in his own way. For some there is no problem. For others, the word spoken, the intonation used or the atmosphere in which an experience is shared, together with long-forgotten motives of the unconscious, provide the setting for the development of symptoms that ultimately indicate the inability of this person to function adequately under the natural pressures of daily living.

Sigmund Freud suggested that the conflicts that cause mental illness or the factors in personality development that prohibit healthy adjustment are completely unknown and certainly only knowable with great effort and introspection. It is probably for this more than for any other contribution that the world is most indebted to his research. When we speak of the mentally ill and their recovery, we must remind ourselves constantly that the illness may be relatively easy to diagnose descriptively, but that for the recovery and, therefore, for the cause, time, patience and perseverance will be required.

The intricate tasks of ultimate diagnosis, of ferreting out the hidden roots and selecting the appropriate therapeutic measures are provinces proper to the physician of the mind. The doctor of the soul has the equally grave responsibility of being alert to the signs of impending and factual mental illness, of honoring symptoms and referring their subjects and, above all, of offering the quality of support that will make time, patience and perseverance fruitful.

For Further Reference

Cavanagh, John R., and McGoldrick, James B. *Fundamental Psychiatry*. rev. ed. Milwaukee: Bruce Publishing Co., 1966.

Maslow, Abraham H. *Motivation and Personality*. New York: Harper & Brothers, 1954.

Nuttin, Joseph. *Psychoanalysis and Personality*. New York: Sheed & Ward, 1953.

Royce, James E. *Personality and Mental Health*. rev. ed. Milwaukee: Bruce Publishing Co., 1964.

Shaffer, Laurance F., and Shoben, Edward J. *The Psychology of Adjustment*. Boston: Houghton Mifflin Co., 1956.

3 The Mental Apparatus

It would be impossible to bring into clear focus the unconscious and defensive working of the mind of man in the face of stress without first formulating some basic ideas on the interior and dynamic structures of the human psyche. We have to know what goes on behind the scene of a man's life, what really makes man tick. At this point in our discussion a schematic summary of this Freudian contribution to the whole area of mental health seems essential.

The use of Freud's description of the mental apparatus or the structure of the human mind does not imply that it is the only one available.[1] Nor does its use here indicate unconditional acceptance of Freud's entire doctrine. Its selection is based purely on the pragmatic conclusion that it is convenient, generally accepted within scientific circles for its dynamic values, easily understandable by comparison with a theory such as Carl Jung's and that its widespread popularity demands acquaintance with its fundamental concepts. In addition, its graphic nature lends well to an understanding of the material that will follow.[2]

Although it long was suspected that there was a great deal

more to man's mind than merely his conscious awareness, it was Sigmund Freud who originated the concept of a conscious system and an unconscious system. Midway between these two psychic components Freud postulated a preconscious or foreconscious. The "conscious" speaks for itself. It is for all practical purposes equal to awareness. The "unconscious," on the other hand, is mysterious. It is the portion of the human psyche that is totally hidden from man's conscious mind. It is, however, real and dynamic and constitutes the bulk of the human psyche. The "foreconscious" is that grey area which is at times hidden but which can be brought to the screen of consciousness by the subject's own personal effort.

In addition to these functional layers, Freud also conceived of functional divisions to which he assigned the names "id," "ego" and "superego." In describing such divisions it is necessary to keep in mind that they are not entities in themselves. They are abstractions based upon the observation of human behavior and concretized for purposes of convenience. They have no anatomical counterparts. Although it is true that the brain and the central nervous system mediate psychic phenomena and translate thought into voluntary behavior, the mind itself does not have any anatomical definition. To reify such concepts is to misrepresent their basic significance.

The Id

At the moment of birth, and probably for some unknown period of time before this, every human organism is endowed with an id. This functional division is a part of the unconscious system. We ultimately learn of its content and its operation but we never can be consciously aware of its operation.

The id is present at birth and has certain attributes. According to Franz Alexander, one of the early pioneers of psychoanalytic thought in America, the id is the powerhouse of the mental apparatus. Its primary attribute is to serve as the repository of the instincts. These include the instinct for self-preservation and the sexual instinct. In considering the latter, it must be kept in mind that in the psychoanalytic frame of reference anything that produces pleasure is felt to be derivative of the sexual instinct.

It is doubtful that a child at birth has any conscious awareness of its own existence. Nor can the newborn identify the pangs of hunger or, for that matter, do anything about it even if he could make such an identification. The instinct for self-preservation, however, which is a part of the id, operates in the form of a sucking reflex which in part ensures the ingestion of the nutritive material sustaining life. For the young child eating is not a matter of conscious determination. It becomes an automatic function in the form of satisfaction of an id drive.

In the same fashion the newly born, the infant and the young child all instinctively seek pleasurable experiences and avoid those that are unpleasant. This obviously is not a matter of conscious determination during the early months of life but rather a manifestation of the sexual drive. The id, then, is said to operate on the basis of the "pleasure principle," which demands immediate satisfaction of all perceived needs.

The id can be more completely described in terms of its attributes. The id is timeless. The concept of time does not exist at the unconscious level. In a dream, for example, which is unconscious mental activity and sometimes referred to as primary process thinking, we can move backward in time, project into the future or remain in the present. The dimension of time is so completely absent from the unconscious mental apparatus that we can experience the past, the present and the future at precisely the same moment. The infantile character of the id is intimately connected with the attribute of timelessness. The id does not grow nor does it develop. It remains the same as it was at the moment of birth regardless of the chronological age of the individual. The primitive drives and urges experienced by the infant persist in the adult. Although the mature individual develops a highly sophisticated system of satisfying emotional needs, the basic primitive drives remain infantile in character. It is also for this reason that we suggest that the id operates on the basis of the pleasure principle. A newborn infant wants what he wants when he wants it. He is completely unable to postpone the satisfaction of perceived needs. Even a child of three or four does not fully appreciate the demand of reality that he postpone the satisfaction of his ice cream cone until after dinner. The unconscious urges are so strong and the childhood capacity to control them so weak that the youngster is apt to react with a tantrum if deprived of immediate satisfaction. In this connection, one might use as a definition of emotional maturity the capacity to postpone the satisfaction of perceived needs. This, as will be described later, is a function of another portion of the mental apparatus, the ego. The mature person can recognize the unconscious striving and at times consciously delay gratification in order to enhance the satisfaction. The capacity to do this is a measure of one's emotional maturity.

The id is chaotic in its disorganization. It is illogical and it is irrational. There is no orderly process of thought progression observable in primary process thinking. Premises that are mutually exclusive and concepts that are paradoxical in nature can stand side by side in the unconscious system without compromising the individual. Because many urges and drives in the unconscious are diametrically opposed to one another, when they are acted out impulsively the resultant behavior is illogical and irrational.

This is the idea of polarity. In the unconscious there are, for example, forces of love and hate. Because of mature ego functioning, only one of these emotions ordinarily becomes attached to a particular object. If, however, such ego functioning is weak or suspended, as happens in mental illness, the unconscious forces may surge to the fore in toto and even loved ones may be attacked. Under such circumstances an otherwise good and virtuous person could commit murder. The expression "you always hurt the one you love" sums up this polarity.

Another attribute of the unconscious is that it is amoral. The concepts of good and evil, right and wrong, simply do not exist at the unconscious level of operation. Anything that is pleasurable is desirable. Satisfaction of urges is demanded regardless of the attitude of society toward the resultant behavior. Whether a thing is good or right does not preoccupy the unconscious process. It is for this reason that every individual in the process of development must learn to inhibit certain of his unconscious drives since they are bound to bring him in conflict with the society in which he lives. The id subscribes to no ethical system and there are no degrees of emotion involved. Unconsciously, we do not like or dislike, we love or we hate; paradoxically, we may do both at the same time, giving rise to what has been termed ambivalence. On a conscious level interpersonal relations admit to varying degrees of emotional expression. Beneath the conscious surface, there are no such refinements. In the face of an injustice, for example, the impulse to kill might be so filtered as it emerges from the depths of the unconscious id and eventually is controlled by the ego that its ultimate expression is reduced to harmless tongue-lashing.

In the sense that anything that produces pleasure is considered to be sexual, the content of the unconscious is predominantly sexual. Although many of the unconscious drives are libidinal in nature and erotic in character, other drives toward pleasure are subsumed under the heading of sexual drives.

It should be noted that the id has no knowledge of external reality. The unconscious system is incapable of learning. There are no I.Q.'s in the unconscious. It can never become aware of the demands of a culture or society. Because of this handicap, the id never modifies itself. The intensity of its demands and urges is not lessened in the course of time. The id is not capable of self-regulation because this portion of the mental apparatus operates initially and attempts to operate later as if reality were nonexistent.

All of the attributes of the unconscious outlined in the preceding paragraphs are demonstrated in the uninhibited behavior of the newborn infant. At this stage of physical development the infant is operating entirely on the basis of unconscious energy. The ego, which we will discuss next, is in the process of a long development and, accordingly, we observe impulsive primary process activity. The infant and young child do not involve themselves with goal-directed behavior. They are unable to utilize will and intellect still in the process of development and, accordingly, their behavior is unreasoned and frequently irrational. If judged by the standards of adults, the behavior of very young children becomes descriptively psychotic. Since the child's thinking is primarily unconscious activity, he is highly imaginative and even creative in his play and not bound by the sometimes harsh dictates of a reality. When reality intrudes, the child frequently chooses to ignore it and becomes even less rational in his effort to do so.

The Ego

Although the id has been referred to as the powerhouse of the mental apparatus, the ego is a much more important functional division of the mind, especially for the individual who is required to live in a civilized society. Unlike the id, the ego apparently does not exist at the moment of birth but is the product of development and adaptation. Arbitrarily, it has been suggested that the ego requires seven to nine years in order to reach the point of development at which it can operate adequately. This is roughly comparable to the age at which the individual attains the use of reason in many ethical systems. The ego develops as a result of trial and error and as a result of identification. The process of development also may be referred to as reality testing.

The first task of the developing ego is to distinguish self from non-self, to distinguish me from all that is not me. During the neonatal period, the individual is blissfully unaware of the existence of any reality. Reality inevitably intrudes, however, and as a result of this intrusion, the ego begins its stages of development. Initially, we assume that the infant operates at the level of unconditional omnipotence. It is quite likely that based on his experience prenatally, he believes that all of his needs can be satisfied automatically. The infant gradually develops a conditional omnipotence in which satisfaction is not believed to be automatic, but is believed to result from his own thinking. An infant experiencing hunger, for example, may recognize the sensations of hunger as a form of anxiety. Anticipating his need, his mother feeds him, thereby dissipating the anxiety. It is quite likely that the child concludes that merely by recognizing his hunger and thinking about it he has satisfied the need. He is most assuredly unaware of the fact that somewhere there was a cow who ate grass and gave milk. He is equally unaware of the complicated process involved in collecting the milk and packaging it for distribution. He certainly does not attend to the fact that his mother or some responsible adult will further process the milk for his consumption. None of these intermediate steps disturb the child's feeling of omnipotence. At a later stage of development, his conditioned omnipotence gives way to magical thinking and omnipotence through magical gestures. At this stage of his life it is possible that not all his needs are being met through the anticipation of his parents. He may be required to make some sign or give some indication of his need before it can be satisfied.

Many individuals who are chronologically mature continue their futile attempts to operate at this primitive level. This is especially true in the United States where we attempt to interpret reality to young people in terms of romantic notions. In the "land of opportunity" every little girl becomes Sleeping Beauty and every little boy Prince Charming. Several years ago we immortalized the stage of development representing magical thinking in song. One of the top ten was a ballad called "Wishing Will Make It So." If the ego is not well-developed or if no incentive has been offered to encourage realistic behavior, the individual is doomed to a series of frustrating experiences. He knows where he would like to go but in the manner of Walter Mitty and other fictional characters he attempts to get there through fantasy and magical thinking.

Again in contrast to the id, the ego operates on the basis of the reality principle. Although portions of the ego remain part of the unconscious system, much of the functioning of the ego is at the conscious level. Memory, for example, is acquired as a result of conscious experience. Memories are stored, however, at the unconscious level and the ease of recall when the material is necessary depends upon the level at which it has been stored. Information that is vital to daily experience usually is maintained at a level of easy recall. Information that was learned in elementary school and no longer is necessary to daily functions probably can be recalled with some difficulty.[3] Other memories are stored in such deep levels of the unconscious that extraordinary means, such as hypnosis or the use of drugs, become necessary to reactivate them.

Because the ego is partly conscious and partly unconscious, we see the possibility of an individual functioning rationally, according to the reality principle, and, therefore, consciously but with a marked absence of awareness to the total situation at hand. He knows precisely what he is doing at any given moment but is not completely aware of the real meaning of his behavior. In retrospect he says, as frequently is the case, "I wonder how I got into that situation" or "I did it but I did not realize at the time what I was really doing."

In contrast with the id, the ego is logical, intelligent and rational. Thinking is organized and precise and it is the ego that makes possible goal-directed behavior. In this sense, it is the ego which makes a man responsible for his own behavior. Impulsive behavior, which is the result of blindly acting out an id urge, because it is chaotic, illogical and amoral, is not considered responsible behavior. Once the ego is functioning, however, we do assign responsibility and the acts of the individual are capable of becoming human acts.

In addition to the trial and error procedure in which the developing individual learns about external reality, the ego acquires efficiency as a result of identification with the parents. If not the parents, then some other significant adult in the environment will become the subject of identification. As will be described in the section on mental mechanisms, identification is different from conscious imitation. To be sure, the latter occurs when developing children comically, and sometimes with painful accuracy ape the characteristics and behavior of their parents. Identification, however, is an unconscious process in which the attitudes, the values and the prejudices of adults are absorbed by the child. In order for the ego to develop functionally there must be an object of identification. It is not only the verbal communications and instructions of adults which shape the character and the personalities of young people. The unspoken communications are often of greater significance. Attitudes, fears and prejudices are all transmitted and become part of the process of ego development.

The functions of the developed ego are:

1. The ego perceives the internal needs of the individual. Instinctual drives never reach consciousness as such. Ideational representatives of the drives, however, in the form of desires, or wishes, enter consciousness. The first function of the ego is to perceive these internal needs.
2. The ego surveys the environment and keeps the individual in contact by reporting back available data through the instrumentality of the five special senses.
3. The ego must select from the environment an appropriate outlet for the unconscious drive. It must measure the internal need with the yardstick of reality and correctly interpret reality in order to find a suitable means of satisfying the need.
4. The executive function of the ego is to mediate disputes between the unconscious and reality, thereby preserving the integrity of the individual. The ego controls the central nervous system and utilizes the central nervous system to translate thought into voluntary behavior.

Contrary to common opinion, it is not the force of the unconscious drive nor the persistence of the instincts which causes difficulty. Rather, it is the failure of one or all of the functions of the ego, which might result in the person involving himself in the unrealistic and inappropriate behavior that is frequently termed neurosis.

The Superego

The superego is perhaps the most difficult of the functional components of the mental apparatus to understand. It is certainly the one about which the least has been written. Although it is psychoanalytically inaccurate and, admittedly, oversimplified, the superego may be thought of as a functional component of the mental apparatus that comes into existence as the result of a compromise between id and ego. If the id continued to send up drives, wishes and urges to be acted upon consciously by the ego in the form of decisions regarding the wisdom or propriety of voluntary action, the individual soon would become immobilized. His entire energy would be utilized in making constant decisions governing his behavior. It can be assumed, therefore, that a part of the id and a part of the ego merge to form an autonomous functional component known as the superego. This can roughly be compared to conscience and functions largely at the unconscious level of activity. Certain drives of which few of us become consciously aware, drives of an incestuous nature, for example, do not occupy our consciousness because they are acted upon automatically by the superego. Incest constitutes such a strong taboo in most civilized societies and even in many uncivilized groups that it becomes the subject of superego prohibition without ever reaching consciousness. The superego is, in a sense, the incorporation of the dos and don'ts of childhood and the explicit and implicit restrictions placed upon the individual's activity by the society in which he lives. Because of the family constellation and the customs and mores of society many ideas simply do not occur to individuals because the superego censors them out of conscious awareness.

If the developing child cannot find a suitable object of identification in his environment and he has been subject to a kind of pseudopermissiveness on the part of his parents, it is altogether possible that he will develop a poorly organized ego and superego structure. In its most extreme form this results in a sociopathic personality development which was known in earlier times as moral insanity or the absence of a conscience. Such individuals are capable of the grossest forms of behavior inimical to themselves and society and characteristically show very little anxiety, guilt or remorse in connection with their behavior. They cheat widows and orphans and sell the Brooklyn Bridge to unsuspecting tourists without qualms or reservations. On the other hand, if the individual is subject during developmental stages to an excessively rigid type of training or if the society or ethical system to which the family subscribes is excessive or unrealistic, the individual may develop a punishing type of superego which inhibits and restrains his behavior. His superego causes the repression of many things that would be permitted by the society if admitted to consciousness. Many such individuals suffer from forms of scrupulosity and are constantly berating themselves and finding themselves guilty of sin when, in fact, no sin has been committed. In extreme cases they even may confess to capital crimes in which they in no way participated.

The mental apparatus is an enormously complex and essentially spiritual component of the psychosomatic unit. Its parts, if such they may be described, are delicately balanced and the balance must be maintained if the individual is to function in a reasoned, orderly, logical, intelligent, rational manner. Any imbalance in which the superego becomes dominant or id impulses break through because of weak ego development may result in pathology. If the ego becomes dominant the individual will develop into a withdrawn, restricted personality who appears to his fellows to be lacking in all emotional response.

For Further Reference

Blum, Gerald S. *Psychoanalytic Theories of Personality.* New York: McGraw-Hill Book Co., 1953.

Brenner, Charles. *An Elementary Textbook of Psychoanalysis.* New York: Doubleday & Co., 1957.

Hall, Calvin S. *A Primer of Freudian Psychology.* Cleveland & New York: World Publishing Co., 1954.

Hall, Calvin S., and Lindzey, Gardner. *Theories of Personality.* New York: John Wiley & Sons, 1957.

Munroe, Ruth L. *Schools of Psychoanalytic Thought.* New York: Holt, Rinehart & Winston, 1955.

4 Defense Mechanisms

When the patient arrives at that stage of distress where he is looking for help, his mental illness has more than passed the initial phase. He is prepared to take definite steps which signal an admission that he no longer can cope with the problem alone. There have been signs of deterioration and it is necessary that the clergyman recognize these signs for what they are. The mechanisms of defense are among the external signs that indicate a need for help. They are sometimes the last hope of victory; more often they are the weakest line of protection.[1]

Defense mechanisms are not necessarily associated with mental illness. They are employed by everyone at one time or the other. This note of universality suggests other characteristics. The mechanisms are unconscious but learned. We all learn to recognize anxiety as a signal of danger. Detection of anxiety, however, does not necessarily occur at the conscious level. When content from the unconscious system threatens to break through to consciousness the ego seeks means to defend itself. Various defensive strategies may be employed while the individual remains consciously unaware of the fact that he is using them. Some of these measures are successful and with the passage of time and repeated use they become completely automatic. Although they vary in degree of self-deception and distortion of reality, they have as their fundamental goal the allaying of anxiety. Unfortunately, they are never really completely successful, feeding as they do on one another and invariably leading to disorder if their extension is not controlled.

The workings of these defenses are comparable to the homeostatic processes of the body.[2] The body is continually at work to maintain and if necessary restore an inner equilibrium among the varied and complex organs and systems that comprise it. At the same time it is continually adjusting and adapting to the demands and threats from a changing world without. A man's heart, for example, beats approximately seventy-two times per minute when the body is at rest. When he is walking down the street the heart rate may increase slightly. If he suddenly begins to run in order to catch an approaching bus the rate will increase to more than a hundred beats per minute. Ordinarily, he breathes about twenty times per minute. When he is running for the bus, however, the respiratory rate also is increased. These changes are required in order that additional oxygen can be supplied to the muscles used during the period of exertion. The increase in the heart and respiratory rates takes place automatically to meet the emergency. Obviously, the man does not make a conscious decision and voluntary speedup of the two systems involved.

When a pathogen invades the organism such automatic responses are dramatically enacted. Such disease-producing agents are viable at temperatures ranging from 97 to 99 degrees F. As soon as the pathogen appears, a homeostatic rise in body temperature occurs. Bone marrow changes are brought into play to provide more white blood cells to combat the foreign body. This requires more oxygen and hence respiratory and pulse rate alterations take place. The point is that none of these reactions is voluntary. They occur automatically to preserve the integrity and comfort of the organism.

In similar fashion comfort is maintained in the emotional sphere through a series of complex adjustments in the psychic life which also are involuntary and beyond the awareness of the individual.

Prime among these adjustments is the defense mechanism of *repression.* Simply stated, repression is an automatic inhibition at the core of personality. It consists in excluding certain impulses and their ideational representations from consciousness. Through confrontation with the outside world the developing ego awakens to the harsh fact that there is an ego larger and more powerful than itself, an ego with ground rules for living and sanctions for both compliance and obstinacy to its demands. As a consequence, certain behaviors are readily acted out while others are labeled as dangerous and, therefore, capable of arousing painful anxiety if admitted to consciousness. The developing ego excludes, therefore, these inclinations, wishes and ideas from its conscious experience.

This defensive move is both fundamental and normal to the developing infantile ego. During the first years of life intellectual assessment is impossible. Repression is perhaps the best way to handle impulses that may be dangerous. As the ego and eventually the superego develop, the latter component of the mental complex takes this role of inhibition and relieves the ego of this labor. With the passage of time, many impulses and desires are automatically censored and prevented from ever reaching consciousness.

On emergence into this world, for example, the neonate accepts no differentiation between the "me" and the "non-me." The mother and all the world are as it were part of itself. Prenatally, the infant was factually part of the mother. Now, postnatally, the inverse is fantasied. Before long the experience of self-identity commences and is enhanced by a series of self-discoveries. One of these discoveries is the genitalia. The small child becomes intrigued with this presumed new part of himself. In itself this behavior is natural and innocent. Often, however, parents misinterpret this preoccupation and inject their adult standards into the mind of the child. The child gradually is deterred from this pleasure in various ways, depending upon the anxiety of the parents. If he persists in the activity he may be physically punished. As a result of this experience and without realizing it the child represses this tendency in order to avoid pain and to consolidate the acceptance of his parents. When the tendency is completely and successfully repressed, its corresponding mental representation no longer enters the child's mind.

Although repression is normal during infancy and early childhood, the use of the mechanism is not without complications. Since the youngster is not able to discriminate, there may be a spread of repression to include ideas and desires that would not prove dangerous if admitted to consciousness. Repression inhibits behavior in order to ensure comfort and safety. Extension of the inhibition, however, may cause problems. In the example used above, repression of the so-called infantile masturbatory tendency may spread to include everything connected with normal genital function. If the external pressures on the child are severe or the mother's attitude excessively punitive, the child eventually may repress all interest and ideas associated with this part of the anatomy because he thinks it is wrong or evil and thereby become involved in psychosexual difficulties.

Although repression is a normal and necessary mechanism in early personality development, its employment in later years gradually should diminish. The mature ego should be able to face what is in its makeup and intelligently handle id impulses and their representations. Simple intellectual appreciation, however, is insufficient. It is the emotional insight or acceptance that is all important. When this is realized repression becomes unnecessary.

It is, however, anger, resentment and sexual strivings that constitute the mass of repressed matter in adulthood. These emotions and their related data, including earlier painful experiences, are not extinguished but merely inhibited. It is as though the threshold of consciousness was heightened to them. If repressed material occasionally breaks through this barrier into consciousness and causes anxiety, the individual may banish it from his mind by a conscious and forceful act of the will. This conscious kind of defense is known as *suppression.* It usually consists in distracting oneself or becoming deeply involved in some activity and usually is not very effective. To say to oneself, "I shall not think about what I am thinking" or, "I shall not feel as I am presently feeling" is quite impossible. Even if pushed away or crowded out of present experience, such repressed thoughts and feelings, because of their emotionally personal coloration, will continue to badger for recognition. Consequently, since suppression is ineffective, repression always requires further implementation in the form of other unconscious defenses.

Some individuals will resort to *reaction formations,* which consist in the development of conscious attitudes or character traits that are diametrically opposed to those representing the repressed material. The process itself is unconscious and can perhaps best be explained by example. Let us assume that for any one or several of many reasons a person never has been able to express hostility. As a result of almost constant repression of hostile drives, considerable emotional tension has accumulated. Although he does not know the reason for it, this individual needs to avoid all situations involving hostility. He even may avoid reading stories in the newspapers dealing with examples of hostility. As pressure continues to build, he may employ reaction formation. He does this by consciously assuming an attitude of excessive compassion and ultimately may give the appearance of obsequious humility. By consciously showing this face to the public he attempts to convince others, and ultimately himself, that hostility is in no way a part of his makeup. The conscious attitude is developed in order to neutralize the unconscious forces of which the individual is unaware.

To take another example, let us assume that an individual has considerable difficulty with unconscious aggressive drives. They have been subject to the forces of repression for a considerable period of time. In order to demonstrate to the world his complete repudiation of aggression, such a person may become a member of an antivivisection society, or he may become a vegetarian. In this manner he proclaims to the world that anything to do with aggression is alien to him. Having convinced himself, he thereby once again neutralizes the unconscious drives that are seeking expression.

Perhaps the ultimate in reaction formations occurred some years ago when, as a hoax, two advertising copywriters established a society whose objective was to put clothes on domestic animals.

It began with facetious suggestions to dress Caroline Kennedy's horse. In a short time a number of people possessing troublesome sexual repressions joined the society in all seriousness, proclaiming their affront at the "indecent exposure" of domestic animals. They were, in effect, attempting to neutralize what probably were unconscious exhibitionistic tendencies in themselves.

Reaction formation is a well-known mechanism and is readily discernible to the keen observer. It should not, however, be presumed that every vegetarian is employing reaction formation against his aggressive tendencies or that every compassionate individual is harboring unconscious hostility. Snap judgments about the behavior of others could itself be a cover-up for one's own inadequacies. Caution is the dictate in the interpretation of human behavior.

Rationalization is a more universally employed mechanism in the reinforcement of repression. Although it operates at the unconscious level, the process is fairly close to the surface. Through its use we attempt to justify or excuse certain aspects of our behavior of which we are secretly ashamed. The salesman who misrepresents his product, for example, may attempt to justify his behavior by convincing himself that being cheated is a valuable lesson for his victim. In other situations, rationalization is used as a face-saving device following an ego insult. Rationalization could be called the "you can't fire me, I just quit" reaction; or, in other terms, "sour grapes." A person may be discharged from his employment because of incompetence. To preserve his ego image, he needs to deny the fact of his incompetence. Accordingly, he rationalizes his discharge by convincing himself that he did not want that particular job in the first place. One saves face in social situations through the use of rationalization. A young couple disappointed because they did not receive an invitation to the social event of the season in their community, may console one another by suggesting "I'm glad we weren't invited. I would not have gone if we were. The Jones's parties are such dreadful bores. I'm delighted they left us off the list." The individual's use of rationalization often is so close to consciousness that he can be considered to be aware of the process and is, in effect, playing games with himself. Rationalization is not a particularly useful or efficient mechanism since more often than not reality is distorted in the process.

Displacement is an extremely common mechanism of defense. It involves the direction of an emotional attitude toward an object other than that originally intended. In this way the emotional attitude can be preserved and the energy discharged without fear of recrimination. It often results in chain reactions: Mr. Jones is dissatisfied with the burned toast he is offered each morning for breakfast; he becomes increasingly hostile and resentful toward his wife. Unconsciously, he is afraid to express his hostility because of his equally unconscious fear that his wife may retaliate by withholding sexual favors. While he remains completely unaware of this process, hostile feelings continue to accumulate. One morning, while he is on his way to work, some of the hostility escapes in his attempt to beat another driver to an intersection. A collision results which adds to Mr. Jones's problem. Officer Smith arrives to investigate the accident and, having reached the breaking point, Mr. Jones makes Officer Smith the object of all his hostile feelings, including those originating in the burnt-toast episode. He verbally abuses Officer Smith but, because of Jones's prominence in the community, the policeman intuitively recognizes the possibility of recrimination if he responds to the unjustified assault. He therefore attempts to absorb the insults. With a predisposition to express some hostility of his own, Officer Smith is very likely to write a number of equivocal traffic summonses in the course of the day. To carry the example of the chain reaction to its ultimate but possibly absurd conclusion, let us suppose that Mr. Brown receives a traffic summons from Officer Smith. This may trigger a reaction in Mr. Brown who accumulates his hostility and upon arriving home for the evening unconsciously displaces his feelings onto his wife. He criticizes her for the sameness of the menu, makes unkind remarks about his mother-in-law, who never taught his wife how to cook. He feels better after ridding himself of his feelings, but Mrs. Brown now has the problem. At that moment, one of the Brown children walks across the newly waxed kitchen floor with mud on his shoes. Although usually gracious and tolerant about the child's behavior, Mrs. Brown releases her hostile feelings in the direction of a very safe object, her child. While children are more direct in expressing their emotions and use fewer mechanisms, it is possible to conclude this example by suggesting that following his mother's tirade, little Jimmy Brown goes outside and kicks the cat.

Although these examples of chain reactions to initial displacement of hostility may seem rather common, they are becoming less and less acceptable because society today is less prepared to extend empathy in the direction of hostile behavior. There was a time when sexuality was in constant need of most repression. As overt sexuality has become more and more acceptable in our society, disapproval of hostility has displaced it.

Substitution, the mechanism by which we seek alternate objects for strong emotions, is the conscious counterpart of displacement. It occurs in various emotionally-charged areas. A business executive becomes aware of his hostility and tells his secretary that he will be spending the afternoon at the gym. He recognizes the need to dispel his excess energy and works out on the punching bag or spars a few rounds with another member of the club who has similar needs. An individual may consciously substitute the vicarious experience of the erotic novel for an actual sexual experience which is not possible at the time. Similarly, stag films and pornographic art may be used as a conscious substitute for sexual experience. It should be noted, however, that substitution is not always the mechanism involved among those interested in pornography. In many instances, this interest may represent unconscious sexual conflict and serious pathology.

Projection is another mechanism and is seen frequently in mild form. Despite its frequency it is not a particularly effective defense. In its more serious aspects it forms the basis for the paranoid reaction and lays the groundwork for delusional thinking. Essentially, it is unconscious in its operation and permits repressed tendencies or desires to escape. This is accomplished when we attribute our own faults to others. This permits us to react to the projected fault in a socially acceptable manner. Projection usually can be detected in the individual who begins a sentence by stating "If there's one thing I can't stand. . . ." He invariably may be guilty of the very fault he is denouncing in others. This is not, of course, universal and some criticism of the social behavior of others is entirely legitimate. In this way projection may be similar in some respects to reaction formation. In the latter, however, we assume conscious attitudes which oppose the unconscious drives, while in projection we direct attention to others.

An extremely hostile person may be unable to express his feelings because of his unconscious fear of his hostility. As repression begins to break down, he projects that hostility onto others. Instead of admitting "I can't stand him," he projects this outward and states "He hates me." When carried to pathological lengths projection forms the basis for delusional thinking in which the paranoid person actually may begin to defend himself against the imagined persecution of others.

All forms of scapegoating are the result of projection. For example, parents who are negligent in the supervision of their children often will project blame for the youngsters' delinquent behavior onto the manager of the pool hall or the operator of the discothèque. They project their own inadequacies outward and envision themselves and their children as victims of someone else's lack of concern for the welfare of children. It they can find a reason for prosecuting they relax in contentment as they send someone else to jail to atone for their own sins of omission.

Some time ago Robert L. Sears conducted an interesting experiment that indicated that lack of insight was closely correlated with the tendency to project. In it one hundred college students were asked to rate each other on a set of variables, most of them undesirable. Sears then obtained the college's estimate on the particular trait. Next he gathered a rating on insight by means of a self-rating inventory. "Insight" was considered good when one's personal rating equaled the rating given him by the other ninety-nine. Where there was great discrepancy, Sears rated them as "lacking in insight." He found that those who lacked insight had a greater tendency to attribute undesirable attributes to others. They were projecting what they could not face in relation to themselves. Those who were high in insight, on the other hand, tended to judge others as they actually were.

In general, projection is employed to rid oneself of repressed ideas and desires. It accounts for the phenomenon whereby personal faults and even sins are attributed in an exaggerated form to others. Shakespeare gave the clue to its detection when he had one of his characters suggest that "the lady doth protest too much."

The very primitive mechanism of *introjection* is roughly the opposite of projection. When the mechanism of repression fails, the unconscious impulse may be so totally unacceptable that it cannot be directed outward. Under such circumstances it may, through introjection, be directed inward or toward the self. To again use the example of hostility, a person who really wants to say "I hate him" finds this so unacceptable that he resorts to introjection and states "I hate myself." If directed outward, the impulse would produce guilt. The mechanism therefore serves a double purpose: it releases the repressed impulse and it precludes associated guilt feeling. Unfortunately, it often leads to severe depression and is considered the basic mechanism of suicide.

Suicide itself is an extremely hostile act. It is a severe indictment of those in the immediate environment and, in a sense, a strong indictment of society itself. Even greater hostility can be expressed when the suicide leaves a note absolving his loved ones from sin. The suicide note that begins "Please don't blame yourself, you had nothing to do with this," interpreted correctly, is an expression of hostility that means "I hope that you are finally satisfied that you caused me to kill myself."

According to most authorities, *identification* is one of the most important mechanisms of defense. Simply put, it is an unconscious form of imitation. We all use this mechanism and in one sense it is part of individual growth. It is, for example, essential for proper psychosexual development that a son ultimately see either in his father or in some surrogate the characteristics that he finds desirable in himself as a male. Conversely, the little girl must emulate the distinguishing features of her mother or another female model if she is to emerge as a mature, balanced woman. Unfortunately, identification with undesirable behavior, mannerisms, fears or attitudes also is possible. In this instance the child very well may continue and even magnify the unacceptable or inadequate example of those he observes.

Identification usually takes one of two forms: assuming the observed behavior patterns of another—usually to enhance self-esteem—or establishing an "affective oneness" with another person, object or situation. In the first instance it is employed as an unconscious protection against the anxiety that the individual will not attain the maturity or position he observes in others. In the second it is used to reassure the individual that he is attaining at least some degree of the status, if only vicariously. Examples of this type of mechanism so abound that society has evolved clichés to identify them, expressions such as "If you can't beat them, join them," "He's a real name-dropper" and "That's my Pop."

Although it cannot be overstressed that a certain degree of imitation or unconscious identification is perfectly normal and necessary, it must be emphasized equally that the value of such identification ultimately will depend on the model chosen. In other words, it is possible to identify with the "bad guys" as well as with the "good guys."

Regression is an unconscious mental mechanism which is difficult to distinguish from some of those already discussed. In many instances, when we characterize an individual's behavior as immature we may be referring to regression.

Descriptions of this rather complex mechanism are difficult because of the risk of oversimplification. During the formative years, certain behavior patterns develop which are used in solving problems that are of significance at the time. The baby, for instance, solves most problems merely by crying. It announces its need to others and the problem is solved through the intervention of some outside agency, usually a parent. As he grows older, this behavior pattern is no longer appropriate as a problem-solving technique but remains in the unconscious.

During childhood, divide and rule is the usual method of solving problems. If the school-age child can drive a wedge between his mother and father regarding such subjects as homework or how late he may stay up he often triumphs and solves his immediate problem by escaping attention while his mother and father argue. This technique, as employed by a jealous mother-in-law, has become the theme of many a soap opera, which has fascinated many a daughter-in-law as she perceives the regression of the "troublemaker."

There is a tendency to convert patterns of behavior into a kind of reflex and to use those that were successful once in all situations. It is only when these patterns become inappropriate and fail to meet the need or solve the problem that we become motivated to seek new adaptations. Ultimately, when intellectual development is completed, we use problem-solving techniques that involve goal-directed behavior and abstract theory. A person faced with a crisis may exhaust his intellectual abilities and still be faced with the problem. He may at this point turn to others, which would be a mature way of handling the issue. It is possible, however, that he will regress to an earlier pattern of adaptation because of the pressure upon him and attempt to solve the problem in a less mature way. The behavior he uses, however, always represents a pattern that was once successful, although it is no longer appropriate. Even physically mature adults may become so overwhelmed that they simply sit down and cry. At the rational level we understand that crying will not solve the problem directly; by regressing to his infantile stage, however, the person often excites the sympathy of others and receives the help that, were he more mature, he would have asked for.

Sublimation is probably the most effective mechanism. It may be defined as the process of diverting ego-alien impulses into socially acceptable channels in order that they may be expressed. An ego-alien impulse is any desire or wish that fails to gain approval in consciousness. To the honest, law-abiding citizen, a sudden desire to rob a bank would be considered ego-alien. Through the process of sublimation we are able to take the illogical, often irrational, crude, repressed material found in the unconscious and transform the psychic energy attached to it into something socially acceptable and usually even useful and productive. Sublimation resembles the chemical process of distillation. When oil is refined chemically, a crude residue known as coal tar remains behind. This material is amorphous, sticky and particularly foul smelling. By further chemical action, however, it can be transformed into a variety of beautiful and useful products, including aniline dyes, various perfumes and the sulfa drugs. In similar fashion, the mental apparatus can take unconscious drives which, if directly expressed, might be considered reprehensible and through the process of sublimation change them into something good.

Destructive, even homicidal impulses may be sublimated occupationally. An individual harboring such impulses might derive considerable satisfaction from becoming a professional housewrecker. Sexual drives may be sublimated into creative artistry or social enterprise. Indeed, many of the world's masterpieces of art, music and literature may represent sublimated sexuality. Many people who dedicate themselves to caring for children or for the aged may be sublimating maternal or sexual drives. In this connection, it is extremely important to note that sublimated sexual energy does not constitute and should not be compared with sexual deviation. Nor is the end product of the sublimated energy counterfeit. It is distressing to hear people with a superficial knowledge of psychodynamics describe social work and nursing as "merely sublimated maternity." During puberty and before marriage we assist young people to sublimate their sexual energies in the form of social dancing and recreation. There is no reason to consider social dancing as suspect or deviate because it is sexually motivated.

Other examples of sublimation of hostile and aggressive drives may be seen in the choice of professions. The person may be consumed with repressed hostility and aggression with no socially acceptable outlet. Society does not permit him to maim and mutilate. When present, such unconscious drives sometimes find useful and acceptable outlets in the form of surgery. It requires a considerable amount of aggression to perform a surgical incision. This is not to suggest that all surgeons are basically hostile and aggressive people; in some instances, however, this mechanism may be operating. Upon hearing this example frequently offered by psychiatrists, surgeons in turn have suggested that the latter are sublimated voyeurs. They have pointed out that our society does not permit people to peek through keyholes or over transoms; allegedly, the psychiatrist sublimates these tendencies in his practice by delving into the intimate secrets of his patients.

Repetition compulsion is an extremely interesting mental mechanism. In its simplest terms, it implies that during the formative years of childhood each of us makes a long-playing record which we tend to play over and over again throughout our lives. In repeating previous experiences, either directly or in symbolic form, we unconsciously attempt to undo what has occurred in the past and have things come out right the next time.

One of the most intriguing and fairly common examples of repetition compulsion involves alcoholism. The young, attractive daughter who was physically abused and traumatized by an alcoholic father throughout childhood would be expected to stay about as far away from an alcoholic as possible. It is remarkable, then, how frequently someone with just this experience will become interested in a young man whose alcoholic proclivities are well known in the community. In spite of her previous experience she may become engaged to and marry a young man with such a poor prognosis. She does this because the situation symbolically embodies her previous experience. The husband who is alcoholic represents the father. If she can cure him she, in effect, undoes the earlier situation and symbolically redeems her father as well.

The clergyman often has the opportunity to intervene in such ill-fated marriages and continues to be astonished at his inability to reach some of the people involved. It appears almost incredible that such individuals could seriously contemplate repeating an unpleasant experience; it is perhaps less astonishing if one is familiar with the repetition compulsion.

Other examples of the repetition compulsion frequently are seen in multiple marriage and divorce sequences. The young man who was dominated by his mother and can escape that domination only through marriage frequently will select a marital partner whose personality is almost identical to that of his mother. Many of his friends will recognize the similarity but, invariably, the young man will not. While attempting to undo the earlier unpleasant relationship with his mother, he finds himself once again headed for disaster. Although the marriage may end in divorce, curiously enough, a remarriage often will involve precisely the same type of personality. The compelling need to repeat previous experiences, even symbolically, is especially remarkable in that it often is virtually impossible to point out to the individual that he is using this particular mechanism.

Compensation is another frequently used mechanism. It is basically a defense against our feeling of inadequacy regarding some particular field of endeavor. The direct approach involves a deliberate effort to excel in an area where one ostensibly is weak. The obvious danger of this approach is that the goal established is completely unattainable and failure will only result in further reactions of inadequacy and self-rejection. For example, the student who is unable to accept his personal scholastic weakness may attempt scholastic goals far beyond his capacities and failure to achieve them will result in utter frustration.

Indirect compensation will acknowledge inability in certain areas and seek to allay the anxiety induced by such inability by over-achieving in another area. Although the classic example of the physically weak student who determines to become the intellectual wizard on campus frequently produces some mild amusement, it more frequently produces pity and embarrassment in the knowledgeable onlooker.

Because of their close association, *isolation* and *symbolization* may be treated together. They usually work together as the individual attempts to rid himself of a particular anxiety by taking it completely out of context and defining it by means of some particular object. In order to appreciate the significance of these mechanisms one must understand the overwhelming desire of the individual to rid himself of anxiety. In the case of isolation, the person cannot accept the true threat to his security and, therefore, uses a "symbol"—often completely unrelated to the real threat—with which he can deal. He thus avoids the necessity of facing the reality that actually is threatening him and against which he feels completely inadequate. Because of faulty training and lack of education, for example, it is possible for one to grow up with an unhealthy attitude toward sexual activity. He may consider it filthy, dirty and strictly a barnyard activity. In early adult life, normal sexual strivings appear in all people. To those with unhealthy attitudes, however, those normal strivings may prompt considerable anxiety and pose a threat to the ego. Through isolation and symbolization it is possible for some such people to become involved in compulsive hand-washing. By repeatedly washing their hands they are symbolically cleansing themselves of the dirt and filth represented by the unconscious sexual striving. At the same time they are isolating this attitude and allowing themselves to function in other areas.

These mechanisms are observed mostly in truly neurotic or psychotic states. There is always a symbolic relationship between the phobic object or the compulsion and the repressed material. The fact that this is so, however, does not make it easier to discover the symbolism involved. In many phobic reactions and in many compulsions the process is so complicated and the symbolism so exotic that the true nature of the repressed material never becomes apparent.

There is a vast difference between a true phobic avoidance as contained in the mechanisms of isolation and symbolization and simple idiosyncrasy. The conditioned reflex of one who has been bitten by a dog to avoid such animals in the future is certainly not a mechanism. Where there is no reasonable explanation for the presence of a phobic object, however, it may be suspected that the individual has isolated a threat and symbolized it in order to explain his own response at an acceptable level.

Since no one is free from anxiety of some type, we all use the natural means of allaying anxiety, the mechanisms of defense, to some degree. The extent to which they are employed varies with the individual and is governed by his ego-strength and the circumstances that surround his mode of existence.

Within the framework of these defenses, an individual seeks survival and this is something good. It is only when they are used too frequently or as a constant means of escape from the demands of facing reality that they may result in neurotic or even psychotic behavior. There can be no doubt that the type and number of an individual's defenses will be a strong index to the type of personality he possesses. Accordingly, it is most desirable that in moments of controlled introspection he evaluate his use of these protective devices. Since they are essentially unconscious reactions they are difficult to recognize in their actualization. It is only in moments of calm and relative security that one can reassess his progress toward personality development and emotional integrity. If the mechanisms of defense are seen for what they are, tricks we play on ourselves from time to time, then we can turn from them with knowledge in our hearts and perhaps a smile on our lips. If, on the other hand, they become crutches on which we must depend for survival, they can become a crippling influence which destroys as effectively as any physical disease.

For Further Reference

Freud, Anna. *The Ego and the Mechanisms of Defense.* rev. ed. New York: International Universities Press, 1967.

Horney, Karen. *Our Inner Conflicts.* New York: W. W. Norton & Co., 1945.

May, Rollo. *The Meaning of Anxiety.* New York: Ronald Press, 1950.

Morgan, J. J. B. *How to Keep a Sound Mind.* New York: Macmillan Co., 1946.

Nunberg, Herman. *Principles of Psychoanalysis.* New York: International Universities Press, 1962.

5 Symptomatology

The attempts of the body and the mind to allay the anxiety induced by the conflict of human needs and their lack of fulfillment are per se good, valid and necessary. These defensive moves may reach, however, such proportions that behavior becomes distorted and socially or morally unacceptable. These manifestations of internal conflict and frustration may vary all the way from the physical peptic ulcer and facial tic to hallucinatory and delusional omnipotence and grandeur. In all cases, these indications of incompletion are known as symptoms and fall under the general heading of symptomatology.[1]

At the outset of any discussion on this subject it is important to note that there is a little bit of the psychiatrist in all of us. Everyone, for example, becomes intrigued by certain accounts concerning the lengths to which some individuals will go in an effort to solve their human predicament. This understandable curiosity becomes even more pronounced when it comes to the question of human eccentricities and to behavior that is "way out" and decidedly psychotic in character. It cannot be too strongly emphasized, however, that as interesting as this kind of information is, it actually is of secondary importance to the more radical need to appreciate these symptoms for what they are in themselves.

In a very real sense, symptoms are built-in devices by which the entire organism is striving desperately to maintain equilibrium and to communicate its state of crisis. It is crying out for assistance while it makes its final bid against the onslaught of an unknown enemy. Every symptom, no matter how unrealistic to the observer, serves a purpose. They must never become the plaything of the amateur, however sincere, dedicated and well-meaning. It constantly must be recalled that symptoms are defensive behaviors and that basically they are employed to protect the individual from the realization of his inner conflict and its sometimes painful solution. He may not be able to endure that realization at all and no matter how distressing the symptom it ultimately may be preferable to the acceptance of its cause. Moreover, the attempt to cure or remove the symptom as an undesirable interference with integrated living may not be the first order of procedure. The symptom itself may have to be understood thoroughly before its real cause can be detected and treated. Casual removal of any symptom before its meaning is known is always detrimental to the individual.

The Functional Theory of Symptomatology

In the last decade of the nineteenth century the concept of man as a biological unit still dominated medical thinking. The pathologist was preeminent and most accurate diagnoses were made at autopsy. When tissues were studied under the microscope alteration in their structure and appearance was used to explain the disease process. When autopsy failed to reveal cellular change, the disease was classified as one of unknown origin. The concept of a functional disturbance without damage or alteration of the appearance of various cells had not yet come upon the scene. All diseases were considered to be organic in nature.[2]

Even the sometimes bizarre behavior of psychotic patients was believed to be the result of cellular damage. The brain and the central nervous system, which controls voluntary behavior, were considered to be the source of such difficulty. Failure to produce pathological evidence of damage to the brain caused the psychoses to be classified as disturbances of the brain that had no known cause. In many instances patients suffering from disorders that now are known to be functional in nature were considered malingerers or attention seekers. A neurotic disorder known then as hysteria was a common affliction. Even it was considered organic in nature. Although the symptoms most frequently involved were paralysis of the upper and lower extremities, the illness was thought to result from a "wandering uterus" and, accordingly, could be seen only in females. Sigmund Freud's first assault upon the medical thinking of the time involved his then outrageous assertion that males also could suffer from hysteria. It destroyed the "wandering uterus" concept.

As the dynamics of personality were revealed through the discoveries of psychoanalysis, an entirely new concept of functional disability in the absence of demonstrable changes in cell structure was established. Even here, the intrusion of biology is evident since these newly-discovered disorders were referred to as "neuroses." Medically, this implied some connection between the observed behavior and the condition of the central nervous system. In actuality, the nerves and the brain as such have nothing to do with a neurosis. The term *nervous breakdown,* as a layman's expression for severe neurosis or psychosis, contains this biological implication. It is perhaps just as well since some comfort attaches to the belief that a disorder results from injury to some part of the body.

Because of the functional dependence of the human mind on the central nervous system and the sensorium in general there will be, necessarily, a certain number of organically caused mental disorders. Mental retardation, for example, is a reflection of underlying physical pathology. This type of subnormal functioning may originate from a variety of physical causes such as prenatal infections, maternal intoxications, chromosomal abnormalities, birth injuries and postnatal metabolic dysfunctions. Several other mental disorders also have been grouped together under the general title of "organic brain syndromes." The symptoms reflected by these disorders range from simple intellectual and memory impairment to gross psychotic behavior. Senile brain deterioration, cerebral arteriosclerosis, alcoholic poisoning, severe head injuries and brain surgery are examples of the physical factors that may account for the appearance of this type of mental disturbance.

This functional concept of mental disorder should not be so strictly interpreted that it excludes physiological side effects. There is an entire group of functional disorders that are essentially characterized by intense and sustained physical symptoms. They have been technically designated as the "psycho-physiological disorders" and involve some organ system of the body which is usually, if not always, under autonomic nervous innervation. Peptic ulcer, chronic gastritis, mucous colitis, hypertension, migraines, bronchial asthma and sexual impotence are examples of physical conditions that can be traced to emotional etiology. It is a well-known fact that under ordinary psychic tension the autonomic nervous system mobilizes the body systems for emergency duty. But when such an internal state becomes the regular order of life for an individual adverse physiological effects are inevitable. Such organ hyperactivity may cause the stomach, for example, to secrete a near constant flow of digestive fluids. In this way the human being, in the absence of foreign digestible matter, actually can go to work at digesting itself. Peptic ulcers are the result of such a self-digestive process. In similar fashion, sustained chronic tension can cause severe cardiovascular damage in which a man's heart becomes enlarged to the size of a football and his arteries harden to the likeness of lead pipes.

In contrast with these somatic manifestations of inner emotional stress, the symptomatology proper to the psychoneuroses and functional psychoses is decidedly psychic in character. In very general terms, it may be said that a neurotic symptom is an unsuccessful effort on the part of the ego to restore emotional equilibrium which has been disturbed by the presence of unsatisfied or poorly satisfied subjective urges. Stated in another way, a neurotic symptom may be considered an additional defensive move to relieve the anxiety created by unresolved conflicts. When such conflicts are harbored in the unconscious and threaten to break through into the conscious mind, the ego's anxiety level rises and thereby signals the need for additional defensive measures. In this way the neurotic symptom is frantically called upon as an anxiety-controlling and conflict-repressing mechanism. Ultimately, the neurotic symptom is a desperate response to the threat to the integrity of the organism.

Neurotic Symptomatology

Among the various neurotic symptoms surrounding the neurotic conflict one group may be referred to as specific avoidances and inhibitions. Almost any human function can become the subject of an inhibition. Applying the psychoanalytic theory to its founder, Sigmund Freud, we see a most interesting illustration of such a specific avoidance or inhibition. Freud was a self-proclaimed atheist. He considered religion a form of obsessive-compulsive neurosis and propounded the theory that man invented God as a psychological defense. Although he did not actively campaign against religion or religious practices he nevertheless elicited harsh criticism from the Church. Although Freud was a world traveler and was constantly on the move from one European capital to another, it took him more than thirty years to enter the Eternal City of Rome despite his conscious desire to visit. He prepared for the trip on numerous occasions but something, at times something quite trivial, always caused him to alter his plans. It could be suggested that Freud, who called himself "an impious Jew," had many unresolved conflicts about relegating religion to the field of mythology and religious observances to that of pathology. If he did have such unresolved conflicts, it would have been a neurotic symptom on his part specifically to avoid confrontation with Rome.

People frequently avoid certain objects, activities, situations or fields of interest. Sometimes they do this without being aware of it and, at other times, they may have full consciousness of the avoidance involved. They tend to rationalize their behavior by believing that they dislike the object or activity that is involved in the inhibition. They may feel afraid or embarrassed at having to face a specific situation or rationalize that they simply are not interested in that person or that activity. Under analysis, the specifically avoided situation or the inhibited function generally is revealed to have unconscious and instinctual sexual or aggressive significance. It is against this unconscious or instinctual significance that the defense of avoidance really is directed.

Impotence on the part of the male and frigidity on the part of the female most often represent unmistakable evidence of neurotic inhibition in reference to sexuality. The male, who unconsciously fears sexual activity because of a poorly developed attitude, because he identifies the act with a form of aggression or for other reasons, may become physically impotent and thereby render the sex act impossible. He invariably blames his impotence on some physical disability or on his mate's lack of sexual interest or even on her fantasied infidelity. The symptom thus prevents him from engaging in the forbidden activity and at the same time obviates the necessity of seeking in the unconscious the source of the conflict. The specific avoidance is rationalized on the basis of physical disability or one of the other reasons suggested. The same dynamics may be seen operating in the female who suffers various degrees of frigidity.

Neurotic symptoms of inhibition also may affect the aggressive drive. Such inhibitions result from anxiety and guilt feelings in persons whose aggressive tendencies have been deeply repressed. When children in their formative years are not permitted to release any of their normal aggressive drives they tend to develop unhealthy attitudes toward this instinct of self-assertion. They perceive all forms of aggression and competition as dangerous because expression of such feelings would result in the withdrawal of acceptance and affection on the part of their parents. The unexpressed drives continue to build up pressure and it is possible that in later life the impulses may threaten to break through to consciousness. This threat produces considerable anxiety and it becomes necessary for them to avoid all forms of aggression and competition, even those that are normal and healthy. In this connection, certain individuals may avoid all forms of occupational competition with others because for them it represents aggression. They may withdraw from the world and bury their talents because expression of those talents might merit rewards that they consider to be the result of taking unfair advantage of their peers.

The number and variety of such neurotic inhibitions or specific avoidances is near infinite. If oral impulses, for example, have been subjected to massive repression during the very early years of childhood, it is altogether possible that the repressed material will exert sufficient pressure in later life to cause symptom formation. The person involved may develop idiosyncrasies regarding food intake and avoid eating certain kinds of food because, unconsciously, they are reminiscent of the objects desired but forbidden during early life. In certain severe cases of oral inhibition other neurotic symptomatology may be seen in episodes of functional hysterical vomiting or spasms of the jaw which make eating temporarily impossible. The inhibition may even be displaced onto other activities with hidden oral significance, such as drinking, smoking or kissing.

It is imperative to sound certain words of caution at this point. Not all food or oral idiosyncrasies are neurotic in character. Allergic factors or other physiological difficulties may account for this kind of symptom. Moreover, although repressions undertaken as a matter of necessity in the initial years of life later may produce symptoms, this does not justify blaming the parents, especially the mother, for all neurotic symptoms. The suggestion that a child who is inhibited during the formative years will become neurotic later in life has no scientific foundation.

The phobia is perhaps the most interesting and certainly one of the most widespread of neurotic symptoms. Many studiously avoid black cats and walking under ladders while others throw spilt salt over the shoulder and knock on wood. These are harmless superstitions and usually provoke little or no anxiety if they are encountered or omitted. A phobia, on the other hand, is a persistent pathological fear about a specific object or situation. The person with a true phobia always will show marked and visible anxiety when confronted with the phobic stimulus.

The number of specific phobias that are commonplace is literally in the hundreds. Any person, place or object can become invested with phobic qualities. Claustrophobia, as all know, is the fear of closed places; acrophobia is the fear of high places; aeriliophobia is the fear of birds. To complete the list it is only necessary to translate the proper name of every real being into Greek and add the appropriate suffix.

Whatever its name may be and though the fear may appear irrational to the observer and even to the patient, the fear itself is extremely real. A multiplicity of problems may be expressed in the one phobic reaction. In a sense, the person suffering from a phobia places all his eggs in one basket. Rather than be concerned with this situation or fearful of that, rather than avoid this person or that place, rather than worry about the appropriateness of a particular impulse, the person "selects" a phobic object. Having made such a selection, he avoids the anxiety from multiple sources merely by keeping clear of the feared object. Admittedly, this is an oversimplification, but it does serve as a partial explanation.

The problem with all phobic reactions is that they are not self-limiting even though the phobic object absorbs and contains much of the subject's apprehension and preserves him from the pain of "free-floating" anxiety. Once the individual has devised a pattern of living that successfully keeps him from contact with the phobic object, his tranquility is restored. But when and if the unconscious material again threatens to break through it will be necessary for him to select another phobic object. In this way, the process tends to feed upon itself and, as the phobia spreads, other persons and things become involved, thereby progressively limiting the individual's freedom.

The degree of impairment produced by the phobic reaction varies from one individual and from one situation to another. It is quite possible, for example, to go through life and avoid high places without much difficulty. A person need not visit the observation tower of the Washington Monument or the top of the Empire State Building and he easily can locate his living quarters and working facilities on the ground floor. If the person is an urban dweller, however, and his phobia involves crowds, subways or tunnels, then his freedom will be limited considerably. Though he recognizes the whole matter as unreasonable and perhaps even understands the symbolic nature of a phobia, he remains immobilized and helpless to control his fear. During therapy it sometimes is possible to alleviate the condition by establishing the symbolic connection between the phobic object and the repression or inhibition on which it is based. In an equal number of cases, however, such symbolic connections are never brought to the surface.

In addition to feeding upon itself and spreading, the phobic reaction often has a tendency to be the forerunner of obsessive-compulsive symptoms. By definition, an obsession is a recurring idea or impulse that remains in consciousness despite its irrationality. Such ideas intrude upon consciousness without invitation and though they make little or no sense to the patient they provoke a considerable amount of anxiety because of their threatening character. To the patient and untrained observer, these persistent ideas appear to have no relationship to the rest of the personality. In themselves, however, they represent in generally undisguised fashion otherwise repressed infantile impulses within the unconscious mind.

An illustration may be of some help in understanding the nature of obsessive thinking. Almost everyone has had the experience of having a tune pop into his head. It may be the result of a singing commercial on radio or television or it may have no obvious explanation. It often occurs spontaneously and keeps going round and round in one's mind. When this occurs the person frequently attempts to banish the melody from consciousness but instead only reinforces the experience and continues it at even greater intensity. Although this is not an obsession by any means, it is an experience somewhat similar to that undergone by obsessive thinkers.

Obsessive thoughts usually take on one of four central themes. Thoughts of violence are perhaps the most common. For example, without any reason a person suddenly may recognize a homicidal thought concerning his spouse, a child or a parent.

Initially, little attention is paid and routine attempts are made to exclude the unwelcome thought by engaging in other activities. As the thought recurs and does not give way to conscious efforts to exclude it the person naturally begins to react with anxiety. He begins to be frightened that he will lose control and act out the thought. Consciously, the obsessive thought makes no sense because surface relationships with the person who is the target of such thoughts usually are excellent.

Another frequent theme of obsessive thought is sexuality. The person's mind becomes overtaken with a variety of irresistible fantasies involving a particular person or a number of partners. These intrusive thoughts come unbidden and continue to plague the person regardless of the efforts he expends at dismissing them. This invasion and the inability to control it always generates painful anxiety for the person. An extension of this basic theme is obscenity. The person's imagination becomes flooded with representations of vulgarity and even perversity. Since these thoughts are alien to his conscious desires, they always generate a considerable amount of distress and anxiety.

Religion and religious themes are commonly observed. Very frequently these obsessions have as their central core the vengeance of God. People with this kind of preoccupation often are plagued by emotional or pathological guilt and imagine themselves to be great sinners when, in fact, they are free of moral guilt in any connection. There also are those who are plagued with obsessive ideas of an anti-religious nature. In such cases, doctrines believed for a lifetime suddenly are brought into question and in no way can be removed from consciousness. At other times, God and the saints become the objects of painful obsessions in which various types of blasphemy are involved.

The compulsive reaction is a neurotic symptom related to the obsession and frequently accompanies it. A compulsion is a recurring act that develops as a means of relieving the anxiety of obsessions or phobias. Like the obsession, the compulsion is ego-alien or contrary to the will of the individual. In spite of this, he finds it impossible to resist the need to place the act. Compulsive acts frequently are exaggerations or caricatures of social behavior.

At other times, they are totally irrational and are recognized as such by the patient, who often will complain "I know how crazy this is. I don't want to do it but I feel that I must."

Obsessions of a sexual nature often involve unrelieved feelings of guilt. Individuals frequently develop hand-washing rituals as a means of dealing with this obsession. In order to undo the imagined guilt and to avoid contamination, they compulsively wash their hands again and again—sometimes hundreds of times a day. In extreme cases this practice may produce skin lesions due to excessive immersion or exposure to strong detergents. Attempts on the part of the person to resist the compulsion only lead to further anxiety.

These compulsions sometimes involve self-mutilation. In such cases the individual attempts to punish himself for unrelieved feelings of guilt and inflicts minor or even major excoriations, usually on the skin. Once they are begun, he picks constantly at these lesions, which often become infected. In spite of seeking and receiving medical assistance, he may continue to undo the benefits of the treatment. Other common compulsions involve the need to count and to touch certain objects repeatedly or to isolate things from each other or arrange things and events in certain ways. All of these practices take on the character of rituals to the patient and are fantasied by him as possessing some magical quality.

By and large, the phobias, obsessions and compulsions represent the most complicated neurotic symptoms. They produce a condition in which the individual suffers a paralyzing doubt which pervades his entire personality and ultimately controls his behavior. He looks at everything from all sides and finally is unable to make a decision about anything. Initially, he is embarrassed about his condition and will go to great lengths to disguise the rituals involved. As the condition becomes more severe or chronic, however, the ability to hide the compulsive acting-out becomes progressively more difficult and the person tends to rationalize his problem by offering superficial excuses for his behavior to members of his family and close friends. If treatment does not intervene, the patient ultimately becomes completely dependent upon those around him and expects them to compensate for his difficulty.

Another and very prevalent symptom of the neurotic process is the anxiety reaction. Anxiety, which is present in virtually all neurotic conditions, becomes the predominant symptom. In this reaction, no clear-cut and dominant symptoms, such as obsessions, compulsions or phobias, are adopted by the subject to contain the basic anxiety. He simply experiences the painful presence of anxiety at almost any time and under almost any circumstances. This reaction must be distinguished from reality-based anxiety, which is not a symptom but a normal physiological reaction which places the organism in a state of moderate disequilibrium in order to meet various emergencies. The anxiety felt by people in dangerous occupations creates a state of readiness and heightened awareness to meet the danger. In this sense, it is a normal and healthy reaction. When the stimulus is unreal or imagined, however, or can be attributed to some unconscious conflict, then—and then only—the anxiety reaction should be considered pathological.

In the clinical sense anxiety is looked upon as a psychophysiological reaction that points to a more complex and unconscious conflict which threatens to break through into conscious awareness. In the anxiety reaction the subject typically experiences generalized uneasiness and apprehension. Feelings of doom, of impending danger, of "going to pieces" and of helplessness in the face of these experiences of unknown origin overcome the individual. These subjective states always are accompanied by physical alterations such as increased breathing and heart rate, excessive perspiration, often involving the palms of the hands, increased urination, diarrhea, heightened muscle tone and dilation of the pupils. Casual observation reveals that the latter are, in effect, the physiological reactions to fear. In a sense, there is a direct relationship between fear and anxiety. Once again, however, care must be taken to distinguish the normal from the pathological. An illustration might serve to point up the relationship and the difference between normal fear and pathological anxiety.

If a person who is walking down the street suddenly is confronted by an armed robber he reacts to this external threat with fear. The adrenal gland is stimulated, causing a discharge of adrenalin into the bloodstream which, in turn, produces an acceleration of heart and respiratory rates and increased muscle tension. What is happening, in effect, is that autonomically and involuntarily the body is being prepared for fight or flight. If one substitutes some unconscious conflict threatening to break through to the surface for the armed robber, the stimulus has been internalized. The physical reaction, however, is precisely the same. In this way, anxiety and fear are related. Anxiety is basically a capacity to be afraid. When a person habitually lives under the threat of such a breakthrough he naturally is in a constant state of tension, ready to fight or flee from the impending threat. Since he is unaware of the source of his anxiety, he frequently tends to attach it to something in his immediate environment. His job, his state of life and the people with whom he works or lives are likely targets for indictment as sources of his anxiety.

Obviously, such a state of habitual heightened tension may give rise to a variety of physical complaints, aches and pains. At times, this constant physical readiness for fight or flight may become such an ennervating process that a state of chronic weakness and excessive fatigue, sometimes to the point of exhaustion, sets in. When this physical state becomes the predominant symptom and the person is genuinely distressed and afforded no secondary gain from his physically depleted experience the neurotic reaction known as neurasthenia has replaced the more generalized anxiety reaction.

The conversion reaction is another neurotic reaction that manifests itself in a predominantly physical manner. The patient unconsciously converts his anxiety directly into a physical handicap or functional disability. In this way he is relieved of painfully unpleasant responsibilities and anxiety-provoking situations. At the same time, he enjoys the secondary gain of sympathy from others. For example, he unconsciously and without deliberate intent may develop a convenient paralysis which inhibits him from going to work or performing activities that are threatening to him. He even might become temporarily blind or deaf before personally disturbing objects or persons. These hysterical conversion symptoms are real and the person is in no way malingering about their presence. But they never have any organic foundation and can be removed quite easily under hypnosis, or even transferred from one part of the body to another while under the state of hyper-suggestibility. Hysterical fainting, facial tics and speech disabilities such as stammering and stuttering are probably the most commonly employed of the conversion symptoms. Such people always manifest a remarkable coolness concerning their physical impairment.

The dissociative reaction and the depressive reaction are two additional neurotic symptoms. In the former, certain emotionally charged aspects of the personality are set apart from the totum of conscious living. A person may become unaware of his real identity or even of an entire portion of his life. At other times, these segregated aspects may usurp the field of consciousness to the exclusion of the normative stream of conscious living. In the fugue, for example, a related series of ideas and emotions that are habitually excluded from consciousness can assume the dominant role and be acted out without the conscious self being aware of it. In extreme cases, this dissociation process can be so effective that it results in alternating or multiple personalities with each personality being unaware of the identity of the other. Somnambulism is a prevalent type of dissociative reaction. Like the other forms, it often represents a return to a past place and time where gratification was maximal or an escape from a frustration-filled present. At other times, it may represent an effort to master some unresolved situation in the past or to realize some unfulfilled wish of the present.

In the depressive reaction, the individual is overtaken by an overwhelming discouragement in his battle with internal conflict or is submerged by grief in the face of a real external loss. An overpowering sadness which eventuates in a state of mental and physical retardation is the principal characteristic of this type of reaction. The entire reaction, however, is altogether disproportionate both in time and in intensity to the real situation. The death of a spouse or parent, physical separation from a loved one, a deflating social failure or financial loss may trigger such grief that convulsive methods of therapy sometimes become the only effective remedy. Whenever this condition is left untreated the possibility of suicide as a desperate measure of relief is an ever-present threat.

These symptoms reflect the presence of an inner conflict and, when severe, constitute the illness of neurosis, a particular kind of mental illness which interferes with a person's living and impairs his efficiency and productivity without necessarily disabling him completely or alienating him socially. The frequently employed observation of the parlor-variety psychiatrist that "We're all neurotics" is emphatically erroneous. We are *not* all neurotics. We all do have, from time to time, some expressions of neurotic symptomatology. Everyone, for example, occasionally suffers from conversion reactions—the tension headache and nervous stomach. Everyone has those unexplainable "down in the mouth" days, those unaccountable moods, odd fears and unreasonable worries. But the clinical symptoms of the genuinely neurotic person coalesce into a behavior complex that makes life painful and partially crippled. His symptoms comprise but never resolve the needs that are in conflict. A conscious decision to deny the one and satisfy the other is never reached. The disturbing and ego-alien impulse continues to be repressed, but remains alive and dynamic. In this way, the conflict continues unsettled.

Even more drastic defensive measures may be employed by an individual in his struggle for adjustment to internal and external stresses. When this pattern is followed and behavior becomes markedly out of step with reality, it indicates the illness of psychosis. There are variations of opinion among the professions concerning the precise difference that exists between neuroses and psychoses. Some theorists contend that there is a "qualitative" difference, an "abyss," between normal and neurotic behavior and psychotic symptomatology. This theory is propounded especially by those who adhere to an organic explanation of mental illness. Advocates of the more dynamic or functional explanation do not as a rule subscribe to this contention of qualitative difference. For them, the concept of the defense mechanisms as ineffectual compromise solutions at the expense of personality growth and development extends to both neurotic and psychotic conflict. The difference is considered more "quantitative" in nature, with a more massive break with reality occurring in the psychoses than in the neuroses. In the psychoses the perceptual functions of personality are so radically disturbed that the individual's view of himself and the world beyond him fails to correlate with the objectively real. His problem is fundamentally cognitive in essence, whereas the neurotic's difficulty is essentially emotional. Neuroses, therefore, frequently are referred to as "nervous" disorders and psychoses as "thinking" disorders.

Psychotic Symptomatology

Schizophrenia is by far the most frequent form of the "thinking" disorders. In the early days of research into the nature and causes of mental illness one method of investigation was to trace the course that different disorders followed. By this procedure it was discovered that some disturbances were not truly deteriorating in effect. They appeared to follow a "come and go" pattern in which the persons who were afflicted were assured of a return to reasonably normal functioning after and in between their episodic bouts. Another group of disturbances were found to be essentially deteriorating in character. They exhibited a slow and insidious onset only to terminate in a "burned-out" mental and emotional state. Emil Kraepelin, a pioneer in the classification of mental ills, assigned the designation of dementia praecox, or premature insanity, to this group.

A short time later, another psychiatrist, Eugene Bleuler, discovered in many dementia praecox patients a fundamental peculiarity of thinking and emoting conjoined with a bizarre type of behavior. He also observed that progressive deterioration was not the common fate of all these patients. By de-emphasizing the latter note and stressing the basic thinking and feeling discrepancies he found in these patients, the illness now known as schizophrenia was segregated and specified. Bleuler assigned the name *schizophrenia* to this illness because he detected in the patients a radical "splitting of the mind." To him, the mental functions of these persons—intellection, perception and feeling—remained unintegrated. Bleuler concluded that it was this fundamental disorganization that rendered the schizophrenic's behavior so incomprehensible to the normally adjusted observer.

The dream state of the normal person is perhaps the nearest psychic phenomenon to the schizophrenic's mode of thinking. In general, there is a lowering of sensory thresholds and a suspension of logical thinking and control during sleep. In the dream state, fantasy and emotion take the ascendance and, in the absence of the corrective services of the outer senses, the inner world of personal experience assumes the role of objective reality. Under these conditions, the subject is cut off from the facts of space and time.

In the face of stress, the schizophrenic individual relies heavily on the defense of withdrawal. As he gradually loses interest in the world about him he becomes more and more absorbed in his own inner self. This autism often expresses itself in obsessive preoccupations with specific and frequently abstract problems which serve to reinforce the schizophrenic's escape from the external world. When this self-absorption becomes intense, outer reality can soon lose its corrective influence. Symptoms in the form of dereistic thinking may occur in which only the inner world of thought is employed as a criterion of truth. As the individual's thinking process becomes a law unto itself, unacceptable and even bizarre ideas can replace rational thoughts. As his private world prevails, he forms conclusions about his environment that are comprehensible only to himself. Events receive private interpretations which have no objective foundation. The words and actions of his family, his associates and even of strangers are judged by the schizophrenic as having special reference to himself. These misinterpretations can trigger emotional outbursts of rage and fear that startle and bewilder those about him. When autism is extreme it may lead to delusions or false judgments that someone is out to get him or that some unseen force is at work against him. At other times the person may believe that he has a special mission to fulfill in life or that he is very important or famous.

Because of the natural connection between thought and language, verbal oddities may appear in the schizophrenic. These language peculiarities will vary according to the corresponding thought disturbances. At first there may be only a certain evasiveness about his conversations or a tendency to persist in the same abstract topics and terms. These may appear quite impressive at times, but on close examination they can be seen to be empty and inappropriate to the situation at hand. When the disturbance of thought is more severe the person's sentence sequence may become entirely incomprehensible and sound like a kind of "word salad."

The schizophrenic himself, however, understands the meaning of it all because he alone knows the associations that he has formed in his inner world of thought. In extreme cases he even may put together or abbreviate conventional terms and produce neologisms, which are meaningless to others. On the other hand, the withdrawal may result in such verbal "blocking" that mutism occurs.

A further consequence of this self-absorption is manifested in the person's affective reactions to life. Life and work appear to have lost all interest. Regular activities are reduced to a minimum and he has to be pushed to perform the routine tasks of life. He appears to have gone into a shell and a general apathy pervades his personality. Because of his inner misrepresentations of outer reality his emotional responses at times may be completely inappropriate and incongruous to the external facts. Objectively unaccountable suspiciousness of others, unreasonable anger and sometimes depression to the point of stupor may characterize his behavior. These inappropriate emotional responses may become so bizarre that he laughs at reports that pain others and, inversely, cries when others are brought to laughter.

This fundamental retreat from reality into self-absorption may become so pronounced that the discriminatory or reality-testing ability of ego fades. The person actually may misidentify objects present to his external senses. A coat hanging on a costumer may seem a menacing villain or an umbrella under a person's arm may be seen as a shotgun. The hallucinations of the schizophrenic are even more bizarre. The inner world of schizophrenic fantasy is projected into reality so that voices are heard and objects clearly seen by the schizophrenic in the absence of any objective stimuli. Unreal accusations may be heard and nonexistent lethal "rays" may be experienced.

In spite of all these mental symptoms the physical behavior of the schizophrenic patient is often undisturbed. Here too, however, oddities may be detected in the form of peculiar mannerisms, posturing and impulsive and meaningless gestures. In extremely advanced states of the disorder, there may be uncontrolled and frenzied motor activity. At other times, there may be an amazing condition of physical passivity known as "waxy flexibility," in which a patient can put himself, or be put by another, into incredibly awkward positions and remain in them for hours until someone comes to his assistance. Under hypnosis such a patient may lose these symptoms completely only to resume them immediately after the hypnotic transaction has been terminated.

The symptoms of schizophrenia do not appear in equal measure in every case. Accordingly, it has been traditional to subdivide the general disturbance into four types: simple schizophrenia, hebephrenia, catatonia and paranoid schizophrenia.

Simple schizophrenia is characterized by a slow and insidious onset. The individual gradually grows indifferent to usual interests and limits his life as much as possible. He prefers to stay at home and to himself and refuses to engage in social functions. Apathy and poverty of thought content characterize his personality. Although there are no bizarre hallucinatory or delusional symptoms, his overall behavior is lifeless, inadequate and inappropriate to the demands of everyday living. In general, positive and dynamically healthy attributes of life are replaced by listlessness, detachment and indifference.

The *hebephrenic* reaction is far more disintegrative and this is reflected in its bizarre symptomatology. The person's total behavior may become inappropriate. Although the mood is most often apathetic and detached, infantile giggling and incongruous smiling sometimes occur. In fact, the entire disturbance has been designated as "the insanity of silliness." There may be kinesthetic delusions to the extent that parts of the body are thought to be wasting away or their positions to be shifting. Language disorders amounting to "word salad" and neologisms are common. Hallucinations, usually pleasant in content, may occur. In the final stages of this illness regression to infantile living may become so great that the patient curls up and assumes a fetal posture.

The *catatonic* reaction of schizophrenia predominantly is characterized by a motor symptomatology. The patient exhibits either excessive physical excitation or marked motor retardation. In the former, physical overactivity usually is aimless and unrelated to environmental stimuli. Symptoms may range from facial grimaces and distortions to purposeless movements of the arms, shoulders, hands and legs. Inversely, in the retarded, activities are reduced to a minimum even to the point of stupor. The patient's face may become expressionless. He may become excessively suggestible or even negativistic concerning the wishes of others. A bizarre manifestation of this kind of catatonia has been termed "waxy flexibility." Here the patient cannot will or simply refuses to move himself or change his position and for prolonged periods of time may maintain postures into which he has been passively impressed. Often he cannot communicate with others and when he does he often simply repeats questions placed to him or answers he has already given.

In the *paranoid* reaction of schizophrenia the extreme personality disorganization of the two previous types is absent. Characteristically, these individuals are suspicious, jealous, antagonistic and go about with a chip on the shoulder. Their main defense is projection, which is the ground for the formation of psychotic delusions which are practically always persecutory in nature. The principal feature of these delusions is that they are always poorly rationalized. The paranoid schizophrenic believes that strange things are happening to him or taking place; that he has been victimized and that people are out to get him. These false beliefs very often are coupled with corresponding auditory hallucinations which aggravate the situation and make the patient potentially dangerous. In general, however, this type of symptomatology is restricted to a narrow segment of the patient's life. As a result, his overall functioning remains intact and his socialization is for the most part unhampered.

Many other features of schizophrenic symptomatology are,

in a sense, schizophrenic in themselves. Although the onset of the disorder, for example, is usually gradual, in many cases the illness breaks through quite abruptly. Some of those who are afflicted decline steadily to ultimate deterioration while others may have only one attack, which can be self-limiting. In other instances, the episodes may be spaced with periods of health. Classically, schizophrenia begins to manifest itself sometime after puberty. Deviations may occur, however, with the illness turning up as late as the forties and as early as the first year of life. Therapy that works in one case may not be successful in another. Therefore, recognized treatment methods can be equally effective at different times and with different patients.

Two other main bodies of psychoses round out the functional division of psychoses: *the manic-depressive* disorders and the *paranoiac* reactions. In the former, the psychic life of the individual either runs wild with elation or is flooded with depression. In either reaction the person's contact with his environment is lost. In practically every case, these moods overtake the individual without any observable or reasonable stimulus in his public life. In the case of depression, the person simply slips into a state of overwhelming sadness. His spirit can sink to such depths that both mental and motor activity come to a standstill. Under such emotional sadness, suicide quite frequently becomes the individual's only solution. Conversely, a person may reach such heights of elation that all control over activity is lost. For no apparent reason he approaches life as though it were going out of style. He talks excessively, which is a reflection of a wild and uncontrollable "flight of ideas." Motor activity and other physical involvements may become so intense that the only way to feed such a person is to serve him on the run. Often, his only salvation is utter exhaustion. If this fails, death may result. Sometimes the two phases of depression and elation occur in succession. The disorder then is referred to as circular in nature.

In the psychotic paranoiac reaction the individual retains his overall reality orientation except for a single well-ordered delusional system concerning some segment of his life. As a result of some actual happening that he misinterprets, he draws a series of logical conclusions which evolve until a practical but erroneous idea dominates his mind. In this way, he may live under the false belief that he is being unjustly persecuted or victimized. Those so afflicted often engage in a certain legal compulsivity or "court-hopping" behavior. They seem to be forever leveling charges against others or attempting to prove their case even though it has been overruled by juridical decision. They are the letter writers, the complainers, the compulsive critics of society. Their delusional system sometimes assumes a more positive but still bizarre function. When this happens they appear as the proclaimers of a mission especially entrusted to them or as "inventors" who believe their ideas eventually will revolutionize the time. Of the four types, the latter is the least frequent and almost always manifests itself in persons of high intelligence. The key to the disorder is always the original premise, which is out of touch with the facts as they objectively existed.

Personality Disorders

Considered in themselves, alcoholism, drug addiction, antisocial behavior, sexual deviation and various other personal and social inadequacies do not necessarily reflect any of the symptoms characteristic of the neuroses or psychoses. As a consequence, these maladjustments frequently are grouped under the heading of "personality or character disorders." This general heading has been adopted because these disturbances seem to stem from the very structure of the individual's personality. The problem is definitely not the result of an overdevelopment of controlling substructures and mechanisms. Rather, it is due to an underdevelopment or deficiency in these critical areas of personality. The confidence man or professional forger, for example, can swindle and steal from the innocent and never experience any remorse. If he is apprehended by the law and punished for his crimes he may immediately revert to his antisocial practices on his return to society. The fundamental problem, and that of the other disturbances just mentioned, is a structural flaw or deficiency in character and personality. To a great extent this is simply the way these people are, whether through nature or nurture.

Conclusion

A survey of this type is admittedly quite schematic and by no means exhaustive. Its objective is to point up the significant characteristics of the major ills of the mind and to indicate the principal indices of their presence. Proficiency in the art of diagnosing these emotional states is achieved only after long years of specialized training and practical experience. The reading of one book, or even a few books, does not make one a diagnostician nor license him to embark on a semiprofessional career of mind healing. It may, however, provide a degree of knowledge that will facilitate the detection of the actual existence of emotional illness or the possibility of it in a particular instance. In every such case, detection of the illness remains the prime requisite in the entire process of effective recovery. Because of the many advances that modern research has made in determining the nature and treatment of these psychic problems this hope of recovery is now within the reach of even the most seriously disturbed. The symptoms of the emotionally ill signal the desperate need for this new experience of hope; detection offers the possibility of its attainment.

For Further Reference

Arieti, Silvano, ed. *American Handbook of Psychiatry*. Vol. 1. New York: Basic Books, 1959.

Noyes, Arthur P., and Kolb, Lawrence C. *Modern Clinical Psychiatry*. Philadelphia: W. B. Saunders Co., 1963.

Overholser, Winfred, and Richmond, Winifred V. *Handbook of Psychiatry*. Philadelphia: J. B. Lippincott Co., 1947.

Strecker, Edward A. *Fundamentals of Psychiatry*. Philadelphia: J. B. Lippincott Co., 1944.

6 Interviewing

A theoretical discussion of symptoms easily might lead one to the misconception that they are always and everywhere obviously identifiable. The fact is that they are more frequently obscure and can be known in their total significance only when the person chooses to reveal them. This revelation occurs most meaningfully in the context of a personal meeting or what is technically termed an interview with a professional whom the troubled individual has approached for help.[1]

The interview is essentially a free-flowing exchange between the client and the therapist for the purpose of obtaining information about a person's problem. It is a dialogue in which both participants attempt to discover symptoms and assess their significance in relation to a specific mental illness. It is most certainly not a question and answer period, although the nature of the interview does not exclude questions which easily stimulate a relevant response. The communication that is sought often is achieved not only by what the person does say, but more especially by what he seeks to conceal and the manner in which both positive and negative reactions are given.

The primary matter to be discussed is what the person himself readily volunteers—not because it is always the essence of his problem but because it constitutes a point of departure and, not infrequently, provides the client with a sense of confidence in the helper which enables him to reveal more and more of his problem and its severity. Accordingly, it is often necessary for the therapist to be satisfied with meager, casual and apparently unrelated remarks before this type of confidence is reached.

In securing this optimal relationship, the helper who has been sought out is the crucial figure. His entire personality and attitude toward the troubled person determines the ultimate outcome of the meeting. In the final analysis what the person is willing to tell and what steps he is willing to take in solving his problem depends upon this fundamental relationship of the helper and client. The significance of this intimate personal relationship cannot be emphasized too strongly. In an extraordinarily large number of cases both diagnosis and treatment hinge upon it. Failure in this relatively simple yet essential operation accounts for much ineffectiveness in the care of patients. The secret of success in the care *of* any troubled person is in caring *for* the person.

The professional whose assistance has been sought must be keenly aware of the psychological dynamics beneath such an intimate relationship. The individual who comes with a problem does so because he trusts and believes in this other human being. Invariably, this belief and confidence is amazingly uncritical, even naive. Although the person may know very little about the professional himself and his skill in handling this precise problem, he regards him as all-wise and virtually infallible. Even the highly intelligent and sophisticated become surprisingly docile and trusting in this regard. The first response of the therapist to such implicit faith should be that of a "best friend." He should be wholeheartedly prompted to genuine concern for a human being who is in need and have a sincere interest in his problem in its entirety.

In this role, the interviewer-therapist must possess a patience and generosity of self and time surpassing that of mere friends. Where other friends sympathize with the person in his troubled condition, the wise and true friend is empathic to the entire situation. He enjoys and communicates the willingness to understand;

even when he cannot, he makes the effort to do so. His acceptance of the person is complete, though in the course of time he may hear things he himself does not approve. As "best friend," the good interviewer-therapist makes certain he remains detached from emotional involvement in the problem and its account in a way that family and other friends are not apt to do. His approach to the problem is different also in that it is free from the impulse to judge, advise and apply immediate remedies. This quality is rooted in his deeper freedom from prejudice, bias and legalism. The satisfaction of his own personal needs is placed second to the ultimate good of the person making the effort to unravel a difficulty.

The helper also must be keenly sensitive to the predominant emotion of fear that so often adds to the patient's discomfort at the initial interview. Very often this fear is successfully concealed beneath a facade of bravado, poise and sophistication. At other times it is pitifully obvious. Such fear may have a wide range of origins. It may be fear of the helper himself, of what he will think and how he will react. Will he be understanding and easy to talk to or will he be stern, sarcastic and threatening? It may be fear that his problem is insoluble or that its solution will be beyond his present powers of acceptance and endurance. It may be fear of disclosure of previously concealed and shameful thoughts, actions and traits of character or fear of being branded a weakling and coward in the face of a problem. Whatever its origin, such fear is real and the good therapist moves rapidly to dissipate this obstacle to effective communication. He does this at the very outset by his own self-composure and professional yet genuinely friendly manner. The interviewer-therapist must ask himself continually: "How would I feel if I were in this person's shoes at this time? How would I feel if I were treated in an offhanded and brusk manner?" Such self-questioning provides the stimulus both for an initial empathy for the client's difficult circumstances and for the verbal reassurance of readiness to understand and help.

Before all else, the one who is approached for professional assistance and advice must be attuned to the basic dynamics of how he, as an interviewer and helper, appears to and influences the client. As a result of the conditioning process that has taken place within the patient because of his earlier relations with significant authority figures, especially his parents, the interviewer is subsumed by the client under the parental image. By this phenomenon of transference the helper becomes a surrogate for previously known authority figures and automatically is invested with the emotional characteristics that the client associates with the original parties. This results in a certain degree of role distortion whereby the client views and relates to the professional helper as once he regarded and related to his own parents. The client's misperception also leads to a projection of the expected responses and reactions of his own parents onto the therapist. In other words, the client behaves more or less as though the therapist were the duplicate of his parents.

The interviewer-therapist always must be aware of and keenly appreciate the potentialities inherent in this phenomenon. This will enable him to realize that in the initial meeting the person is not truly himself and will help him to avoid premature and faulty categorizations of the person. If the person is overly frightened, tearful and self-effacing; if he is excessively dependent, solicitous of near-magical assurance and needful of approval and acceptance from the outset or if he appears suspicious, cautious, seductive and bribing of special concern, the wise helper will assess these and similar characteristics impersonally and objectively as indices of how this individual perceived and related on previous occasions to parents and other persons of importance in his life. This affords the interviewer the first ingredients of a personality impression and immediately signals the presence of basic needs that must be met if the person is to tell his story without obstruction.

Over and above this, the good interviewer must be conscious of how he himself, under the influence of this unconscious phenomenon, affects the patient's behavior. By partially duplicating these authority figures he triggers previously ingrained reflexes of a child-parental or subject-authority nature. In this way the personality and whole approach of the helper may partly or even totally jar that portion of the cilent's mind that views the therapist as an expert and helpful friend to whom he should communicate his story. Everything from physical appearance, age, simplicity or sophistication of manner to a smiling, placid or stern countenance will affect the person's decision as to what is safe and useful to tell at this particular time. The more the interviewer reminds the patient of earlier authority figures, the greater the potential of role misperception.

The client's conception of the authority role of the therapist will greatly condition his initial reactions and behavior. He cannot help but feel some degree of uneasiness and lowliness before the authority role of the interviewer who is invested by his unconscious mind with power to weigh and judge, recommend drastic measures and execute painful decisions. Here, certainly, the therapist is subsumed under the father image, which for the client may mean tyrant, policeman, judge, teacher or protector. Indeed, all aspects of the therapist's behavior evoke these and related experiences borne in the client's unconscious since early days. If the interviewer's manner is brusk and conveys annoyance, if he appears too busy or anxious to get on with some other business or seems impatient and pressures with questions, these provide the stimulus to evoke earlier built-in, hampering and conditioned reflexes.

The interviewer-therapist must have a serious regard for himself and the role he plays in the patient-therapist relationship. He must be aware of what he himself brings to the interview. In each personal meeting and plea for help the client responds to everything the interviewer does and says but above all to everything the interviewer is. The troubled individual will talk and unburden himself according to his unconscious expectations of how the therapist will be but eventually according to how the therapist concretely is. Much of the success of the interview and subsequent meetings in search of a solution rests in the person of the helper. It is essential, then, that the interviewer from the very outset present those personal qualities of understanding and professional competency that alone can dissipate the interfering aspects of the client's fantasied expectations and, at the same time, sustain his initial inclination to seek help. In these two attributes—genuine concern and humble competency—the troubled person finds the motivation necessary to disclose his story and the assurance that he is telling it to someone who has more to offer than can be found in ordinary social circles.

The interview itself must proceed along a definite path if it is to succeed as a meaningful technique. Its entire success ultimately depends upon the interviewer's ability to help the person to talk freely and to channel his thinking and expression into topics that will reveal the nature of his trouble and contribute to the formulation of an evaluative judgment.

From the start, the interviewer manages and directs the entire process. It is he who initiates the interview by making those overtures of friendliness and respect that are necessary to make the client as relaxed and comfortable as possible. Unless the client himself begins to relate his story, the interviewer should tactfully start him off by making some reference to the purpose of his coming and by encouraging him to talk about his difficulty in his own words.

Since the interview is not designed to subject the person to a painful ordeal, the interviewer should be especially sensitive to the client's anxiety level in these early moments. Some anxiety is inevitable and when moderate should simply be observed and studied by the therapist. This can afford him an index to the patient's homeostatic adaptive powers in a difficult situation and at the same time reveal the nervous mannerisms and gesticulations the client unconsciously employs when under stress. During subsequent phases of the interview the appearance of these same nervous habits can be a clue to the therapist that the topic under consideration is touching a "nerve" in the person's psychic life.

When anxiety is severe, however, it must be reduced to a minimum. Otherwise it will only sabotage the free flow of communication which is so necessary. To eliminate this obstruction the interviewer may simply say: "You appear to be very upset. Is it that you are afraid of me and how I will react to what you want to tell me? If so, try to remember that we are here to work together and try to find some solution to your problem. So, try to be more at ease and tell me what your difficulties are." Remarks to this effect not only stimulate confidence but, more important, deflect the client's anxiety away from the therapist and toward those other persons and events that have driven him to seek help.

Once these initial jitters have been overcome, the interviewer must keep every avenue of communication open and relevant. In his approach to a physical disorder the medical practitioner has at his disposal X-rays, fluoroscopes, blood pressure indicators and a variety of other instruments which give an immediate entree into and revelation of the inner disposition of the organism. Psychic interiority and its status are not so accessible. Only the individual's own revelation through verbal and nonverbal communication can convey what is going on within these hidden and private precincts. Consequently, the expert interviewer must be a master at being a good listener.

Within the framework of the interview, however, being a good listener does not imply passive receptivity. The therapist should not resemble an eternally patient father in his rocking chair or the man whose shoulder provides a crying post for anyone with a problem. His role involves a very active and definite kind of involvement. Through a genuinely dynamic interest and personal concern for the entire situation, the interviewer provides a feedback of energy which stimulates the narrator to continue in his monopoly of a dialogue that flows to the design of the interviewer. The therapist knows precisely what he must know and subtly but skillfully draws this information into the open.

The interviewer's techniques range all the way from common sense to professional craftiness. No one, for example, wants to talk to a bored audience or a disinterested party. The situation becomes even more difficult when the one who must do the talking is not too sure himself what he should tell, yet knows that his listener is looking for something definite. The interviewer always must be an interested listener. By appropriate facial expressions and such simple gestures as nodding his head and leaning forward on hearing particular points of importance he both motivates the person by signaling his approval of the account and prompts a more detailed description of special topics. At the same time he encourages and guides the whole narration by verbally registering his interest at precisely chosen moments through such simple statements as "I see" or "I understand."

The interviewer not only knows how to stimulate and maneuver the client's thoughts and expressions, but also is adept at handling pauses and periods of silence. By careful scrutiny of the client's overall behavior and the particular topic he was discussing and its special significance to him, the skilled interviewer knows when to keep quiet and when to intercede. When such pauses are obviously efforts at thought-reorganization or recall he simply maintains the silence and gives the person the time he needs. When the pause is pronounced and therefore signals fatigue, indecision as to whether to continue, defensive blocking or the surging of anxiety, the good interviewer answers the need by terminating the silence. Even then his words are few and reassuring: "Take your time, you have been doing fine. Just try to continue to tell me about these things as you have been doing."

The skilled interviewer aims at keeping his client in a talkative mood and at keeping quiet himself. It is perhaps his greatest test of patience and self-control during the interview. The natural inclination during the course of any dialogue is to converse verbally with the other party. The unique character of the interview forbids such participation since the interview is not a mutual sharing of views and opinions. This spontaneous temptation to interrupt may stem from a variety of origins within the interviewer. If, for example, the client adverts to an experience that touches upon the interviewer's personal experience the natural impulse is to interrupt and say "I know what you mean. Take my mother-in-law, for instance. . . ."

The same natural urge may arise from personal curiosities and interests. When the client adverts in passing to his or her sexual life the immediate interior response of the interviewer may be "I wonder what that was all about." In the best interest of the patient, the good interviewer will always hold such curiosities in check.

Perhaps the greatest tempter of all is the impulse to advise and correct. At times this impulse is triggered by the constructive wish to point out and save the person from future harm. At other times it is rooted in the interviewer's conscious need to justify his own conscience in the face of what he hears. Occasionally, it may happen that the impulse to interrupt and immediately admonish has its origin in unconscious repressions within the interviewer which are threatened by the detailed account. Whatever its source, the temptation to interrupt is controlled by the expert interviewer. His sole purpose is not his own good but the good of his client. He knows that good cannot be attained at this time except through a complete ventilation of the client's troubles. He also knows that listening quietly to the entire account in no way implies approval of what he hears or laxity in his own attitude.

It must not be concluded that the interviewer never exercises a direct and more open kind of control. His covert signs of special interest and passing words of reassurance can go just so far. At times his guidance and prompting must become quite explicit. When crucial areas of trouble are merely adverted to or are about to be dropped from the dialogue by the patient he always asserts his need to learn more about these subjects. He encouragingly but explicitly asks the person to tell him more. "Go on," he might say. "You are doing fine but tell me more about this matter."

This kind of guidance usually is provided through the art of questioning. It is an art because even though the question itself is quite simple it leads the person comfortably to an elaboration of even delicate and sensitive areas of his life. The questions are never harsh or offensive. This serves no purpose except to unnerve the person and lessen his confidence in the therapist. In addition, the questions are practically always "open" rather than "closed." They demand an elaboration rather than a categorical yes or no response. Instead of asking "Are you happily married?," he might ask "Could you tell me in your own words some things about your relationship with your wife and family?" As often as possible, the expert inquirer employs the client's own words in the formulation of a question. He will say, for example, "A few moments ago you said 'my mother-in-law has caused us a great deal of trouble.' Could you give me some examples of the kind of trouble she has caused you?" In this way he keeps the patient from interpreting the question as an intrusion, since he himself brought the matter into question.

Above all, the expert investigator is a master at timing his questions. He temporarily postpones delicate and sensitive topics until he is certain that the client has achieved sufficient confidence and assurance to talk freely and safely about virtually anything. This is especially true of matters that relate to the sexual life of the individual. Depending upon the sensitivities of the person, questions of this nature are delayed and even postponed to a later meeting. When they are presented they usually are embedded in less painful questions or prefaced by understanding and reassuring remarks. Instead of bluntly asking "How is your sex life?" the interviewer might say "Many people frequently have difficulties in the sexual sphere. It can be a troublesome area of life for almost anyone. I certainly understand how trying such problems can be." Sometimes a few remarks like these are enough to encourage the person to talk freely. When they are not, the interrogator can simply add "Before, you mentioned some difficulties of your own. Could you give me some ideas about these troubles?"

The interviewer never assumes the role of a district attorney, nor is the interview ever turned into a courtroom drama. He is careful, however, not to confuse tact and thoughtfulness with timidity. Matters that must be investigated and disclosed for the patient's ultimate good are always faced and approached—but in a manner that is both considerate and obviously constructive.

Verbal communication, however, is only one way to tell a story. People are constantly telling us things in many other ways. The skilled interviewer is ever observant of such physical occurrences as trembling, perspiring, flushing, rapid breathing and eye expansions. This type of "organ language" tells him about the anxiety spots in the person's life and the emotional tone that surrounds certain topics in the person's mind. In the same way, smiles and grimaces and tears, pounding and finger-pointing, head-shaking and shoulder-shrugging, are all indices of the importance that certain topics have for the individual.

The interviewer should never panic in the face of emotional

displays nor cut them off prematurely in the name of compassion. By permitting them he gives the patient both the opportunity to relieve himself of much pent-up tension and the chance to tell both himself and the therapist how seriously he has been affected by the whole problem. Since such open displays are rarely tolerated in our culture, the therapist's acceptance of them also solidifies the bond of understanding which is so necessary to the patient-therapist relationship.

During these moments of emotional expression the interviewer studies them in kind along with their perceptual and ideational counterparts and the persons and events intimately associated with them. Occasionally, when he detects in the person's account a highly charged but deeply repressed emotional conflict, he may prudently induce an affective discharge in order to verify his suspicion and test the conflict's severity. Here again, he subtly channels the client's thoughts and expressions into the pertinent area. He could say, for example, "You seem to have had quite a bit of sorrow during your married life. Could you tell me something about this? I know it might be a sensitive and painful subject but I am sure it will help if you talk about it." Because of such understanding reassurance the client will feel safe not only to reveal any sorrows he might be harboring but also to express those emotions he might otherwise suppress.

Through the employment of techniques such as these and by taking careful stock of all that he hears and sees, the interviewer gradually forms an impression of the total situation. He knows beforehand precisely what factors he is looking for and this governs both his management of the interview and the formulation of a final critical judgment. An exposition of his client's symptoms is an essential part of the overall information he seeks, but because he appreciates their phenomenal nature he is interested in more than the mere description and enumeration of them. Their duration and intensity and their onset and progress are the features he seeks to discover and to weigh.

His primary concern is with the profound value of the human person beneath these surface behaviors and the significance of these phenomena in terms of his interior functioning and daily living. Consequently, the interviewer aims at an entrance into the interior life of the person, his personal world of unshared experience. He may, for example, ask himself the question "How is this person living with himself? Is he confused, frightened, overwhelmed, disorganized, anxiety-ridden, depressed, defeated? What are his vulnerabilities and strengths and how does he meet and utilize these? What are his tension zones and how does he cope with them? Are his defenses effective or collapsing? Are they realistic or distorting?"

The interviewer also wants to know the world of persons and events in which the person currently circulates. What are the immediate environmental demands and pressures that he experiences and how weighty and powerful are they? Who are the significant people in his life and are these relationships peaceful or stormy? Here, particularly, the emotions become a prime target of his entire impressionistic search. From the observation and study of their nature and intensity the interviewer penetrates into the perceptual and ideational life of the person. He strives to learn of his world-view, of how he sees and evaluates his outer personal and impersonal environment.

Since every man's life is a continuum and the present a mere child of the past, the interviewer aims at more than an account of recent history and present problems. He also wants to know something of the remote past and those other persons and events that have contributed significantly as predisposing factors to the person's present status. How were his childhood days? How did his parents relate to him? Did he feel loved or rejected? The interviewer works toward a mental absorption of the person in his entirety. By entering into his inner life and history and carefully noting the topics chronicled by the patient he mentally sketches a dynamic portrait of this person and his relations to the world about him.

With the aid of this comprehensive conception the interviewer judges the nature and severity of this person's problem and symptoms, the quantity of his ego-strength and the quality of his adaptive defenses to these stresses and strains and the degree to which all these are interfering with his overall functioning. In the final analysis, the ultimate goal of the entire interviewing process is to gather the amount and quality of data that is necessary to formulate a professional judgment about the person's present status and future needs. At the very least, the meaningful interview should indicate the necessity of referral to an appropriate kind of therapy or the possibility of continued personal contact with someone who can effectively help the person discover himself.

Sometimes one interview is sufficient to realize this goal. Quite frequently more than one meeting is required. When such a judgment cannot be reached with reasonable accuracy and certainty the interview should be suspended and more time assigned for further open-minded investigation. Justice to the troubled individual demands this additional time and effort. Many problems are diagnosed incorrectly and handled imprudently because of hasty judgments and stereotyped attitudes. Accordingly, the investigator must exercise a professionalism that insures an objective appraisal of the reported complaints and behavior. When certain dispositions and kinds of behavior are detected there is a natural temptation to pigeonhole a person immediately and instantly conclude what his trouble is. In the interviewing situation tentative hypotheses certainly must be raised and tested. The helper who is truly worthy of that title, however, never permits himself to become so prejudiced that he attends only to those aspects of the report that fit into his preconceived notions and ignores those details that do not.

When a decision of referral has been prudently reached the next task for the interviewer is to communicate this to the client. Whatever its nature—whether it be referral to a clinic, to a psychiatrist, psychologist, another clergyman or counselor—this decision must be announced with due regard for its possible implications to the patient. A person who is already troubled and anxious naturally will suspect the worst on receiving such news. Consequently, it must never be conveyed in a severe and frightening manner. Since the person has implicit faith in the helper whom he has sought out, he will automatically cling to whatever he hears and however he hears it. He will review it over and over again, draw all sorts of conclusions from it and magnify it painfully beyond its proper proportions. This final decision, then, always must be presented in a way that reveals an understanding of the problem and fosters an optimism for the future.

It is the whole person who must be cared for and not simply the problem. If referral to another is the outcome, the willing pledge of continued personal support in the future can go far in reinforcing the confidence so necessary for a successful adjustment. The bond of friendship that is at the core of every patient-therapist relationship demands this kind of offering in the interest of the one who is in trouble. Ultimately, the goal of anyone who would aspire to help another human with a problem is the humble realization of the motto "To cure sometimes, to relieve often, to comfort always."

For Further Reference

Cavanagh, John R. *Fundamental Pastoral Counseling.* Milwaukee: Bruce Publishing Co., 1962.

Curran, Charles A. *Counseling in Catholic Life and Education.* New York: Macmillan Co., 1952.

Hiltner, Seward. *Pastoral Counseling.* Nashville: Abingdon Press, 1949.

Tolbert, E. L. *Introduction to Counseling.* New York: McGraw-Hill Book Co., 1959.

Wise, Carroll A. *Pastoral Counseling: Its Theory and Practice.* New York: Harper & Brothers, 1951.

7 Cautions

Compassion for the sufferings of other people is a good quality in a human being, not a sign of weakness. It is evidence of presence and openness which are genuine marks of humanity. It is the quality that tells the troubled person that there is someone who cares. This in itself has the power to dissipate much of the aloneness and isolation that accompanies every kind of personal problem. True compassion has an otherness about it which partakes of the true significance of community. In the interest of the well-being of the other, this quality moves a person to offer himself and to do what he can, but always within the limits of his own potential. He is aware of and accepts the boundaries of his competency and this measures the degree of service he offers. Nor is he jealous or critical of what others can offer. It is always the welfare of the one who is in need that governs his concern. Above all, he is willing to listen and to learn concerning how he may be able to administer more effectively to the needs of others.

The fields of psychiatry and psychology obviously have taught us much about the inner workings of man's mind and have contributed greatly to our understanding of human problems. Findings have been shared by these disciplines in a genuine effort to advance the cause of mental health in the world. This knowledge, however, must be employed in a prudent and controlled manner. Certain practical guidelines to governing the use of this type of information will insure that the maximum benefit is derived from it.

One important caution deals with the question of language and labeling. More than forty years ago Dr. Karl Menninger wrote: "The greatest foes of psychoanalysis have been its misguided friends. It has suffered at the hands of amateurs who think or pretend that they understand it well enough to apply its principles. Human behavior is a matter of common interest and therefore verbalisms from psychoanalytic literature have been eagerly pressed into public service. Certain Freudian phrases have, in fact, grown out of all proportion to vocabulary. They are required to hold more meaning than is possible. Their dramatic significance has become inflated far beyond their dictionary proportion and Freudian words taken in this way are dangerous. They are apt to become emotional and ethical dynamite."[1] If the situation obtained then, it is even more true today. Children who are angry with each other have stopped shouting "Stinky!" and "Fatty!" and substituted "Psychopath!" and "Retard!" People with the most superficial knowledge of psychodynamics go about openly calling attention to each other's anxieties, compulsions or repressed hostilities. They include as symptoms of the neurotic process all sorts of behavior that is not, and at times even appear to make unhappiness a symptom of serious emotional disturbance. In such circumstances, the disciplines of psychiatry and psychology suffer a serious loss of control.

Perhaps the most significant problem involved in labeling people or attributing to them a neurotic symptom is that it creates the opportunity for the person to rationalize his behavior. Once a label is attached, the individual tends to perpetuate the behavior and call attention to the fact that it is the result of his repressed hostility or pent-up libido—or, in the current vernacular, one of his hang-ups. Attaching labels also may lead to the person feeling that he has been relieved of all responsibility for his own behavior; to the expectation that the rest of the world should tolerate and even make allowances for his rude or otherwise outrageous actions. In this way individuals can use psychiatric terminology to exploit their own dependency needs and have the rest of the world compensate for them.

Closely related to this practice is the equally unfortunate tendency in some untrained people to develop a fascination for psychiatric techniques and to engage in a somewhat ruthless pursuit of pathology. They gain a superficial knowledge of psychodynamics and see pathology where it does not really exist. As has been stated earlier, almost all neurotic symptoms are caricatures or exaggerations of otherwise normal behavior. When the fascination of psychodynamics becomes an end in itself even normal behavior tends to be regarded as pathological, which can create a dangerous situation.

Although a knowledge of psychodynamics would appear to be indispensable to the clergyman, such knowledge should not be interpreted as a license to root about clumsily in the unconscious of those seeking help. Such knowledge is acquired with relative ease but it does not endow the individual with the skills of therapy, which can be developed only through long periods of formal training.

Many who dabble in psychopathology make the serious mistake of erroneously assuming that because they may be able to see behind the behavior of a troubled individual the person himself should be capable of knowing and accepting the explanation of that behavior. If this assumption were true, the person would never have had to assume the symptom in the first place. One of the reasons why training in the science of professional psychotherapy takes what appears to be an inordinate amount of time is the need for the therapist to develop a capacity to evaluate the ego-strength of the patient. Paradoxically, the most important knowledge to be gained in psychotherapy is the knowledge of when *not* to treat a troubled person.

As an example, there is the psychoanalytical construct that latent, repressed homosexual drives underlie paranoid projections and even form the basis of paranoid schizophrenia.[2] If the professional therapist discovers that this theoretical explanation is profoundly at work in a particular patient he does not immediately and indiscriminately uncover this situation. Rather, he carefully assesses the individual's ego-strength and judges its sufficiency to recognize this and to explore its unconscious content. He does this because he realizes that without the needed ego-strength the patient could be destroyed. More important, perhaps, is the fact that it is altogether possible to treat the individual without necessarily confronting him with such repressed material. This, however, is the talent of the professional and the skill of therapy. In the efforts of the untrained, such a venture can result only in the kind of cure that is worse than the disease. In this connection, it is again necessary to point out the temptation, at times almost irresistible, to remove a symptom merely because it is so obvious. As has been noted repeatedly, symptoms have meaning and until the meaning is fully understood the symptom should not be removed. To do so would create a vacuum and thereby intensify the insecurity of the person. The most serious threat is the possibility of the person selecting another symptom far worse than the one just removed. It is also important to understand that there is a relationship between neurotic symptoms and overt psychosis. This is perhaps best understood through a concrete illustration.

A Marine Corps drill sergeant who had received an allotment check for his wife for several years after her death failed to notify the paymaster. The error eventually was discovered but his exemplary record saved him from court-martial. Instead, repayment was made to the government on the basis of a garnishee against his salary. Consciously, he accepted this decision but unconsciously he saw it as an injustice and concluded that if he were not to be paid then he would not work. As a consequence, he suddenly developed an hysterical aphonia and his case was diagnosed as completely emotional in nature since no physical basis for the paralysis could be determined. Psychiatric care ensued and an accurate diagnosis was made by an astute intern. Unfortunately, because of his lack of experience the intern was unable to measure the importance of the illness to the sergeant who was using it to explain his unconscious rejection of the imagined injustice. The intern's use of hypnosis and posthypnotic suggestion removed the symptom and the sergeant's speech became normal. At the unconscious level, however, this intrusion was intolerable because the sergeant immediately concluded that nothing had been wrong with him and that all his fellow Marines would regard him as a "goof-off." Overwhelmed with guilt and convinced that he had been unmasked as a charlatan, he experienced within six hours a complete break with reality in the form of a psychotic episode. Delusions, hallucinations and disturbed conduct forced his restriction to a psychiatric ward. Medication gradually brought him back in contact and after re-hypnosis he was given back his symptom, which eliminated the psychosis. After a long period in psychotherapy he was permitted an insight into his illness at which time he discarded the symptom voluntarily.

It is cardinal principle that illness and symptoms must be respected. Supplementary to this principle, it can be said that there are few psychiatric emergencies. Certainly, an emergency situation exists whenever a person is imminently suicidal or otherwise constitutes a danger to himself or to others. Other persons, however, even though they have lived uncomfortably for quite a period of time, need not be treated and cured within twenty-four hours. While early referral is desirable, panic should not be the rule. Some estimates indicate that more than fifty percent of all those who are referred to psychiatrists are not accepted for therapy. Either they are not suitably motivated or their symptoms, for one reason or another, do not make referral desirable or useful. As a general rule, unless the symptoms are interfering with the person's overall functioning and constitute an impediment in his private, social or family life, psychiatric intervention is rarely indicated. When functioning is disrupted, however, the degree of disruption should be the criterion in dictating the urgency of referral. When a person is hallucinated or delusional, immediate referral is the only sensible course. In lesser situations, the best course to follow is to listen attentively but objectively to the story as it unfolds. Strictly speaking, no general rule can be set down regarding individual referrals since they are so highly specific in nature. When one recognizes that he is reaching the limits of his competence and the need for more specialized help is evident then the correct course is to begin motivating the person to seek psychiatric assistance.

The implication behind these remarks is not that the psychiatrist or psychologist is the only one capable of helping the emotionally troubled person. The mass of help for those in the general population who are troubled must come from those other professions that are dedicated to the personal and social welfare of men. These practical suggestions should not lead one to the belief that he must assume so nondirective a role that he fails entirely in providing assistance to the troubled individual. There seems to be a good deal of misunderstanding among some counselors and advisers trained below the level of clinical competence regarding the whole topic of nondirective therapy. All therapy, by definition, must be directive. If the therapist, for example, has no goals toward which he leads his client, however subtly, he really has no excuse for being involved in the first place. Any idea that leads to a totally passive listening in the expectation that after the client has talked long enough he will have cured himself is part of the considerable mythology that has grown up around the subject of mind-healing.

The all-important role of empathy cannot be stressed too strongly. Empathy is quite distinct in both nature and effect from sympathy. Simply feeling sorry for persons in trouble really does not constructively help them, and in some instances it actually may increase their difficulty. Merely to sympathize and to engage solely in environmental manipulation in order to achieve an instantaneous solution is not very effective in dealing with emotional problems. To do so essentially is to identify wholly with the person, which makes an objective evaluation of the problem virtually impossible and renders the counselor impotent. On the other hand, complete objectivity, or the impression of it, must be equally avoided. Such a stance will only be interpreted by the troubled individual as indifference and will inhibit the development of the effective relationship basic to therapy. In other words, the middle course of empathy must be achieved, the capacity to understand, and more importantly, to accept the problem precisely as it is without feeling personally responsible for it. Through empathy one may know about a person's feeling in a vicarious way without necessarily going through or having gone through the experience itself. It is this capacity to accept the human person and to understand his plight that seals the therapeutic relationship. It is fundamentally a gift, and when fully developed it is the key to successful counseling.

PART TWO

8 Alcoholism

"Would ya' like another drink? Aw, come on, just one for the road. . . ."

These and similar exhortations have become so commonplace in American society that it is estimated they are among the first words heard by the child learning to speak. What these words imply, however exaggerated the extension of the reference, is that the average American citizen is becoming more and more attuned to the use of alcohol. Almost inevitably a tremendous increase in the number of those afflicted with the illness known as alcoholism has resulted.

What is alcoholism? There are many definitions but none is completely satisfactory. There is always an "X-factor" that cannot easily be identified since its outward manifestation varies with the individual. Some of the definitions that have been proposed are descriptive, some quasi-scientific, some almost romantic. All contain the germ of an idea and the sampling that follows is listed so that common elements may be extracted in order to provide a working definition, if not one that will satisfy completely.

The National Council on Alcoholism states: "Alcoholism is a complex disease, having psychological, physiological and sociological implications."

The Yale Center of Alcoholism Studies says: "Alcoholism is drinking to escape problems created by drinking."

The American Medical Association's Archives of Industrial Health asserts: "Alcoholism is reached when certain individuals stop bragging about how much they can drink, and begin to lie about how much they are drinking."

Mark Keller, managing editor of the *Quarterly Journal of Alcoholic Studies,* points out: "Alcoholism is a chronic behavioral disorder manifested by repeated drinking of alcoholic beverages in excess of the dietary and social usage of the community and to the extent that it interferes with the drinker's health or his social and economic functioning."

Giorgio Loglio, a New York physiologist, states: "Alcoholism represents the abnormal survival in adulthood of a need for the infantile normal experience of unitary pleasure of mind and body. The alcoholic rediscovers this experience in the course of intoxication. He cannot resist its gratification–however illusory or temporary it turns out to be."

From Skid Row come these words of an alcoholic in a medical interview: "One drink is too many. Twenty are not enough."

Alcoholics Anonymous tells us: "It is an obsession of the mind coupled with an allergy of the body."

The World Health Organization: "One becomes an alcoholic when he begins to become concerned about how activities may interfere with his drinking instead of how drink may interfere with his activities."

A Japanese proverb says: "First the man takes a drink; then the drink takes a drink; then the drink takes a man."

Father Ralph A. Pfau, a recovered alcoholic, writes in his book *A Priest's Own Story*: "The alcoholic drinks because he has to. The drunkard drinks because he wants to. Once the alcoholic starts drinking, he can't stop. The drunkard can stop whenever he feels like it. When the alcoholic drinks, all he can think about is when he will get his next drink. When the drunkard drinks all he wants to do is get high and enjoy himself. Most alcoholics start out as social drinkers but who knows where the responsibility for his becoming an alcoholic lies."

In Tennessee Williams's play *Cat on a Hot Tin Roof,* we read this definition: "A drinking man is someone who wants to forget he isn't still young and believing."

Marvin A. Block, chairman of the AMA Committee on Alcoholism, says: "The drinker who uses judgment alone allows his body to utilize the drink he has consumed before he takes another. But the alcoholic continues to drink—unable to control his compulsion. Many an alcoholic would literally drink himself to death if nature did not interfere by causing unconsciousness. It is difficult to recognize when social drinking ceases and alcoholism begins."[1]

These authoritative statements all seem to hint at one distinguishing characteristic of the alcoholic, no matter where he is found, no matter what his class in society. That characteristic is the purpose for which he drinks. Some people drink to fulfill a religious ritual, others to be polite, others for a good time or to make friends; some drink to experiment or show off, to get warm or cool or quench thirst, or because they like a particular alcoholic beverage or want to go on a spree. None of these is the purpose of the alcoholic, although he may claim all or any to satisfy a questioner.

The alcoholic drinks because he *has to* if he is to go on living. He drinks compulsively; that is, a power greater than rational planning brings him to drink and to excessive drinking.

Many alcoholics hate liquor, hate drinking, hate the taste, hate the results, hate themselves for succumbing—but they cannot stop. Their drinking is as compulsive as the stealing of the kleptomaniac or the continual hand-washing of a person with a neurosis about cleanliness. This compulsive, obsessive element, which is constantly present in alcoholism, suggests that alcoholism is a pathological condition. Research has led to its being labeled a disease in the true sense, with specific symptoms. A study of its etiology reveals these fundamental elements in the bona fide case of alcoholism: (1) an effect upon the brain caused by a metabolic change induced by the excessive use of alcohol which, in turn, reduces the tolerance of certain individuals for the poison (physiological factor); (2) the excessive use is itself employed as a defense against the individual's inability to solve life's problems under ordinary circumstances (psychological factor). The breakdown of alcohol as a defense has the reverse effect of no longer permitting the alcoholic to function at a reasonable level because of it. These two factors—the physical inability to absorb alcohol and the psychological inability to adjust to the demands of everyday living—are present in every case of alcoholism. They must be present concomitantly for the disease to flourish. As long as either factor is absent the individual will not present the classic manifestations of the disease.

The question "Can anyone become an alcoholic?" is often discussed. There is some divergence of opinion but most authorities today hold to the view that potentially any person can develop the disease. One psychiatrist with vast experience in treating alcoholics puts it this way: "For each one of us there is a horizontal line—indicating our individual tolerance for alcohol. There is on this line a point of no return where tolerance is destroyed and we develop the physical factor in alcoholism. This point may be the terminus of a relatively short distance, or it may be comparatively, a very long way from the starting point. But make no mistake about it—anyone of us, under the proper circumstances of the abuse of alcohol, can reach this point where he can no longer function physically as an integrated person without dependence on this sedative. This, coupled with problem-stress, will undoubtedly turn such a physically dependent person into a classic alcoholic. Once this point is reached, there is no question any longer of cure. There is only control."

Symptoms

There are many armchair analysts who after the fact say with some tinge of self-satisfaction of the alcoholic: "I saw it coming for years. He never could handle the stuff and should have stopped when he first started to miss work on Monday mornings."

It's easy to second-guess any situation, of course, but actually there are certain clear indices that may indicate the onset of alcoholism and which, if properly understood and quickly perceived, may prevent much of the grief and hardship inevitably associated with it. It is not suggested here that these symptoms are the causes of alcoholism; that is another problem entirely and deserves special consideration. The concern at this point is with those signs that suggest that the patient easily could become an alcoholic or already is at that point.[2]

A physical dependence on alcohol is among the most obvious symptoms. This does not express itself in one moment or even on a series of occasions. There comes a time when the stage of social drinking has long since passed and the use of alcohol has become a crutch upon which the individual must depend in order to face crises or daily tensions that ordinarily are solved within the framework of perfectly normal, healthy anxiety-reaction. At this point it is no longer possible for the potential alcoholic to face up to the vicissitudes of everyday living. This is further complicated by his refusal to recognize his growing dependence. He disguises, rationalizes and finally denies the motivation that drives him to seek solutions in a bottle, glass or cocktail shaker. The unconscious guilt associated with the fact he refuses to acknowledge manifests itself in the secretive manner in which he drinks. The "secret drinker"—the one who feels compelled to explain his drinking or hide it from others—displays a danger sign which is soon followed by a compulsion to drink at odd hours. The need for an "eye-opener" in the morning is such a distress signal and invariably is followed by the alcoholic "coffee break," the liquid lunch and the early cocktail hour. At this point there are rarely overt manifestations of drunkenness and the patient is still functioning at a reasonable level of efficiency.

Other and more significant indications of the inevitable descent toward oblivion follow. Problem drinking—the occasional "binge" that becomes more and more frequent—begins and there are days when the person does not appear at work in the morning and appears late at home in the evening. The road down takes a sudden dip at this point and before long the drinking binges are extended to the point where normal work and living become impossible. Sometimes hospitalization, and quite frequently medical treatment, is required before there can be any hope of sobriety. The state of physical compulsion coupled with psychological dependence completes the picture of the incurable alcoholic whose best hope now is "control."

Unfortunately for too many, these external symptoms coincide with a physical deterioration which runs the gamut from ptosis of the eyelids through hyperemia to edema and swollen tissue and finally to gastritis, esophageal varices and cirrhosis of the liver. The physical appearance of the alcoholic, which has provided many a comic with a characteristic routine, betrays the very unfunny physical corruption that is directly traceable to the abuse of alcohol. Anyone who has witnessed the final stages of decay of such a victim invariably considers such a routine to be in poor taste and finds himself substituting an uneasy grimace for the expected burst of laughter. There is nothing funny about the memory of such a person's final end.

Despite the abundant and practical evidence regarding the dangers inherent in this depressant poison, the number of alcoholics gradually mounts until it is the number four health problem in the United States today, preceded only by mental illness, heart disease and cancer. It has been estimated, for example, that six to eight million—or approximately one in fifteen of the adult population in our country—are or will become chronic alcoholics. Since most alcoholics live in families, this means that at least twenty million, and probably more, are immediately and adversely affected by this dread disease. The National Safety Council states that alcohol is a cause in about 50 percent of the road accidents fatal to drivers and in about one-third of the accidents fatal to adult pedestrians. The Council goes on to say that recent evidence strongly suggests that alcoholism as such is an ever-increasing factor in these accidents. Statistics also show that alcoholics attempt and complete suicide at a much higher rate of frequency than nonalcoholics. Significantly, most alcoholics do not come from underprivileged areas but are found in good homes, private business and offices and not infrequently possessed of exceptional skills and talents.[3]

These brief statistics, which may be somewhat surprising in view of popular misconceptions, give some insight into the problem of postponed diagnosis. Despite the dangerous symptoms that precede its onset, alcoholism often is already a disease in an active stage before it is detected.

What are the factors in human existence that bring about this condition? Is it merely a medical problem? Is the solution completely in the hands of physical medicine? What is the "X-factor" that makes one person incapable of absorbing alcohol while another may drink for a lifetime, even at times to excess, and never suffer from alcoholism, properly termed?

Although frequently guessed at as a result of the "controlled experiment," the causes remain to a certain degree a mystery. There are, however, certain things that seem to suggest a predisposition to the disease even if they do not in fact actually cause it. These "contributing causes" invariably are present in the personality disorder generally classified as alcoholism. The degree to which any one or all are present may vary with the individual but their presence consistently offers a point of departure for a discussion of descriptive causality.

There are almost always personality weaknesses among the compulsive drinkers which lead to instability and a limited capacity for enduring stress. These weaknesses invariably manifest themselves in terms of immature selfishness, self-pity and resentment at the apparent capabilities of others as compared to the person's own inadequacy. The latter characteristic usually gives rise to insecurity and fear which the individual seeks to escape through reliance on drink.

What might be termed a social cause of alcoholism is also frequently present. The individual's relationship with others is poor even though he frequently is not thoroughly aware of it. This may be reflected in home background, with some reversal or loss or with strained family ties with which the person cannot bring himself to cope.

The physical craving of the body for alcohol usually represent a dependence. There are theories of etiology that relate this craving to nutritional or biochemical deficiencies, to endocrine disorders, brain pathology or some form of allergy. As has been pointed out, this need is not born of pleasure from the taste or ingestion of the alcohol. Nor is it developed because the patient enjoys the effects produced. That quite the opposite is true has been clinically and experimentally demonstrated.

Despite the fact that there is no definite "personality type" to fit the profile of every alcoholic, certain personality factors are consistently present. The underlying dependency and inadequacy that traditionally have been attributed to the alcoholic are almost universally discovered. Other socio-cultural factors help to complete the picture. In those cultures where strong alcoholic beverages are part of a way of life, alcoholic addiction is much more prevalent. On the other hand, it is less common among Jews and Moslems, where drinking is associated with religious practice and restricted almost exclusively to that purpose. In countries where taboos are rigidly observed, the ratio of alcoholism is proportionately reflected. In Scandinavian countries the ratio of alcoholic addicts is about twenty-three to one in favor of men. In the United States, it is about three to one (a ratio that is rapidly diminishing) and in England, it is reported as two to one. Studies have shown that the social mores governing the custom of women drinking is completely in accord with these statistics.

Another factor determining the propensity to alcoholism is quite naturally the "parental model." Children imitate the adjustive patterns of their parents and accordingly children with alcoholic parents tend under stress to become alcoholics. Clinical observation shows that most alcoholics come from families where there was a drinking problem or where there was an unnatural and unreasonable rejection of any use of alcohol.

In attempting to specify some causal relationship between antecedents and this type of addiction, some students of the problem describe a genetic-nutritional condition as essential and all other factors as merely "precipitate." These authorities place heavy stress on hereditary factors as predisposing the individual to a particular constitution or metabolism which ultimately renders him prone to the craving for the effects of alcohol. This way of thinking emphasizes a certain chemical affinity and even need for the drug once the system has been affected by its depressing effects. These theorists maintain that without this so-called genetic-nutritional inadequacy the patient never would become an alcoholic despite the presence of stress.

After all the research has been sifted through certain accepted facts remain:

1. The disease of alcoholism is due to a combination of a physical and a psychological deficiency, which remains for the most part a mystery.

2. While there are no specific "personality types" who become alcoholics, all alcoholics display a very definite attitude of insecurity in the face of even the normal stresses of everyday living.

Cases

Dolores is an attractive woman in her late thirties who has this story to tell: "My father was a drinker from way back and my earliest recollections of my parents involve constant fighting and confusion. As I grew older I saw their financial problems, caused by his drinking, drive them further and further apart until there was a permanent divorce. I resolved that such a situation would never enter my life. But on a dare at age seventeen I took my first highball. I remember now how I disliked the taste and wondered how anybody could possibly drink enough to get drunk. Three years later I found out–and my future husband and I were off and running. After our marriage we became steady and eventually inveterate 'boozers' and all our friends thought it mildly amusing. I had my own business, a beauty parlor. We had no children and were living high off the hog. At one point I remember having to sell my business for a fraction of its worth to pay for our drinking habits. Most of the next ten years is vague in my mind because I can only remember 'coming off it' with the help of friends and going to various 'drying-out farms,' with or without my husband. Finally he disappeared and I woke up in the psychiatric ward of a city hospital and was told that I had slashed my wrists in a vague attempt at suicide. It was then and there that I resolved 'never again.' I joined AA and must go to meetings seven nights a week in order to maintain the sobriety I achieved six years ago. Somewhere, someplace, there is a man who is my husband—and I don't know where to look for him. He's one of us, and I must live every day with the knowledge that all this might have been avoided. My business does well. I have a comfortable living. But I know that in one instant I can blow the whole thing. And so I just go to meetings. My friends tell me it's not much of a life. They don't understand it's the only one I've got."

Bob, a twenty-seven-year-old mechanic, came to a session of group therapy for alcoholics in a large metropolitan hospital. When questioned by the director as to his reason for coming he announced: "I can't understand it. Everybody says I'm such a nice guy. And I am—even-tempered, generous and sociable. But the other day—actually it was New Year's Eve—I had been drinking all day and went home with the intention of going to a party with my wife. Now understand, I've been drunk before, even had a black-out or two, but this was something completely different. I lay down for an hour and she called me to get ready for the party. I woke up, took two more 'shots' and the next time she spoke to me I just belted her. She screamed and her parents, who live downstairs, came running to her aid. When I saw them I grabbed my shotgun from a closet and blasted away. Luckily I hit nothing but the wall and destroyed some furniture and lamps. The cops came and since nobody pressed charges, I merely was told to sober up. I can't understand it, because everybody thinks I'm such a nice guy."

The director asked for opinions. None were forthcoming until one veteran of many years of therapy turned to Bob and tore into him: "So you think you're a nice guy. Let me tell you, you're a son of a bitch. You are one son of a bitch. And until you begin to understand that you don't know anything about yourself.

You'll always be an alcoholic. So am I, and I know it because I used to think I was a nice guy too. Now I sit here in my chair each week in this class. And you know what this chair is? It's my kindergarten chair, and I'll sit in it the rest of my life if I have to. But I know this: When I have even one drink I'm no longer a nice guy and neither are you."

"We'll never beat it, any of us, we're hooked for good," was the way one fifty-six-year-old man put it, describing the influence of alcohol in the life of an addict. "The sooner we admit that simple fact to ourselves, the sooner we have a chance of recovery. Until we do, we're just going to go on stumbling and staggering through life, destroying ourselves and those who have to put up with us. Take myself for instance. I was a twenty-seven-year-old lawyer in New York City before I had my first taste of hard liquor. I had a promising career with a Wall Street firm and they told me that within a matter of a few years in a specialized field of law I could write my own ticket. Within thirty-six months I couldn't even get back to work after lunch. My wife left me and took our two children with her. I was eventually disbarred (about the only bar that really threw me out) and found myself living in a flophouse along the waterfront of Brooklyn. I went to a priest for help. (Actually I wanted the price of a drink.) He told me he'd give me the pledge for one day and then to come back and see him. I insisted that I take it 'forever' and he threw me out when I became obnoxiously insistent. He said something I'll always remember: 'You're not ready yet. You haven't been really hurt. You haven't bounced. The day you find yourself picking up cigarette butts from the gutter, come around to see me.' Six months went by and then it happened. I had run out of cigarettes, my welfare check was completely consumed and nobody would give me a dime. I saw a 'clippie' that had a few good puffs in it on the pavement and as I bent down to pick it up to smoke, his words hit me between the ears. That was the beginning of sobriety for me—after nearly thirty years of being drunk. I look back at a wasted life and realize now how much I've lost—a family, an honored profession, a chance to be somebody. But you don't know how good it feels right now just to be 'anybody.' "

A careful study of these examples of real people with a drinking problem will reveal the basis for some type of therapy to offer hope or cure for this dreadful illness. In each of the instances cited, there came a moment of crisis when the person had to do something or perish. At that point he came to a realization described by Alcoholics Anonymous as the understanding that "he was powerless over alcohol" and his life was "unmanageable."

The clergyman frequently will encounter the addict at this point either through personal contact or through association with a member of the family involved. It is, however, impossible to attempt any meaningful communication with the patient while he is "under the influence." The first problem to be solved is to get him sober. This usually requires referral to a physician. It may demand hospitalization. Ordinarily it requires twenty-four to forty-eight hours before sobriety can be attained. The usual hospital stay for "drying-out" periods does not exceed a week.

When the patient is able to talk with some understanding of his illness there remains the second and most crucial task of the road to health, i.e., to have him convince himself that he must never drink again for the simple reason that he can never drink again without developing the complete alcoholic syndrome in its active stage. This is not an easy admission to make. It is surely not an easy resolution to keep. However, it is the key to the whole problem and unless the patient accepts this simple fact, further attempts at a cure will be relatively useless. This is not to suggest there should be no further therapy. Nor is it to suggest that there may not be an underlying cause for the "symptom" alcoholism. But the resolution of this psychological problem must wait until the person can readily understand and accept the involvements. Unfortunately, too many alcoholics want to know *why* they can't drink before they are willing to submit to the undeniable fact that they cannot.

The presentation of motives for not drinking is a difficult and tedious task that must be accomplished with the greatest of delicacy. One false word or intonation at times can destroy the whole effort. Usually these patients are intelligent persons, not infrequently gifted, whose sensitivity to their surroundings causes them many more anxieties than the ordinary person with a personality disorder. Invariably their illness itself is associated with a certain degree of complexity within the framework of their personality. Hence, it becomes the work of a sensitive nature to restore the confidence that they need to face the problem they are attempting to escape or the difficulties to which they cannot easily adjust.

How this is to be accomplished will vary to some extent with the personality and background of the patient. Anyone who attempts it should be aware of certain ground rules that should be observed since violation of them has proven disastrous.

1. The initial encounter with the patient after he has attained sobriety is a crucial one for it will establish, or destroy, a sense of confidence and rapport which is essential for providing the motivation necessary to "take the first step." Accordingly, a patronizing tone, a censorious manner or any lack of sympathy will immediately cause the patient to "turn off" and the interview not only will not accomplish anything, it will provide another reason for drinking to escape an additional unpleasant adjustment that could not be made.

2. This does not imply that the therapist should try to ignore the facts of alcoholism or the disruption of a life, or many lives. The patient is painfully aware of these facts and to gloss over them or explain them away will never inspire the confidence that must be present for progress. A realistic, reasoned and friendly relationship should be established before any attempt is made to analyze or prescribe.

3. The person—who should always initially be described as someone with a "drinking problem"—must be gradually set in the direction of accepting the fact of his illness. Indiscriminately blunt reference to this fact may cause withdrawal and complete failure. The stress should be on the fact of an illness that can, and must, be cured to avoid the dire consequences and destructive influence it has caused and will continue to cause.

4. In this connection, emphasis must be placed on the necessity of ignoring the cause of the disease. One therapist-psychiatrist puts it well: "We can talk about who took Teddy or who stole the red wagon later on. Right now we have to get you on your feet and well."

5. After the initial establishment of confidence on the part of the patient, the therapist should convince the patient that his view of the future must not include "never drinking for the rest of my life." The matter of time should be minimized in terms of resolution of the difficulty and the cure of the disease. "I must not take the first drink"—that's all. If constant reference is made to a week, a year or a month, the patient may become discouraged at an obstacle which at first seems insurmountable. Even worse, he may believe that all he has to do is not drink for the given period, after which he will be perfectly free to return to his old ways and habits.

6. The patient also should be made to realize that there is no moral guilt involved in alcoholism as such. It is a disease, an allergy, completely devoid of any personal responsibility for its presence. He should be informed that this could, and does, happen to people of every walk of life. This emphasis will help to eliminate the insecurity that is involved in the problem he must face. He should be completely familiarized with the services offered by groups such as Alcoholics Anonymous, which, practically speaking, have made a fraternity of those afflicted with this disease.

7. As with every habit there must be some replacement when the habit is eliminated. For example, when a person stops smoking after some years of the habitual use of tobacco he must find–at least at the beginning—some substitute for what could be called an oral fixation. Chewing gum is frequently suggested. With the alcoholic there must be something to which he can direct his interest that will distract his attention and in which he will find some gratification and sense of accomplishment. The practical application of this principle will depend upon the back-

ground and temperament of the individual. But one thing is certain: The liquor must be replaced and the energy involved in maintaining a habit of years must be sublimated in a useful and satisfying direction. Whatever the direction be—hobbies, works of charity, community projects—the therapist constantly must keep in mind that the type of personality who becomes an alcoholic is frequently somewhat compulsive and, therefore, if properly motivated can expend great energy for the achievement of worthwhile goals.

8. Finally, the religious potential of the patient should be actualized by confronting him with the support and challenge that his religious beliefs offer. Reliance upon prayer—a significant suggestion of AA—would be accepted easily as a proposal from the clergyman, and specific prayers or methods of religious formation would be regarded as a therapeutic pattern naturally to be proposed by the religious representative.

In all of these suggestions for initial attempts at the rehabilitation of the alcoholic addict the common note is definitely one of pragmatism. "If it works, use it" is pretty much the rule to be followed. The major objective is to keep the patient sober in order that he then may submit himself willingly to further professional therapy in order to discover the underlying cause of this symptom. Some authorities are of the opinion, however, that if a test of ego-strength reveals that the person is incapable of accepting the reason for the symptom, then it would be better to continue with motivation for not drinking rather than run the risk of nonacceptance of the real reason for drinking. This test involves technical knowledge and is completely beyond the scope of the average clergyman. In many instances the psychotherapist will realize that the clergyman can provide even more significant motivation than he and will refer the problem back to the priest, minister or rabbi for supportive care. This involves familiarity with local programs designed for the treatment of alcoholics and a thorough understanding of the dynamics involved in this type of person-to-person relationship.

The clergyman also should understand his constant opportunity to be of help and service to the family—the wife and children—of the victim of this disease. Sympathy, practical advice and charity will require much time and patience. But more than that is required if those intimately associated with the problem in terms of family life are to be educated properly concerning the nature of the illness and their role as aids to recovery. Organizations such as Al-Anon (for husbands or wives of alcoholics) and Al-a-Teen (for the teen-age children of alcoholics) offer much in the way of practical understanding of the problem presented by this disease and the adjustment that must be made because of its presence in a family.

Recommendations for Families

DO'S

1. Learn the facts about alcoholism. A variety of authoritative booklets for the layman are available through the American Medical Association, Chicago, Illinois, the National Council on Alcoholism, 2 Park Avenue, New York, N. Y. 10016, and other organizations. Attend meetings of AA and Al-Anon family groups with an open mind to learn and benefit from the experience of others.

2. Develop an understanding attitude to match the facts you have learned about alcoholism and the alcoholic.

3. Test this attitude by taking an honest personal inventory of yourself in respect to such questions as: Are you convinced that alcoholism really is a disease? Is your approach to the alcoholic one of love, indifference or rejection?

4. Discuss the situation with a clergyman, social worker or friend, or an individual who has experienced some phase of alcoholism, either as alcoholic or family member.

5. Take it as a matter of course if the alcoholic stops drinking either as a result of self-help or of formal treatment. Abstain completely from alcohol; drinking on the part of the nonalcoholic mate is unconsciously resented by the alcoholic and may make him resume doing so himself.

6. Establish and maintain a healthy atmosphere in the home, with a place in the family circle for the alcoholic member.

7. Encourage new interests and participate whenever possible in recreational or occupational activities enjoyed by the alcoholic. Encourage him to see old friends.

8. Be patient and live one day at a time. Alcoholism generally takes a long time to develop and recovery doesn't happen overnight. Accept setbacks and relapses with equanimity. Keep on trying.

9. Approach the alcoholic about drinking only when he is sober, the best time being shortly after a bout when hangover, depression and remorse are prominent.

10. Discreetly place injurious objects out of sight and attempt to withhold car keys when the alcoholic becomes intoxicated.

11. Explain the nature of alcoholism as an illness to children in the family; try to spare them from seeing the alcoholic parent in an extremely intoxicated state.

12. Alert local bartenders and police to the alcoholic's condition in order to help prevent community incidents and embarrassment.

DONT'S

1. Don't preach, nag, lecture and assume a holier-than-thou attitude; with the alcoholic's characteristic low tolerance of frustration, these probably will cause him to escape more and more into alcoholism.

2. Never use emotional appeals, such as "if you loved me," which only tend to increase feelings of guilt and the compulsive need to drink.

3. Be sure not to make threats you don't intend to carry out or will not be able to follow through on.

4. Do not look upon the alcoholic as a moral weakling or completely take over his responsibilities, leaving him with no sense of importance or value.

5. Don't shelter the alcoholic from situations where alcohol is present. Don't hide bottles or pour liquor down the sink. Such acts only impel him to establish a secret supply hidden from you and certainly do not aid him in facing the everyday temptation of drinking in our society.

6. Never extract promises or place the alcoholic in a position where he or she must be deceitful; pledges are readily given and readily broken, intensifying the alcoholic's guilt feelings and loss of self-respect.

7. Be sure not to argue or put pressure on the alcoholic when he is drinking or intoxicated. The response is usually one of negativism and even violence. Never resort to physical violence or punishment.

8. Never be overconfident or expect an immediate one hundred percent recovery.

9. Don't cover up or make excuses for the alcoholic.

10. Try not to be a martyr, feel ashamed or at fault; these attitudes will only serve to destroy objectivity and usually are sensed by the already remorseful and suspicious alcoholic.

11. Avoid making an issue over or standing in judgment of the method of recovery selected by the alcoholic.

12. Never use the children as tools or turn them against the alcoholic in an attempt to cope with your problems.[4]

Some Special Problems of Alcoholism

In recent years special problems connected with this disease have arisen within our society and deserve particular mention. The first of these is the astonishing increase in teen-age drinking and the second the equally phenomenal growth of alcoholism among housewives, particularly in affluent, suburban areas.

In a certain sense the increase of alcoholic consumption among teen-agers is not a surprising statistic since there has been a tremendous increase among all ages in recent years. Nevertheless, the availability and social acceptance of drink among the young now poses the new problem of education as to the proper use of this potentially dangerous threat to the physical and psychological well-being of young people. Studies have shown that youngsters who develop drinking problems invariably come from homes where alcoholism was prevalent or there was a poor relationship between parents. The reason for drinking was to solve some problem or escape its consequences. There was a high degree of hostility toward authority-images and group drinking was a substitute for the lack of any close family relationships.

These circumstances present the basis for poor psychological development at best and for poor reactions to the use of alcohol at worst. Ordinarily, teen-agers do not become alcoholics, but perhaps the only reason is that they have not yet had enough time in which to reach the point of no return. Potential alcoholics are always present and the telltale symptoms should be noticed immediately lest they develop into a condition that can only result in the regret and misery already known by too many. Educational programs should be proposed in which the proper use of drink as a social amenity can be presented for the information of all and the protection of the inevitable few.

At first glance the case of the housewife-turned-alcoholic has all the ingredients of a successful soap opera. The tragic reality, however, is all too widespread to suggest the escape that an afternoon soap opera might provide. The culture in which we live and the socio-economic status we attempt to achieve and defend offers much of the explanation as to why the traditional gap between three alcoholic males to one alcoholic female is narrowing. A housewife easily can begin drinking alone without fear of detection because she is in her own home a good portion of each day, unobserved. The taboo that prohibits her appearance unescorted in the local tavern reenforces the possibility of her solitary drinking. The loneliness that many suburban housewives face while the children are at school and her husband is at work induces many women to find temporary relief from boredom and ennui by drinking.

If the tragedy of the husband-father alcoholic is immediately evident, the catastrophe of the wife-mother alcoholic should be even more so. The children whose formative years are spent largely with the mother are the obvious victims. The husband, who tradition and statistics indicate is a much less lenient and understanding mate of the alcoholic, frequently will not tolerate such a condition and the break-up of the home is much more likely.

The solution to this constantly increasing problem is again one of education and cautious observation. The use of drink as a value must be emphasized. The discernment of its potential abuse should be labeled immediately and the precautions invoked without hesitation.

For Further Reference

Fox, Ruth, and Lyon, Peter. *Alcoholism: Its Scope, Cause and Treatment*. New York: Random House, 1955.

Jellinek, Elvin M. *The Disease Concept of Alcoholism*. New Haven: Hillhouse Publishing, 1960.

Mann, Marty. *New Primer on Alcoholism*. New York: Holt, Rinehart & Winston, 1958.

President's Commission. *Task Force Report: Drunkenness*. Washington: U.S. Government Printing Office, 1967.

Roche Laboratories. *Aspects of Alcoholism*. Philadelphia: J. B. Lippincott Co., 1963.

9 Drug Addiction

"I am a failure and this setup is my last chance. I was a loser almost from the moment I was born. Two parents who hated each other brought me into a world which I grew to hate. I wanted to show my hatred and since they gave me no reason for believing in happiness over the rainbow, I wanted to hurt them as well as myself.

"The first problem was drink. Too much, too soon, too young. I was hanging around bars ready for anything when I was sixteen and by the time I was a year older I was getting 'help' from a friend who had turned me on with marijuana. From that it was an easy ride to the big 'H' and in no time I was a mainliner. The habit started to cost and the only way out—an easy one for a drop-out from humanity—was prostitution.

"But I was luckier than most. I met someone who directed my steps toward a recovery program and put the whole scene in focus for me. I don't know how long I'll last but this is better than nothin', or as they say in skid row, 'you can't fall off the floor.' "

The author of this horror story is an attractive twenty-three-year-old girl named Dea who is trying to make a comeback from dilemma and addiction. She may make it, but she doubts it. So does everyone else.

"I was an altar boy. I went to a parochial school. I came from a good Catholic family. My father was a church worker and the pastor was a visiting friend of the family. But I got hooked—but good. My friends dared me and I fell for it. From smoking pot and sniffing glue I went for the 'white stuff,' finally to the tune of forty dollars a day. I'd do anything to get a fix. There was nothing I wouldn't steal, nobody I wouldn't hurt. Physically I was small but I'd take on Gargantua if it meant a good ride. I even belted my father one night in an effort to get out and get going.

"I stole cars and tools and clothes and purses and anything you can name. One day I stole a doctor's bag from his car and took an overdose of morphine. I woke up in a hospital and it finally crashed in on me–still a baby, haven't grown up. That's why I'm here, trying to produce, tryin' to grow up, hoping I'll learn. But you know the terrible part is that when I turn the light out at night and I'm in my room all alone after everyone else is asleep, I know that I would probably do it all over again. Unless I hold on tight, very tight."

Frank, nineteen, white, upper middle class, lived in a New York suburb—a typical profile of a young American drug addict. He admits candidly that he had every chance, that he was "given the best," that by the rules of the game he never should have had to spend the next two years trying to break a ruthless habit and find meaning in his life without the artificial stimulus of drugs. But there he is and with the complete realization that the struggle in which he is engaged is one in which he may become an overwhelmed victim.

These cases could be multiplied many hundreds of times among the interviews held with drug addicts of various sizes, shapes, colors and backgrounds. The amazing statistic is that drug addiction is not just becoming more evident, it is actually becoming an accepted practice like dancing or smoking or going to the movies. It is one of the most obvious social problems facing our nation and the effective clergyman must be thoroughly familiar with it and his role in any possible solution.

Statistics

The experience of anyone who attempts an accurate picture of the extent of drug addiction at the present time is one of utter frustration. This is due largely to the constant change in the actual number of people using drugs as well as the improvement in the techniques of reporting statistics of this type. The problem is further complicated by the fact that no generally accepted definition of the word *addict* exists. With these limitations in mind we attempt here not *the* final picture but a sketch, suggested by even the most conservative estimates, of the frequency of what within the past five years has grown to the number one social evil.

Within any statistical analysis there must be a consistent return to the principle that statistics alone do not solve a problem or even give an accurate representation of its involvement. There must be an awareness of the personalities that make up these numbers. Whether there are five addicts per one hundred population or ten times that number is not the matter of greatest significance. What is more important is the undeniable fact that any use of this type of psychological support indicates a certain personality inadequacy. This ultimately is the tragedy. If official records state that there are 57,000 or more opiate addicts in the United States at the present time,[1] this, for the clergyman, means that there are 57,000 personality problems some of which he most probably will be called upon to deal with. If, more realistically, as some authorities strongly suggest, the number is ten times this official count, then the extent of the problem is multiplied that many more times.[2] The problem presented by the disturbed personality invariably touches upon an inestimable number of others in terms of family and social relationships which, in turn, must affect the life and working contact of the clergyman. This must be our point of emphasis as we approach the drug abuse problem as it exists in our time.

Tangible evidence of the massive proportions of the drug abuse problem in the United States is reflected in the number of crimes that are reported as related to the illicit use of drugs. In

New York City alone—sometimes referred to as the heroin capital of the world—it has been estimated that narcotics users steal over 500 million dollars each year to support their habit. In the same city, approximately 20 percent of the crimes against property are perpetrated to support drug habituation and 80 percent of the prostitutes arrested are drug addicts, with the majority of them engaging in prostitution as a means of maintaining their expensive habit of drug abuse.[3]

John E. Ingersoll, director of the Federal Bureau of Narcotics, indicates that the problem of drug abuse has exploded into frightening proportions and is currently mounting at a startling rate throughout the country. He observes that from 1961 to 1968 the arrests for drug-related offenses increased by more than 300 percent while juvenile arrests for such offenses over this same period increased almost 1,900 percent. From 1960 to 1965, approximately 300 persons died from heroin-related causes in New York City alone. In 1969, however, more than 900 people died of such causes in New York City and of these 224 were teenagers. Ingersoll also gives the incredible statistic that heroin in one way or another is currently causing more deaths among those between eighteen and thirty-five than automobile accidents or disease.[4]

This numerical increase is only a part of the entire picture of the drug problem today. During the 1930s and 1940s most use of marijuana, for example, was restricted to depressed areas and most users were members of minority groups, specifically Negroes, Puerto Ricans and Mexicans. Today this use is common among youngsters of affluent, middle class and residential communities. Not so many years ago this type of drug use was expected in areas that offered little in the way of social acceptance or prestige, to say nothing of vocational opportunity. Today, the so-called better homes and gardens are producing more than their share of those who cannot or will not accept the necessity of facing life and its problems without the sustaining force of chemical supports. This should certainly cause the thinking person to question the oversimplified explanation that this kind of inadequacy is caused by social deprivation. Or perhaps more accurately, it should cause him to reevaluate the whole structure of a society that can offer so much materially and yet cannot provide those basic elements in personality development that would prevent recourse to such abuse from becoming painfully commonplace.

Despite the tons of material that makes its way to the newsstands regarding drug abuse there seems to be little agreement as to addiction as such. Some emphasize physical dependence and others psychological dependence, while still others insist that the ultimate norm of addiction is the extent of the usage and the kind of drug that is used.[5]

The axiom "Once an addict always an addict" is rejected by many authorities because it is felt that through proper training and motivation an addict can be brought to the point where he can readjust his needs and values so that drugs no longer will provide "supportive attraction." Conversely, there are those who constantly refer to the empirical cliché that less than 5 or 10 percent of genuine drug addicts are ever completely rehabilitated.[6]

In a sense, such disagreements and debates remain academic for our purposes here. When we use the word *addict* we refer to a person who through usage of a given drug is physically and psychologically disposed to become dependent on the support the drug supplies. Most authorities are agreed that there must be some psychological inadequacy before addiction or dependence can ensue. Not just anybody can become an addict, for addiction in the truest sense is a symptom which immediately suggests a breakdown of the ordinary defenses. It is an effort on the part of the individual to allay the anxiety that results because he cannot adjust to the demands that daily living makes upon the resources with which he is endowed. Place him in another set of circumstances and the need might never arise. Place someone else in his position and drug abuse becomes completely meaningless.

This concept of individual need should not be misunderstood as a justification for personal inadequacy. Nor should it be concluded that the abuse of drugs must be accepted as a necessary crutch for the weak. Too often, those who discuss the concept of addiction place the total emphasis upon dependence without spelling out the fact that this dependence has a point of origin within the totality of the addict's life. How this weakness manifests itself has been described by many observers. In 1957, the World Health Organization of the United Nations defined drug addiction as "a state of periodic or chronic intoxication detrimental to the individual and to society, produced by the repeated consumption of a drug (natural or synthetic). Its characteristics include: (1) an overpowering desire or need (compulsion) to continue taking the drug and to obtain it by any means; (2) a tendency to increase the dose (tolerance) and (3) a psychic (psychological) and sometimes a physical dependence on the effects of the drug."[7]

First, it is a state of intoxication. This results when the chemical is introduced into the system and eventually results in a poisonous condition which, in turn, alters psychic and somatic equilibrium. In general, these alterations or effects are regarded by the drug user as pleasurable, producing the experience of muscular relaxation, warmth or a dreamlike state in which all anxieties vanish and all problems cancel out. With some drugs there is a feeling of exhilaration, pleasurable excitement or drive. This state of intoxication can be induced by the drug abuser at more or less regular intervals or it can be a steady ongoing affair which occurs daily and continues for years, sometimes terminating only with the death of the person. The individual who is psychologically dependent upon marijuana, for example, might only turn to its intoxicating effects on specific occasions of stress, whereas the hard-core heroin addict will begin every day with an injection which serves as his "eye-opener."

The description of addiction, as the WHO's significant and reasonable analysis indicates, involves more than one element or aspect. Obviously, one act of abuse of drugs can hardly constitute addiction in the technical sense of the term. Compulsion, tolerance and dependence very well may be the ultimate results of the first introduction to the intoxicating effects of drugs, but a casual chance meeting would hardly suffice for a permanent, lasting association.

A compulsion is an irresistible and intrusive urge to perform an act that is contrary to the individual's conscious wishes or expectations. No matter how much the person tries to control the drive or rid himself of its influence, the compulsion continues to exist and gnaw away at consciousness. Invariably, the only way to drain off the anxiety that always accompanies such psychic insistence is to perform the particular compulsive act. In the instance of drug abuse, the addicted personality has, for the time at least, lost his freedom and, therefore, his control over drugs. He needs drugs now. He no longer simply takes drugs. Drugs have taken him. The specific impelling need behind this compulsion is not the point here. The point is: The addict has no real choice. He will do almost anything—literally anything—in order to satisfy a force that more often than not he cannot even explain to himself.[8]

As the compulsion to the satisfying effects of the drug feeds upon itself, a tolerance for the particular drug gradually is built up within the system. The practical result of this is the necessity to take more and more of the drug in order to achieve the desired effect. The body keeps step with the drug and adjusts to specific dosages. This in part explains the phenomenon commonly known as withdrawal symptoms, or more technically as the abstinence syndrome, which is more fully explained in terms of certain drugs themselves, especially the opiates. When, for example, the body ingests heroin on a regular and frequent basis a physiological adaptation to the drug is built up through the process of homeostasis. It ultimately causes a larger dosage to be required to achieve comparable results. Through this process of adaptation, the physiological mechanism is forced to function in a manner that is diametrically opposed to the natural effects of the drug. With a drug like heroin the body adapts to the presence of the drug by a compensatory type of activity. When heroin is regularly taken into the system the body reacts by stepping up its processes in order to offset the lulling effects of the drug. It is precisely this adjustment that brings about the obvious symptoms of withdrawal. Tolerance, then, is a physiological phenomenon. With the continuance of the drug it becomes an ongoing, expansive type of adjustment which requires that more and more of the drug be taken to satisfy the psychological dependence involved.

According to the WHO's definition, the final characteristic of the addict involves "psychic and/or physical" dependence which will vary with the drug taken and the amount, frequency and duration of its usage. For all practical purposes physical dependence can be equated with the withdrawal syndrome. The individual frantically adheres to his drug habit to avoid the physical distress that withdrawal of the drug necessarily will involve. Although withdrawal symptoms have often been the basis for successful dramatization, in our country, where the opiates especially are quite diluted or "cut," the symptoms themselves usually resemble those commonly associated with a heavy case of the flu. They include such inconveniences as headache, running eyes and nose, bodily aches, chills, nausea and vomiting. This is not to minimize the somatic effects of physical drug dependency but merely to state the facts and clear the air of popular misconceptions. Although threatening presentations of the symptoms of withdrawal are often effective deterrents to drug involvement, their misrepresentation must be clarified for those who would help the drug addict who perhaps might postpone recovery out of fear of undergoing some serious and severe physical malaise. The stress here is not so much on the danger of physical dependence, but rather on psychic dependence, which in the long run is far more devastating though less obvious.

The psychological dependence involved in addiction establishes a pattern whereby the individual drug user will never really mature. He cannot face the challenges that life presents, for he does not want to recognize the opportunities they offer. For the addictive personality there is only one solution to any difficulty and that is escape. He employs the ordinary mechanisms of defense and when these fail—as with his type of personality they surely must—to protect him from the demands of everyday living he develops more elaborate systems of defense which ultimately include drug usage resulting in behavior that is completely unacceptable socially.

The real disaster is not so much that his mode of escape is unacceptable. It is that he will never realize the opportunities for achievement that are his unless he becomes willing to submit to the calculated risks that are inherent in the process of daring to meet responsibility head on.

The dangers to health from physical dependence, the dangers to society from the need to support drug dependence, the dangers to individuals that result from tolerance and the concomitant need for more drugs—these are the points of emphasis that constantly are made. But the negative destructive force that prohibits the actualization of potential because of psychic limitations must remain inestimable. It is precisely this force that needs to be reexamined in order to understand the actual damage of drug addiction.

What, then, is the key to the personality of the addict or one prepared to let himself become habituated in such a way that total dependence eventually ensues? Fundamentally, the addict, like everyone else, seeks what is best for him in a given set of circumstances. People do not throw themselves into problems, especially problems they know spell self-destruction, without some reason. Some unfulfilled need, some unsatisfied drive, some flaw in the program of maturing is always present. No man rises in the morning and while viewing himself in the shaving mirror asks such questions as "What awful thing shall I do today?" or, "What can I think of to hurt myself or my future or ruin my family?" People do not act that way. Neither does the drug addict. He has a problem which has led him to rely on drugs for only one reason: he knows of no other way of escaping from its demands. Fight for some reason is impossible, so he has recourse to flight. This is not to justify his reaction, merely to specify it. His personality is characterized by inadequacy, dependence, uncertainty—all of which add up to immaturity. Add to this a sizable portion of compulsivity and the picture is almost complete. There remains only the first flirtation with drugs as such, and it is almost certain that the full flowering of addiction will follow.

Description of Drugs

There are many arbitrary divisions of the various types of drugs. The Task Force Report on Narcotics and Drug Abuse prepared by The President's Commission on Law Enforcement and Administration of Justice, published in 1967, presents the following division:

A. NARCOTICS
  1. The Opiates
  2. Cocaine
  3. Marijuana

B. DANGEROUS DRUGS
  1. Stimulants
  2. Depressants
  3. Hallucinogens

The Task Force points out that "drugs liable to abuse" are usually put into these two classifications of "narcotics" and "dangerous drugs" and the people who abuse them are usually called "addicts." Whatever the refinements of this classification or the concomitant use of the word *addict,* the division will serve for purposes of identification.[9] The accompanying chart (page 121) lists the more common drugs, their use, symptoms and common designations.[10]

Certain of these more commonly used drugs deserve special consideration in terms of their relative importance and the dangers to those who abuse them. Among these are marijuana, heroin, the amphetamines, the barbiturates and the strong hallucinogens.[11]

Marijuana

It is estimated that nearly 90 percent of all heroin users and addicts started their habit by using marijuana.[12] Nearly all those questioned confessed that their first experience with this form of drug was due to environmental influence and that they were willing to "take a chance" or "meet a dare" because they were

Drugs, Medical Uses, Symptoms Produced and Their Dependence Potentials

Name	Slang Name	Pharmacologic Classification	Medical Use	How Taken	Initial Symptoms	Long-Term Symptoms	Physical Dependence Potential	Mental Dependence Potential
Heroin	H., Horse, Scot, Junk, Snow, Stuff, Harry, Joy Powder	Depressant	Pain Relief	Injected or Sniffed	Euphoria Drowsiness	Addiction, Constipation Loss of Appetite Convulsions in overdose	Yes	Yes
Morphine	White Stuff, Miss Emma, M, Dreamer	Depressant	Pain Relief	Swallowed or Injected	Euphoria Drowsiness	Addiction, impairment of breathing	Yes	Yes
Codeine	Schoolboy	Depressant	Ease Pain and Coughing	Swallowed	Drowsiness	Addiction	Yes	Yes
Methadone	Dolly	Depressant	Pain Relief	Swallowed or Injected	Less acute than opiates	Addiction	Yes	Yes
Cocaine	Speed Balls, Gold Dust, Coke, Bernice, Corine, Flake, Star Dust	Stimulant	Local Anesthesia	Sniffed, Injected or Swallowed	Excitation Talkativeness Tremors	Depression, Convulsions	No	Yes
Marijuana	Pot, Grass, Locoweed Mary Jane, Hashish, Tea, Reefers	Depressant, or Hallucinogen	None in U.S.	Smoked, Swallowed or Sniffed	Relaxation, Euphoria, alteration of perception and judgment	Usually none, but currently under study	No	Yes
Barbiturates	Barbs, Blue Devils, Candy, Yellow Jackets, Phennies, Peanuts, Blue Heavens, Downs	Depressant	Sedation, Relieve high blood pressure, epilepsy, hyperthyroidism	Swallowed or Injected	Drowsiness Muscle relaxation	Addiction with severe withdrawal symptoms, possible convulsions	Yes	Yes
Amphetamines	Bennies, Dexies, Co-Pilots, Wake-Ups, Lid Proppers, Hearts, Pep Pills, Ups	Stimulant	Relieve mild depression, control appetite and narcolepsy	Swallowed or Injected	Alertness, Activeness	Delusions Hallucinations	No	Yes
LSD	Acid, Sugar, Big D, Cubes, Trips	Hallucinogen	Experimental Study of Mental Function, alcoholism	Swallowed	Exhilaration, Excitation Rambling Speech	May intensify existing psychosis, panic reactions	No	Yes

convinced that marijuana could not be addictive. The fact that so many advanced drug users begin in this fashion certainly seems to make it possible to label marijuana as the vestibule of drug addiction.

Marijuana has had a long history. It was first mentioned in Chinese medical documents nearly three thousand years before Christ. In India, in about 800 B.C., it was valued for its intoxicant, euphoric and supposedly aphrodisiac properties. Its source is the leaves and flowering tops of the female hemp plant which can be cultivated in nearly any part of the world.

In the United States it has become popular for many reasons, primary among which are its availability, its relative inexpensiveness and its simple administration. It is usually taken in the form of cigarettes which are popularly called "joints" or "reefers." It is also frequently referred to as "pot," "weed," "tea," "grass," "Mary Jane" and "Boo."

Marijuana acts almost entirely on the central nervous system and the user retains the smoke in his lungs as long as possible in order to gain the greatest effect. There is an initial experience of exhilaration which manifests itself in heightened sensibility to sounds and colors coupled with frequent giggling. The reduction of natural inhibition sometimes brings about an increased feeling of sexual urge and power. However, marijuana is not aphrodisiac in effect because prolonged or continued use usually decreases sexual drive and in some instances even may cause impotency. Despite the initial excitation the net effect of this drug is as a depressant which produces a feeling of contentment, relaxation and pleasant drowsiness.

The so-called high that results from the use of marijuana lasts from thirty minutes to several hours. There are striking variations in its manifestations from individual to individual which seem to add to its enticing character. These variations are explained generally in terms of the conditions of use and the predispositions of those involved.

Although authorities insist that this drug is nonaddictive in the sense of physical dependence, there can be no doubt about its ability to prepare the habitual user for more potent forms of drugs. In this sense it certainly can be said to induce a definite psychological dependence which in many instances may prove more dangerous than the obvious physical dependence.

Heroin

Heroin is a semisynthetic derivative of morphine known as "H," "Horse," "white stuff," "Harry" and "joy powder." It is the opiate most frequently employed by drug abusers. A more potent, more euphoric and more available substitute for morphine, heroin is consequently more addictive. Although its manufacture and importation are illegal in the United States and there is tight supervision by federal and local authorities, it is estimated that profits derived from its illicit sale in this country approach $700 million annually.[13]

The heroin employed by the abuser is always diluted or "cut" with lactose or quinine and sold in capsules or paper as a white crystalline powder. The average individual packet or "fix" costs the abuser about five dollars and contains only five grains of 5 percent heroin; however, these figures hardly can be guaranteed.

Although the ingredients often are sniffed or taken as a "snort," the powder most often is heated and dissolved in water and then injected under the skin, which is called "skin popping." The next step is intravenous injection, called "mainlining." The high, which is determined by the degree of addiction and the strength of the dose, consists of a feeling of relaxation and freedom from the inner and outer world of problems. Despite the usual droop of head and eyes and body slump associated with the heroin addict, other hard-core addicts who use the drug have the unusual reaction of actively engaging in work and still others take the drug almost constantly to avoid withdrawal symptoms.

Dangerous Drugs

STIMULANTS. Recently there has been a tremendous emphasis on the dangers involved in the extended use of certain of the amphetamines, particularly methedrine, popularly referred to as

"Speed." Authorities have become so concerned regarding the deleterious effects of this stimulant that the slogan "Speed Kills" is now popular even among the most vocal advocates of the liberalization of drug laws.

In general, the amphetamines, as central nervous system stimulants, have many beneficial medical uses, among them the reduction of weight by curbing appetite, the stimulation of people in mild depression, the implementation of psychotherapy and as an antidote to narcolepsy, a disease characterized by an uncontrollable desire to sleep. These drugs do not cause physical dependency and therefore may be interrupted without the usual withdrawal symptoms associated with this aspect of addiction. Their overemployment, however, may lead to such long-term effects as high blood pressure, cardiac symptoms and liver and brain damage. Sudden cessation of the drug may terminate in deep depression which may lead to suicide.

The amphetamines, which as a class are known as "pep pills," "eye-openers" and "ups," are used in excess invariably by emotionally frustrated and immature people who are constantly looking for a lift and seeking thrills. The user usually becomes alert, talkative and vivacious and can fulfill a work load that otherwise would be impossible. Frequently, these abusers can go through long periods without sleep or food, but eventually experience the inevitable results of fatigue, collapse and malnutrition. Despite the apparent lack of physical dependence there is no question that psychic or emotional dependence can and does occur. But even more dangerous is the fact that when taken without proper medical supervision these drugs may instigate a rundown physical condition which may prove fatal. They sometimes also produce dangerously violent and antisocial reactions. When excessive daily doses have been taken over prolonged periods of time an acute psychosis is possible with auditory and/or visual hallucinations.

THE DEPRESSANTS. This category comprises mostly the barbiturates, commonly designated by users as "barbs," "goofballs," "sleeping pills" and "downs." They are central nervous system depressants and one of the most useful classes of drugs in medicine. Some medical uses are to calm patients suffering from nervous tension and anxiety, to aid in reducing high blood pressure, to induce sleep in insomniacs and to prevent convulsions and seizures such as occur in epilepsy.

In spite of their depressant action on the nervous system they are not narcotics. Generally, they do not cause addiction. In repeated and massive doses, however, they may induce physical dependence. In such cases abrupt withdrawal from the drug can be dangerous and demands immediate medical assistance. Drug users turn to barbiturates to relieve themselves from the pressures of everyday living. When he takes very large doses the user usually appears to be drunk. He has all the signs of being drunk except for the characteristic liquor odor. At times, barbiturates are taken in conjunction with alcohol in order to intensify the effects of each and procure a so-called cheap drunk. Whenever one encounters an unconscious apparent drunk who is carrying unidentified drugs, it is well to keep in mind that his unconsciousness could be due to the combination of alcohol and barbiturates. He may not be drunk at all. Any barbiturate user who is unconscious should receive immediate medical assistance.

THE HALLUCINOGENS. The hallucinogens are also referred to by physicians as psychotomimetic drugs and by others as psychedelics or "mind-manifesting" drugs. Some hallucinogens date back to Aztec times while others have been synthesized as recently as 1953. In general, these drugs upset the subject's perception of reality. They induce hallucinations and sometimes ecstatic states. They also can produce reactions of a psychotic type.

LSD-25 (D=Lysergic Acid Diethlyamide) is the most potent of the hallucinogens known to man. It was synthesized in 1938 by Albert Hofman who also accidently discovered its psychic properties in 1943. It is derived from the rye fungus ergot. Users refer to it as "the Hawk," "the Chief," "the Cube," "the Big D," "25" and, most frequently, "Acid." It is usually taken orally as a liquid or as a saturated sugar cube. It takes only twenty micrograms, which amounts to 1/7000-millionth of an average man's weight, to produce noticeable effects. In the form of powder, this amount is almost invisible. More striking is the fact that when even an ordinary dose, which would be about 50 to 200 micrograms, is taken, this small amount leaves the brain rather rapidly and the effects do not commence until thirty minutes to an hour have elapsed. From such a small amount, the effects may last from four to eight hours. The hallucinogen apparently sets off some physiological process that causes a chemical reaction or release which is the immediate instigator of the psychic effect.[14]

Certain effects of LSD are reported frequently. Sense impressions are perceived more vividly. Colors become more intense and sounds normally imperceptible become audible. Synesthesis, which is the transference of sensations from one sense modality to another, is often experienced. The integrating of sense perceptions is disabled. If one touches his nose it is difficult to discern which member is touching the other. Often, time seems to have no meaning. One sees things, as it were, for the first time. Time seems to stand still. Reactions to pain are diminished and muscular coordination is reduced. Learned and elaborately acquired behaviors seem to dissolve. Emotional repressions are released and people act more fundamentally, whether for better or for worse. Hallucinations ranging from those recognized as no more than pure phantasy to total absorption in an unreal world may occur. This drug seems to separate the user from his ordinarily experienced world and opens up to him the hidden world of his own unknown, unconscious mind.[15] Contrary to the defense offered by its advocates, LSD actually constricts or narrows the scope of consciousness rather than broadening or widening its contact with reality.

At times, LSD has been employed as an adjunct to psychotherapy and as a research tool in psychology. In such controlled situations it seems to have some value. In the hands of amateurs, and certainly in the case of drug abusers, it has caused some terrifying experiences. The drug is definitely capable of producing both temporary and prolonged psychotic reactions in persons with a pre-psychotic but latent psychological disturbance. These reactions are referred to as recurrences or flashbacks. For literally months after the ingestion of the drug into the system the terrifying experiences of what drug users call a "bad trip" can recur with all of their initial force. These occur as "rushes" which the individual is totally incapable of controlling. Under such conditions medically prescribed drugs are the only effective means of control. Such flashbacks may occur after only one trial run with the drug.

Most serious of all is the possible genetic damage that this drug eventually might cause. Chromosomal breaks have been definitely detected in babies born of girls who had been on LSD immediately before pregnancy or during the early days of the gestational period. The precise implications of such genetic alterations are not clear and will not be for some time. As of the present, there does not seem to be any truly documented case of congenital physical anomolies after LSD ingestion, as occurred with the drug thalidomide. Studies with mice and hamsters, on the other hand, reveal that when LSD is injected early in the animal's pregnancy a marked reduction in the number of offspring occurs. Many of the young are born abnormally small and often die shortly after birth and many of those who do survive eventually suffer physical anomolies. Such studies are, of course, only in their initial stages and are being reported slowly and cautiously in scientific journals and by word of mouth within professional circles.

Legal Aspects of Drug Usage

A natural outgrowth of the tremendous increase in the interest in drug usage in recent years is the reevaluation of the present status of laws governing it. The federal and local governments have taken constant and consistently more stringent steps to protect the individual and society from the ill effects of improper usage of drugs and narcotics.[16]

The Harrison Law of 1914 was the first dramatic step taken by the federal government to restrict the illicit importation, sale or possession of narcotic drugs. In 1937, marijuana was brought under the same federal restrictions by the Marijuana Tax Act.

Local communities have followed suit and there is hardly a state that does not have some legislation that makes it contrary to the law to dispense or use specific drugs without proper authorization. The basic purpose behind all these prohibitions is one of protecting the common good.

In recent years, however, there has been an upsurge of criticism of the position taken by authorities and lawmakers in establishing laws and enforcing them. It holds that they are infringements on the rights and freedom of citizens to enjoy the good effects of at least some of the proscribed drugs. In the case of marijuana, which enjoys the questionable distinction of being one of the most commonly used drugs in the United States, many advocates of a more liberal approach to its use have launched campaigns to "legalize pot." They argue that since marijuana is not a narcotic, not addicting in the sense of inducing physical dependence and never has been proved to cause any true or lasting physical damage it should be permitted in much the same way as are nicotine and alcohol. Those opposed to such a position prefer to hold the line until the drug has been scientifically proved to be noninjurious physically. They also assert the undeniable fact that although marijuana is perhaps not technically addictive in nature it is definitely habituating and that there are very few hard-core drug addicts who did not first experiment with marijuana.

Other proponents of a relaxation of the restrictive influence of narcotics and drug laws suggest that there should be a clinical method of treatment of what all are agreed is essentially a medical problem. They argue that since addicts are sick people they should be treated as other sick people are and put on a regular therapeutic basis, not have their problem treated on a punitive basis. In a sense these protagonists miss the point of restrictive legislation. It is not the purpose of the laws to punish sick people but to eliminate the possibility of obtaining drugs and narcotics for illicit purposes. All admit that for any disease to flourish there must be present a living subject, a germ and suitable environmental circumstances. The analogical argument that immediately suggests itself is that if the germ is eliminated the disease will not spread. Empirically, it is known that where drugs and narcotics are not available there is no addiction.

It is also frequently suggested that the British system of treatment, whereby medical practitioners care for drug-dependent persons by dispensing narcotics to those they believe would be incapable of leading normal lives without a small supply, be adopted. Under this system there are no penalities except for illicit importation or sales. The obvious advantages pointed up by proponents are the "more humane treatment of sick people" and the elimination of both the profit motive of the unscrupulous and the criminal enticement for the helpless victim. This again is to compare incomparables, for the addiction problem in Britain is nothing like our own. There are at least fifty times more known addicts in this country. Nor is Britain plagued with a black market in drugs dominated by gangsters. It has, moreover, been the experience of the British that such a procedure only results in the development of tolerance and the increased appetite of the addicts for larger dosages of drugs. In addition, the British program is not intended for everyone but only for those who have failed in prolonged efforts at withdrawal. A further distinguishing characteristic of the program is that responsible physicians restrict themselves only to those addicts who are seriously interested in overcoming their sickness and living a normal well-adjusted life.

The supportive program that has been attempted with regard to those addicted to heroin has had some interesting results but the program is apparently too new to be properly evaluated. Essentially, it consists of a series of substitutions for the heroin, notably methadone. This produces something of the effect of heroin but is less addictive and the hope is present that the addict gradually may be weaned away from the more potent drug.

Narcotic Antagonists

Anti-drugs or narcotic antagonists which tend to build up a contrary tolerance and ultimately destroy the habit are also being attempted. At this early stage of the experiment, however, there is always the danger of a mere transference of dependence and a certainty that mere maintenance of the drug addiction syndrome will never be cured unless the basis for the "symptom" is discovered and eradicated.

When the Boggs Law was enacted shortly after World War II to punish drug traffickers, the hope of eliminating the source was a realistic one. Since that time the hope has dwindled considerably despite large sums spent on enforcement and control of illicit drug trade. It is estimated that more than twice as much opium, for example, is produced than is needed for legitimate use. International bodies such as the United Nations have directed their attention to the problem with funds, studies and proposals. Federal governments throughout the world and local governmental agencies have joined forces in communal efforts to stem the tide of this destructive influence. But all their efforts have proved woefully inadequate in view of the constant pattern of frequency of addiction.

Laws in Existence

The basic federal law controlling drug abuse in the United States is the Harrison Narcotic Act of 1914. This is a tax statute, forbidding the manufacture, importation, sale or transference of narcotic drugs without proper registration and taxation. Unauthorized possession, whether or not the drug is intended for personal use, and unauthorized sale or purchases are criminal offenses under this statute. Unauthorized sale or purchase are also criminal acts under the Uniform Narcotic Drug Act, the control statute in most states. The Harrison Act is concerned with opium and cocaine and all their compounds and derivatives. In 1922, the Jones-Miller Act was passed by Congress, leveling heavy penalties for violation of the Harrison Act. In 1937, marijuana was brought under federal control by the Marijuana Tax Act. According to this law unauthorized possession, sale or purchase are criminal offenses. In 1956, the Narcotic Control Act was passed to increase penalties for drug abuse. Under this law both possession and sale of narcotic drugs including marijuana are punishable by sentences ranging from two to forty years (for first through third offenses).[17] More recently, in an attempt to curb the traffic in dangerous drugs, the federal government enacted the Drug Abuse Control Amendments, which became effective on February 1, 1966. This statute is the principal federal law controlling amphetamines and barbiturates. It limits manufacture, sale and distribution of any controlled drug to certain designated classes of persons such as registered wholesale druggists and licensed physicians. It requires that inventories be taken and records of receipts and dispositions be maintained and places restrictions on the refilling of prescriptions. Such violations as the manufacture, sale or distribution of these drugs by unauthorized persons are subject to set criminal penalties. The first offense is a misdemeanor; the second a felony. Possession of drugs for personal use is not an offense under this statute. All of the amphetamines and barbiturates are specifically designated in this statute. Although the hallucinogens were not specifically identified in this amendment, their control was left to the disgression of the Secretary of Health, Education and Welfare. Early in 1966 such potent hallucinogens as LSD were specifically named and brought under the law by the Secretary.

The most significant development among recent legislative efforts in the drug abuse field is that of civil commitment. This approach has received wide public endorsement and has assumed proportions approximating a general movement. It certainly represents a greater flexibility in handling the problem and manifests a spirit of compromise. Generally speaking, civil commitment means court-ordered confinement in a specified rehabilitation facility. This phase, designed to handle withdrawal difficulties and overcome psychic dependence, is followed by a controlled outpatient status in the community. If abstinence is maintained for a period of time, discharge is granted. If a relapse occurs, reconfinement is demanded. The entire program extends over an indeterminate period of time which ideally should not exceed a prescribed maximum term. In addition to this involuntary or compulsory method there are provisions in many instances for voluntary commitment to treatment programs in lieu of criminal prosecution and a possible jail sentence.

Civil commitment legislation was initiated in the early 1960s with California and New York leading the way. Since then, other states have followed and in 1966 the federal government enacted a national civil commitment law in the Narcotic Addict Rehabilitation Act. The rationale of all such legislation is the view that drug addiction is basically a medical and psychological phenomenon and not criminal in essence.

In spite of such efforts, there remains a minority that argues, among a myriad of objections, that compulsory commitment violates civil rights; that mere proof of addiction is insufficient evidence that one is a threat to himself or to others and that the entire program is subterfuge, offering the promise of an effective method of treatment and a reasonable hope of cure, which they claim simply do not exist.

Although many arguments of a pragmatic nature are advanced in favor of the legalization of narcotics and drugs, those opposing such liberalization of the present laws appeal to common sense and the principle repeatedly enunciated by the American Medical Association: "Any method of treatment which permits the addicted person to dose himself with habit forming narcotics and drugs placed in his hands for self-administration is an unsatisfactory treatment, begets deception, extends the abuse of habit-forming drugs and causes an increase in crime." The revolving door of drug abuse has yet to find an acceptable solution in an open-door policy.

Recommendations

Among habitual users of drugs it is an accepted fact that the clergyman as such will have little or no influence. The obvious reason for this is that a person seeking surcease from the pressures of the problems of life by the use of drugs surely will not place himself in the presence of one who represents authority, censure, disapproval. Consequently, the priest, minister or rabbi must first approach the person and the problem as one sincerely interested in the welfare—physical, psychological and social—of the addict. He must become the Good Shepherd who seeks, actively, the lost sheep caught in the bramble of his own inadequacy. In performing this work the clergyman must expect a cool reception, perhaps even open hostility. But if he persists in extending friendship the patient will eventually recognize a need, then a dependence and ultimately an awareness of the good than can come from his own surrender.

But good will and all the dedication and personal self-sacrifice in the world will not suffice if the clergyman is not equipped with specific information as a background for his personal suggestions and recommendations.

1. To be an effective instrument of peace in the lives of drug users the clergyman must be thoroughly aware of his position and that of the addict in this most intricate of relationships. He must be as "wise as the serpent" while remaining in his own dedication as "innocent as a dove." He must realize that in common parlance the addict is a "con artist" by virtue of the very obvious need he has. The clergyman easily may be taken in. He must be certain to reassure the addict that while he is "hip" to all his wiles, he is also most sympathetic to all conflicts.

2. Since the addict's first hope for rehabilitation is a withdrawal period, the clergyman must not make the unfortunate mistake of imagining himself a technically qualified therapist. The clergyman is not a physician, no matter how well-intentioned. He should prescribe only one thing, professional service. He should therefore know of the facilities available in his community that offer the treatment needed for withdrawal. He should be thoroughly conversant with the time required, the expense involved and the public social services present.

3. The clergyman should know when to make such a referral and, therefore, he certainly should be capable of recognizing the physical and psychological manifestations of drug use or addiction. It is to be hoped that the current practice of extensive lectures in this area of social psychology in many seminaries will continue, since it seems to be more and more a part of the professional life of a clergyman.

4. Most larger communities are making such information available in a whole program of public education. No group should be more obviously represented than the clergy, for they can offer much in the way of supportive care, which is painfully lacking in the life of the addict. The clergyman should therefore support community efforts in this direction not only for his own personal information but especially for the purpose of encouraging others to become aware of the problem and resolved to aid in its alleviation.

5. The clergyman is also in a unique position with regard to the propagation of related information within his own congregation. Movies, lectures and demonstrations on the evil effects of drug misuse can easily be arranged and will help in the tremendous task of educating the public to this social problem.

6. There must be a clear-cut program for the addict during and after recovery. If the clergyman were to be described in this context by a single word it would surely be *hope*. He must become the hope of the patient during the period of recovery when all seems to be covered with a pall of despair. Frequent and regular visits should be arranged when at all possible so that the relationship between clergyman and patient will grow from a natural friendship to a meaningful understanding. If these visits are physically impossible, the clergyman should keep in touch by letter or telephone. But abandonment must never be suggested by one in whom the addict has placed his confidence. This would only serve to aggravate the feelings of inadequacy which underlie the whole emotional confusion which, in turn, partly explained the drug addiction in the first place. After the patient recovers, the clergyman should use his efforts and influence to find employment for him. This employment should be specifically related to the talents of the individual and should give him a sense of accomplishment which again will help him to rediscover his latent potential and, ultimately, some sense of security.

7. The family of the addict should receive the careful consideration of the clergyman who attempts to help in this area. It is obvious that the family probably will be the first to refer the

case of misuse or addiction to the clergyman, since, as pointed out earlier, the patient himself is unlikely to approach a source of suspected reproach. The clergyman should examine with the family the causes of the condition and explain the need, for the future, of a great deal of understanding. Censure at this point will accomplish little or nothing. Understanding does not necessarily imply weakness or lack of resolution. Instruction as to the necessity for strong family ties will help, since this is one of the weakest links in the chain that leads the immature addict to experiment with drugs as a means of escape.

Studies have shown that addicts consistently have a poor relationship with their parents and frequently turn to drugs as an expression of their acceptance of peer-relationship in preference to family relationships. Accordingly, it is essential that the clergyman speak well and often from the pulpit, in the meeting room, in the office or wherever he has a chance, of the role of parents in relation to their children. The need of proper expression of affection as an insurance of security, the need of good example which will lead to inevitable emulation, the need for reward for achievement—all of these aspects of this fundamental social relationship, which is the first in the experience of any human being, must be stressed constantly.

Given the fact of addiction or habituation, the fundamental rule must be that the panic button should not be pushed. The family should be made to realize that this is an illness and must be treated as such. They must be made to understand that there is hope of cure and that the fall, like any specific deviation, may offer much in the form of instruction for the future.

A Dozen Questions That Clergymen Ask

1. What should be my attitude in dealing with the drug addict?

Answer: You are not a district attorney. You are not a psychiatrist. You are not a physician. You are a clergyman. As such you have something distinct to offer to the drug addict who approaches you for help. Therefore, your attitude should not be one of censure. It should not be one of analysis. It should be one of sympathetic understanding similar to that which you would register with anyone with any problem who seeks your advice. What makes this case different is that some technical knowledge is required. You should readily recognize the symptoms of drug addiction or abuse. You should be on your guard against the uncanny methods that an addictive personality may have developed almost as a mechanism of defense.

2. What should be the tone of my advise to the addict?

Answer: You should avoid preaching to the addict on the physical, social and psychological damage he is inflicting on himself and others. He has heard this before. He looks to you for a fresh viewpoint which will offer him some hope for the future. Your words must be positive. They must reflect the sincere concern and the sincere hope that you have that no matter how powerful this addiction seems, it can be overcome. This should not involve a Pollyanna approach. You should be realistic and your advice should indicate clearly that you are prepared to help if help is really what is sought.

3. What is the first impression that should be left with the addict?

Answer: He should be convinced that in the clergyman he has found a friend, a confidant whom he can trust above all others. He must be able to see and hear in the words of the clergyman a source of belief in himself. He must come from the meeting with the firm conviction that he will not be punished for violating a law but will be helped to health from an illness.

4. When and to whom should referral be made?

Answer: When it is ascertained that true addiction is present the person should be referred immediately to a physician to obviate the possibility of severe withdrawal symptoms, especially convulsions, which could prove a serious physical threat. The patient then ordinarily will be referred for psychiatric care either at a rehabilitation center or at an out-patient clinic.

5. If there is not true addiction, as in the case of the so-called beginner, should any referral be made?

Answer: That depends. If there has been any drug abuse whatever, an attempt should be made to investigate the history of the individual. His age, background, educational level and social and vocational interests should be established. His family background should be explored. If there is no apparent concern expressed by the person about the danger of drug abuse, then referral to a psychiatrist should be made. If, on the other hand, the person has a good background and shows a clear understanding of the dangers involved and an attitude of repentance, it is unlikely that immediate referral is required. If there is a poor achievement background and evidence of consistent failure and relapse regarding drug abuse, there may be a masked psychic problem and referral is strongly indicated.

6. How should referral be made?

Answer: Referral to the physician should be made on the basis of physical protection: "Perhaps you need some supplement for the correction of a body deficiency. This easily could be remedied by your doctor once he has the chance to examine you." Referral to the psychiatrist is a matter of much more delicacy. It might be made on the basis of helping the person to appreciate the need to know more about himself and to give the clergyman a chance to have more complete knowledge for his proposed assistance.

7. Should the addict ever be encouraged to identify either his drug companions or his source of drugs?

Answer: No, unless he wishes to do so and is willing to initiate the process himself. Otherwise, you may lose the immediate confidence of the user and many others who ultimately might seek help. The clergyman should remain completely concerned with protecting the confidence of the person who seeks his help. He also should warn of the danger that might result from such a revelation. If the clergyman is asked directly whether such a report should be made it is best to answer with the question "What do you want to do?"

8. Should the clergyman actively seek out drug users?

Answer: Not as a first recourse. He should encourage the

contact with attractive programs in the parish and in that way gain their confidence. However, if this technique fails, he should seek them out not as a "preacher" but as a friend who wishes only their personal welfare.

9. What should he do about "pushers" in his area?

Answer: If the pusher seeks out the clergyman he should be treated in much the same manner as is the user. An offer of help coupled with a guarantee of anonymity might go far in establishing a satisfactory relationship. If he must be sought out, he should be contacted on some pretext and dissuaded by moral persuasion. If none of these procedures works and report to the authorities is used as a last resort, it should be done anonymously in order not to lose any possible influence with other addicts.

10. In the case of a minor, should the addict's parents be notified?

Answer: This should be the aim, but always with the addict's consent. An effort should be made to convince the addict that knowledgeable parents might provide the help and understanding that will enable him to overcome his habit. To obviate any fear of punishment, he should be reassured that his parents will be properly prepared by the clergyman.

11. What attitudes should the clergyman cultivate in the addict's parents?

Answer: Essentially, the clergyman must instill a determination that whatever the causes of the unhappy situation they must be ferreted out and eliminated. The parents must be convinced that a punitive attitude or one of rejection will accomplish little. They must be made to understand that the reason for their child's failure may have been their overseverity or overpermissiveness, which engendered unconscious reactions of rebellion and confusion. In either case, it undoubtedly was due to their desire to be "good parents" and as such they now must face the task of helping their child in distress.

12. Should the clergyman use the language of the addict?

Answer: Only to the extent that he will be convinced that the clergyman is familiar with the circumstances of his situation.

There must be no indication that the clergyman will lower his position or relinquish his control. If this happens his influence will be completely lost.

The removal of drug abuse, which darkens the lives of so many of our citizens and threatens the future mental health of our country, has become a major national project. This project must not fail. Its success, however, is contingent upon many factors, among them continued research, careful implementation and coordination of national and local programs, increased economic support and improved law enforcement. But the ultimate victory is in dedicated manpower. The clergyman must respond to this need. Flesh and blood and spirit are at stake and these are magnets to our ministry.

For Further Reference

Ausubel, David P. *Drug Addiction: Physiological, Psychological, and Sociological Aspects.* New York: Random House, 1958.

Bier, William C., ed. *Problems in Addiction: Alcohol and Drug Addiction.* New York: Fordham University Press, 1962.

Louria, Donald B. *The Drug Scene.* New York: McGraw-Hill Book Co., 1968.

———. *Nightmare Drugs.* New York: Pocket Books, 1966.

Laurie, Peter, ed. *Drugs.* Baltimore: Penguin Books, 1969.

President's Commission. *Task Force Report: Narcotics and Drug Abuse.* Washington: U.S. Government Printing Office, 1967.

10 Sexual Problems

There is not a clergyman with any years of experience who has not encountered individuals with personal problems whose basis is the fundamental sex drive. What priest, rabbi or minister has not been asked to counsel someone who is struggling with a conflict that cannot be resolved until his whole orientation toward sex has been clarified and matured? In many instances, the problem is not apparently connected with or related to this force. Upon further analysis, however, the resolution of the conflict will occur through a proper adjustment to the demands this powerful and significant force makes in every life. This is not to suggest that the Freudian concept of sex as the basic source of all energy is necessarily true and valid. It is to suggest most emphatically that a great step forward was made when the Freudian concept of personality development proposed that sex is a much more dynamic element in human life than had been imagined previously.

Unfortunately, what we are witnessing today is an inversion of a valid principle. As a result, the emphasis placed upon sexuality has become out of proportion. The pendulum seems to have swung in the direction of obsession or compulsivity as opposed to the previous reaction of avoidance based on fear or ignorance. Today, sex is used to sell everything from automobiles to soap to potato chips to tuna fish and there seems to be no end in sight. It is employed overtly as a means of encouraging interest in areas ranging from national politics to conservation. It is everywhere, and too many Americans approve in lusty tones and with ready cash as the hedonism of our times continues to make rapid progress and permanent inroads on American culture. It is not surprising that with this obvious emphasis and, at times, distortion, there have been many confused minds and disturbed personalities who have not been able to cope with the frequent misrepresentation of this vital segment of life.

It is not the purpose here to moralize, but rather to suggest that an honest evaluation of the "sex revolution" cannot be made until we understand the significance of the sexual drive and its relationship to the many causes of mental illness that plague our society. The clergyman, who will be called upon to deal with this problem many times and in the most personal of circumstances, must understand the natural basis for discussion and the scientifically accepted terminology and concepts that have been incorporated into the process of diagnosis and therapy.

Anyone who would work with the emotionally upset who come for help must understand adequately the problems involved in sexual maladjustment and realize that many other problems not obviously sexually related can be appreciated and solved only within that framework. This will not be achieved easily unless there is an openness to the fact that sexuality and its overt expression are determined by the nature and nurture of an individual and do not immediately become matters of moral turpitude or degeneracy. The drive will vary in intensity and expression in accord with the physiological structure and psychological strength of each person. The success of the adjustment that must be made will vary according to how the person has been trained and given values that enable him to control this dynamic force which in itself derives its worth from the purpose to which it is put.

This does not imply that the clergyman should reduce imputability completely because of the presence of an internal or external factor. It is in no way suggested that a more complete knowledge of the influences that cause or exacerbate sexual problems will obliterate moral imputability. These problems *do* have moral implications. They should be recognized and dealt with in terms of the principles of moral theology. However, the application of the basic principles of moral imputability must take into account the many natural and real factors of the human situation without relinquishing the equally fundamental and real bases provided by these principles.

The principle toward which the clergyman must strive as his point of departure may be stated through an illustration. One of the most perplexing problems and sources of suffering in the area of sexuality is that of sexual inversion, more commonly referred to as homosexuality. In recent years this manifestation of poor psychosexual development has moved from the point where it was condemned as complete degeneracy to being regarded as a manifestation of sexual deviation which society has no right to condemn merely because it does not follow a pattern previously accepted. Nevertheless, mental health authorities who have arrived at some explanation of the condition we know as inversion cannot label it in any other way than as a perversion of the natural function of sex.

Homosexuality

A major problem which demands initial consideration in any discussion of homosexuality is that of definition. A study of the literature concerning homosexuality discloses a wide spectrum of opinion not only on this but on many other questions related to the problem, with each view supported by many ardent proponents.[1] With this diversity of opinion in mind, and with our own practical intent as a guide, what can we say constitutes the condition of sexual inversion?

Some authorities consider homosexuality from a "quantitative" point of view. They look upon it as an aggregate system of attitudes, emotions and reactions that are present in all persons to some degree and become most obvious in the behavior of those who engage in overt homoerotic activity. According to this theory, homosexual patterns are universal and dynamically present even in the most heterosexual individual. This view is a reflection of Freudian influence and at present is the most prevalent theory in psychiatric circles. According to its proponents, the term *homosexual* is not necessarily restricted to overt homosexual behavior per se. It is employed to cover a number of behaviors ranging from actual and direct genital contact with members of the same sex, regardless of how transitory or how long ago it occurred, to those who currently limit their sexual expressions exclusively to their own sex. Some carry this loose designation so far as to include under the label homosexual any closeness or intimate contact with the same sex, even such simple pastimes as playing cards with the same sex or being a member of an exclusively male or exclusively female club or organization. Anyone who lives a solitary life and avoids the opposite sex, even though he in no way is involved in sexual intimacies with his own sex, also falls under the designation "homosexual."

Such usage, however, is criticized by other specialists as lacking scientific precision. Their principal search is for a concept that will demarcate the point at which a person becomes a homosexual in a more operationally qualitative sense. This trend is exemplied by Dr. Irving Bieber, who says: "A homosexual is one who engages repeatedly, in adult life, in overt sexual relations with a member or members of the same sex."[2] This definition avoids the quantitative vagueness inherent in the previous view and emphasizes the operational element. Bieber's position narrows the applicability of the term *homosexual* by excluding the universal and predominately unconscious factors commonly referred to as "latent" homosexuality. By his insertion of the qualifying terms "adult life" and "repeated" activity, he also omits from the designation sexual activities with members of the same sex that occur at certain stages of development and periodic or situational homosexual behavior. In other words, homosexual acts that take place occasionally during adolescence and in segregated situations where the population is exclusively of one sex, such as prisons, schools and the armed services, are not strictly considered to be truly homosexual.

The factors that more precisely determine this distinction are contained in the more "qualitative" definitions. In addition to the conscious and operational notes, these stress the motivational character of the homosexual behavior. Hence we read Judd Marmor's estimate that "a homosexual is one who is motivated, in adult life, by a definite preferential erotic attraction to members of the same sex and who usually (not necessarily) engages in overt sexual relations with them."[3] Here, the key to the label "homosexual" lies in *preferring* such behavior even when alternative partners are available. It implies a dominant attitude or way of thinking and emoting about sexual involvement. The homosexual experiences from his "nature" a spontaneous and powerful sexual movement toward his own sex in much the same manner as the heterosexual is inclined toward the opposite sex.

Given these varying and representative views, homosexuality would appear to consist of many variables, extending from totally unconscious and nonconsequential dispositions, common to all persons, through transitory and/or situational conscious experiences and behaviors, to persistent and preferential adult activity. At one end of the spectrum is so-called latent homosexuality. It is totally unconscious, extremely ambiguous and, for the most part, nonoperational. Since the sexual love-object is initially nonspecific, any person has within him the potential of becoming homosexual. The determination of this object is primarily a matter of training and environmental factors and if these are faulty poor identification must be expected as the natural result. Because the initial and early environments of all are populated by both males and females this identification process is never unilateral. Dual identification with both sexes always occurs. Hence there is something of the female in every male and something of the male in every female. Everyone, then, may be said to be a latent homosexual. In some, this latency is more pronounced but still unconscious, and very often involves traits not conventionally attributed to the sex in question, such as exaggerated passivity and timidity in males and over-aggressive emotional and physical traits in females. Because the identification process was predominantly with one's own sex, however, the love-object will be a member of the opposite sex. The person basically and consciously strives toward heterosexual involvement.

There can and does occur in some individuals a conscious experience of homosexual attraction. When this is totally controlled by the ego and forbidden overt expression, it remains concealed from others and may be termed "covert" homosexuality. It may involve mere fleeting thoughts or more constant and bothersome fantasies. It may be due simply to deprivation of heterosexual stimuli and/or to homosexual segregation. Under the impact of these conditions, one actually may enter into overt behavior with a member or members of the same sex. This type of behavior is "accidental" or "situational." As long as the individual basically, spontaneously and, therefore, preferentially, is geared toward heterosexual involvement these happenings are not strictly and essentially homosexual in nature. When, however, these inner preoccupations and overt behaviors are not triggered by such external circumstances but are expressions of the sexual character of the person–to the degree that they are what he truly desires—the condition is truly homosexual.

True and absolute homosexuality, then, is to be differentiated from homosexual behavior. A perfectly heterosexual individual may on occasions engage in homosexual conduct. Conversely, neither the absence of overt homosexual behavior nor the presence of heterosexual involvement precludes the possibility of homosexuality. In the former instance, the condition may be covert because of strong inner controls; in the latter, heterosexual involvement may be a defensive move against the basic sexual orientation. This often occurs in marriage in which case the individual may be labeled bisexual.

In its essential form true homosexuality is persistent and preferential sexual orientation toward the same sex. Operationally, it consists in the acting out of this sexual orientation by physical, genital involvement with the same sex.

A number of illustrations may further clarify these distinctions.

Absolute Homosexuality. John, forty years old, is a successful advertising artist. He admits to his homosexuality. He states that he fought it throughout adolescence and into young adulthood. At one time, he went to a psychiatrist but claims it did him no good. Now he has given up, is in love with a man younger than himself and is living with him. He cannot understand why he and people like him are ostracized and not granted the privilege of a marriage that would be legal and approved by God. For him, there is no other way for mutual and intimate love.

Bisexuality. Don is forty-seven years old. He is married and a professional man. He is the father of three children. He was an only child and his father died when he was seven years old. His mother was extremely strict with him when he was growing up. To this day, he must call her up every day or there is trouble. In his sexual relations with his wife, he reveals that he always has had a strong desire for anal intercourse. He knows a co-professional who is a homosexual. Don admits that he has entered into masturbatory acts with this person. These feelings were with him during his adolescence, left him during the first years of his marriage, but returned and are now overpowering him.

Covert Homosexuality. Bill is a college student and is troubled because he sometimes has thoughts and images of nude males with accompanying sexual stimulation. He goes out with girls and admits that he "makes out" with them on occasion. He has never actively engaged in sexual activities with males. He hopes to marry someday and have a family but is severely disturbed over his recurring sexual fantasies involving males.

Because of the many distinctions and the obvious need to conceal one's homosexual identity, precise figures as to the incidence of homosexuality never have been accurately determined. There are estimates, however, and though these vary the most conservative of them indicate that in America today there are anywhere from two to four million males who for most of their lives are exclusively and predominantly homosexual.[4] In his treatment of the "homosexual explosion," *The Sixth Man,* Jess Stern suggests that every sixth American male is a sexual invert. When taken to task by scholars and heterosexuals in general, homosexual groups reacted by saying that the figure was too low. The more scientific although often criticized statistics of Alfred Kinsey indicate that homosexual "behavior" at least is much more frequent than ordinarily supposed.

Whatever the exact number, the male population of true homosexuals in America has developed an extended and somewhat loosely related "contact network." Evelyn Hooker of the University of California, Los Angeles, has made a complete and objective study of this aspect of homosexual living.[5] Dr. Hooker reports that in addition to what homosexuals themselves call "the Swiss Alps" and "Boys Town" communal dwelling in apartment houses operated by and usually rented exclusively to homosexuals, there are network clusters made up of friends and acquaintances from far and wide. The three most common forms of cluster are the tightly knit clique made up of "married" homosexual couples and some select single members who are most often heterosexually married; looser clique structures comprised of larger numbers and less restricted membership and extremely loose networks of friends and acquaintances who casually meet at public gathering places adapted to a homosexual clientele. The most important in the latter category is the "gay" bar. Such places as steambaths, gyms, beaches, coffee houses, restaurants, public toilets, parks and streets also serve as centers for this specialized subculture. Such private cliques and public meeting places offer to the homosexual, who in our social structure must ever guard his sexual identity from the world at large, a setting where he can be comfortable, safe and "gay" in his social and recreational life.

"Cruising" and the "one-night stand" are standard and characteristic features of these loosely structured groups. Both practices are essential features of "sex without commitment or obligation." Cruising, as might be expected, is bar-hopping, and the "one-night stand" the actual engagement in some form of homosexual activity. This sexual involvement is sealed by the "glance," a unique form of eye-to-eye communication which every homosexual knows and recognizes, which reveals mutual recognition of sexual identity and intent to the point of mutual contract. It is standard wherever homosexuals gather in the United States. Such centers also provide opportunity for making friends and exchanging gossip and news within the homosexual world.

There are common understandings within the homosexual society. It is understood, for example, that success in the homosexual subculture is enhanced by physical appearance, that youth is essential, that anyone past thirty-five may have to pay in order to "make out," that being seen too frequently is not the thing to do, that familiar faces are suspect and every "stand" is necessarily a meeting of strangers.

This public and visible part of the homosexual world has its counterpart in the private and secret activities of the closely knit cliques, where long-term and established relationships between homosexuals are found. These people rarely, if ever, go to public places because of the possible effect upon an established homosexual relationship. Most frequently, they include persons of professional and high socio-economic status who cannot afford the exposure to the threat of detection and arrest that always prevails in the public centers.

There is, however, no such thing as a "homosexual personality." This is a misconception as absurd as assuming that all heterosexuals are alike. Personality variation among homosexuals is as great as among the heterosexual population, encompassing the introvert and the extrovert, the timid and the aggressive, the sociopath and the morally scrupulous, the brilliant and the borderline mentally defective. It is true, however, that in general neurotic patterns of behavior tend to be more prevalent among homosexuals than among heterosexuals. Most authorities attribute this to interaction with social, legal and moral proscriptions and views rather than to the condition of homosexuality itself. Such circumstances obviously create intense inner tensions in many homosexuals, especially those who find themselves incapable of accepting their sexual identity because it lessens their self-image and destroys their social status.[6]

This neurotic tendency, usually born of the inability to adjust through acceptance of the condition, is further aggravated by a fatalistic attitude toward the condition. Most homosexuals are of the belief that they were born such or made such by familial or other environmental determinants. They are convinced that since the condition exists without choice or control the possibility of changing or adjusting is extremely remote. Consequently, for them to fight against their homosexuality would be to battle their own "nature" in its essential form as they experience it. This prompts the question: What precisely is the teaching on the causality of homosexuality? All available evidence points strongly to exogenous factors in the genesis of homosexuality. Genetic studies involving identical twins have been conducted without any decisive or reliable conclusions. The possibility of hormonal causation also has been investigated, but in most instances the evidence thus far obtained does not support such a contention.

This latter or organistic school stresses the androgens and estrogens since both are found in male and female alike, and asserts that a preponderance of either in the inappropriate sex results in homosexuality. These hormones in fact fulfill a threefold function: they govern the growth of the sex organs, they determine the secondary sex characteristics and stimulate the sex drive by increasing sexual end-organ sensitivity. They are, however, nonspecific in terms of sexual object-relationship. If there is an excess of estrogens in the male he may be somewhat "girlish" in build, even to the point of breast formation and sensitivity. This oversupply of estrogens may intensify sexual strivings as such. As has been observed in certain cancer cases where hormonal injections are employed, however, the sex drive is increased but its object is unaltered. Dr. William H. Perloff, supervisor of Endocrinology and Reproduction at the Albert Einstein Medical Center in Philadelphia, concludes from his research that large doses of estrogens administered to normal males actually decrease the sex drive in some instances but never increase the attraction to other males. He further reports that large amounts of andogrens given to normal women may increase their libidos but never change their sex-object orientation. Homosexual patients may react to the administration of andogrens by an increase in sexual behavior but always in the direction of a homosexual object.[7]

Among the exogenous factors that have been studied, the family constellation proves to be the most potent. It has been demonstrated repeatedly that sexual attitudes are formed long before the person acquires definite factual knowledge about sexual activity. At the roots of these attitudes are the "identification" process and "castration fear" process described by Sigmund Freud. In the "identification" failure, a detached, indifferent, rejecting, passive or punishing father may bring into effect an obstacle in the boy's process of identifying with him. In the need to identify with someone, the boy may become attached to the mother and unconsciously mold himself and his inner emotional life according to her female dispositions. She becomes the one to "be like" rather than the father, who becomes an object of fear or hate. A somewhat similar but inverse process often occurs in the case of Lesbians.

With "castration fear" the fault lies in a domineering, aggressive, henpecking or emasculating mother. The boy identifies with the father but develops a generalized fear of women and of involvement with them because of his initial contact with them in the person of his mother. The ultimate and unconscious thought pattern emerges that "If you love at all, never love a woman for she will rob you of your manhood." When homosexuality does not eventuate from this basic female hatred, the heterosexual orientation usually becomes marred by a hostile and punishing type of behavior toward the female mate. Once again, with appropriate modification, these equivalents may be seen at work in many Lesbians.

These two interpretations of the genesis of homosexuality have received wide acceptance because of their continual recurrence in clinical records. Many experts also stress a basic temperamental makeup characterized by such features as extreme timidity and passivity and excessive gentleness. They believe that with this type of constitution, one is more likely to become a homosexual, especially if certain environmental factors are present. Even in the absence of such a constitution, these same environmental circumstances of themselves may lead to a homosexual formation. Among the circumstances are:

1. Unrealistic and harsh parental sexual prohibitions. Constant injunctions such as "Stay away from girls" and "Girls get you in trouble" may impede and block normal heterosexual development. It could happen that sex is not interpreted as bad in itself, but bad only in relation to girls.

2. Parental rejection of the boy precisely because he is a boy. In their unfulfilled desire to have had a daughter, some parents stress female activities to the point of even dressing the small boy as a girl. In such cases, the boy may either conceive of himself as a girl or believe that it would be better if he were a girl.

3. Continual berating of a son as not "rough and tough" enough. The boy who is reared in such circumstances may come to feel that he is not a real man and never will be attractive to females or able to satisfy them.

4. Female sibling rivalry, with girls always preferred and favored by the parents. The boy may interpret this as rejection and unconsciously think "If I were a girl, I too would be favored and accepted." He may then begin to take on female qualities.

5. Constant rejection of a boy as a "sissy" or "weakling" by older boys and men. Under these conditions, the boy may adopt a feminine role and in this way attempt to gain the acceptance that he sees these male figures accord girls and women. Above all, if such a boy suffers the misfortune of being abused by an older male, he unconsciously may conclude "Older men accept and like me because of sex. Acceptance by men apparently demands of me sexual activity with them."

These many possibilities of homoerotic etiology make it clear that the homosexual is not a person who has deliberately chosen or consciously planned his homosexual orientation. In a real sense, he became what he is, a homosexual, because of the people with whom he lived when he was young. He was less fortunate than his heterosexual brothers.

Here are some of the questions most frequently asked about homosexuality:

1. Is homosexuality a disease?

Answer: A number of prominent psychoanalysts regard homosexuality as an illness that is incompatible with a reasonably happy life and which is to be treated and corrected. Freud himself did not consider it an illness. The latter is the opinion of most authorities and psychiatrists, who hold this view especially when no other symptomatology is in evidence. In itself, homosexuality is usually regarded as a personality disturbance which involves a fixation at or regression to an earlier and immature level of development.

2. Is homosexuality ever overcome?

Answer: There is evidence that homosexuality is a potentially reversible condition. Treatment is long and tedious and the prognosis usually guarded. Success always depends upon the type or degree that is involved and ultimately upon the motivation of the patient. Psychoanalysis is the principal, if not the only effective means of therapy. The most successful time for therapy is the period between adolescence and maturity when sexual orientation has not been fully established.

3. Is homosexuality easily detected?

Answer: Biological and psychological tests are unreliable bases for diagnosis. Even personal observation of homosexual activity cannot warrant the diagnosis of "homosexuality." Strictly speaking, the only legitimate bases for the label of "homosexuality" are the individual's personal admission of the condition and/or the professional therapist's conclusion drawn from personal interview.

4. Is effeminacy essentially related to homosexuality?

Answer: Homosexuals may be effeminate or extremely

robust. Effeminate habits also may be found in the perfectly heterosexual person. There is no necessary connection between the two. Effeminacy is assumed through unconscious imitation of female mannerisms, without any necessary or essential defect in the process of sexual identification.

5. Are homosexuals less trustworthy than heterosexuals?

Answer: This assumption, which is widespread, is based on lack of objective and intimate knowledge of the personalities involved. In general, they are no less in control than are heterosexuals. Homosexuals are neither more nor less trustworthy with their own sex, even with children, than heterosexuals are with members of the opposite sex. The homosexual's dependability should be gauged in precisely the same way as that of the heterosexual; that is, is he a responsible human being—does he have an adequate superego?

6. What emotion constitutes the greatest barrier in homosexual adjustment?

Answer: Fear is the greatest obstacle to the homosexual's adjustment or reversal of pattern. Fear of the opposite sex, adult responsibility and competition with his own sex underlie and perpetuate much homosexuality. It is this same fear, even though not consciously experienced, that hampers resolutions and attempts to abandon homosexual involvement.

7. What is the legal view on homosexuality in the United States?

Answer: In every state, homosexual acts between males (not always females) is an offense. Nowhere (except in Illinois) does consent between parties exempt one from the law. The element of "force," however, is often an important factor. The exact types of acts that are to be punished and the nature of their punishment varies from state to state. For the most part, these acts are called "crimes against nature" and mainly include adult anal and oral penetration and bestiality. In addition to the homosexual proscriptions, most states have "sexual psychopath" statutes. These are aimed primarily at curbing sexual assaults against adults and sexual molesting of children. The homosexual also may be subject to the controls of such legislation. At present, the view of most jurists and physicians that private homosexual behavior between consenting adults should not be brought under criminal headings has not been very well incorporated in remedial legislation.

8. What should be done with homosexuals who are seducing others?

Answer: When this activity occurs privately among other homosexuals where the practice is accepted and there is no threat to the common good, concern should be dismissed. If it takes place outside these circumstances and the security of others is threatened, the homosexual in question must be stopped. If he does not desist after peaceful intervention, recourse to other measures, even the police, must be adopted. This is especially so where the young are imperiled.

9. Is homosexuality synonymous with sexual perversion?

Answer: Homosexuality is only one form of sexual perversion. In recent years, the term *perversion* has been replaced by the designation "sexual deviation," which is the modern equivalent of "sexual degeneracy."

10. What are the other sexual deviations?

Answer: Though many nuances exist, "sexual deviation" refers to any sexual satisfaction that is obtained through practices other than adult heterosexual intercourse. Even this very general definition fails, since masturbation is not classified as a deviation. In general, the deviations may be classified as those of "aim" and those of "object." In the former, the quality of sexual striving is abnormal. The individual is not aiming at intercourse. For satisfaction, he prefers such practices as exhibitionism, voyerism, sadism, masochism, fellatio, cunnilingus and sodomy. Among the deviations of object, the nature of striving is preserved and normal. It is geared toward sexual congess but the object is abnormal. These objects may vary from and give rise to such states as pedophilia, fetishism, bestiality and homosexuality.

Other Sexual Deviations

It must not be concluded that because homosexuality has received extensive publicity in recent years that it is the most significant form of sexual perversion. Some other deviations are more common and frequently indicate a personality disorder that will require professional help.[8] They include:

PEDOPHILIA. This is a sexually-motivated and pathological erotic craving for children. The pedophiliac derives sexual satisfaction from sexual intimacies with children, usually of the opposite sex, but frequently of the same sex. The degree of intimacy may vary from fondling the child sexually to actual penetration. This deviation is more commonly present among men who seek out children and "palpate" the child or cause the child to "palpate" them. With young boys, masturbatory practices and fellatio are the usual procedure.

Those engaging in such practices invariably are psychosexually immature. Ostensibly they are weak, fearful and ineffectual people who have deep doubts concerning their sexual status and fear rejection in any attempt at an adult sexual relationship. Some theorists have suggested that the cause of this deviation may be an unresolved and unconscious desire in childhood to have had parents act toward the pedophiliac in question in the same manner. In such a case the patient may not want his victim to suffer what he considered his own "rejection." Another possible explanation is that the practice may be an hostility outlet in which the patient asserts a "power" influence over another.

CASE: A thirty-eight-year-old salesman, white, from a middle-class family, obtained a rather lucrative position as a company representative who traveled to other cities regularly on company business. Unmarried, he sought sexual satisfaction from children casually encountered in public parks. A first overture to the children was made through plastic toys, a product of his company. Demonstration of the toys required that they come to his car. At this point he would manually molest them one by one until satisfaction was achieved. Departure to other cities made his arrest difficult.

TRANSVESTISM. This manifestation of sexual maladjustment takes the form of a morbid impulse to wear the clothing of the opposite sex. This is quite different from the innocent masquerade or the joke or hoax. The patient who is so inclined desires to achieve sexual satisfaction from the association with the clothing, usually through masturbatory acts. The disposition may be permanent or occasional but always indicates a poor sexual identification. The transvestite invariably exhibits homosexual tendencies but almost inevitably denies homosexual interests and assiduously avoids overt homosexual conduct. As such, tranvestism is a separate paraphilia but with thinly distinguished homosexual overtones.

The condition occurs most frequently in males who have been raised as girls because of their mother's desire to have a daughter. It also may be the result of an overpowering erotic attraction toward the opposite sex which is so intense that the individual wishes to be permanently identified with it. He may depise his own sex and wish to escape from it by idolizing females, which in turn prevents a permanent adult sexual relationship with them.

CASE: A male, age forty, was arrested for the crime of homosexual solicitation. His first sexual experience was at age twelve with another older boy, a cousin. As a boy he was always fascinated by the clothing of his older sister, which he used to wear secretly before engaging in acts of self-abuse. Eventually he wore women's clothing in the streets and began using it as a sexual invitation to other men. He denied emphatically that he was a homosexual.

FETISHISM. This deviation often is an outgrowth of transvestism and something of an extension of it. Sexual pleasure and gratification is sought not merely from association with the clothing of the opposite sex but from objects directly or indirectly related to them. It is a deviation common mostly among men and usually involves personalizing objects either worn by women or used by them. The fetish itself may not necessarily be limited to inanimate objects but may be associated with parts of the female body dissociated from the genitalia. They may be fingers, toes, the chest or locks of hair. The objects are usually women's underclothing and in these instances, as well as in those involving part of the body, there is always a genital reference which helps to provide a source of erotic gratification and relieves both psychic and physical tension. The person usually masturbates on contact with the fetish and the condition must be described as pathological when the activities become compulsive and preferential. Equivalents may be found in homosexuals but, of course, always in reference to their own sex.

Many authorities feel that this deviation is essentially employed as a means of denying the anatomical difference in the sexes, the discovery of which caused an overwhelming anxiety and fear. The object serving as a substitute for the proper sexual stimulus allays this fear and allows the patient to destroy the image of sexual fear and impotence in his own mind. Most of those who have recourse to fetishism are frequently impotent with their own wives or other women.

CASE: A thirty-six-year-old father of two children was arrested for breaking into a house and was found to have in his possession a pair of black panties belonging to the woman whose home he had entered. It was discovered that from age seven he had been stealing female underclothing and using it for masturbatory practices. He "liked the feel of silk" and related this to a childhood fascination with a little girl whom he had had as a neighbor. The little girl moved away and he asked her to give him her panties "to have something that belonged to her." She refused, and later he entered the house and stole a pair from her bedroom. During the following years, he rubbed them against his genitals and eventually developed a practice which lasted into his adult life. The practice was completely occult and unknown even to his wife with whom he had made a fairly successful adjustment. Treatment was delayed because of this and his illness was discovered only as a result of his arrest.

EXHIBITIONISM. This common form of sexual deviation is simply described as the compulsive act of exposing the penis. Psychologically, however, the involvement that this form of abnormality represents is by no means simple. This aberration is the reason why most sex offenders are brought to court and although usually repetitive may occur only once in a man's life. The major element of sexual gratification is the desire to surprise a woman or girl when he is erected and thus acquire a stimulation to masturbate. The stimulation consists in his capacity to observe carefully the psychological reaction of the female. The compulsive and preferential character of the act constitutes its fundamental pathology.

The fact that this is such a common form of deviation is in part the explanation of its entire etiology. Exhibitionism is essentially a hostile act toward members of the opposite sex based upon a castration complex or fear that somehow an adult relationship will rob the offender of his manhood. He must, therefore, reassure himself, as it were, in the presence of the opposite sex that his virility has not been destroyed or in any way threatened. This abnormal fear is usually traceable to a domineering mother. Eventually the son resents this domination but also fears the opposite sex. When hostility becomes a substitute for fear, its expression may take many forms as an outlet. Exhibitionism is one and clearly indicates the domineering influence which too many mothers play in the live of their sons.

CASE: Walter, forty-three years old, is a bachelor who has been arrested on three different occasions for exhibitionism. He delights in driving his car slowly in residential areas as though looking for directions. He invariably attracts the attention of a young mother walking an infant. He calls to her from the car and when she comes to the car to give directions he exposes himself and drives away.

CASE: Harold is an exhibitionist who goes to the trouble of dressing as a woman and entering female rest rooms in subway stations. He derives satisfaction from exposing himself to any woman who comes through the door. He exits quickly and is lost in the crowd. The police of a large city's vice squad eventually traced him in one day to seventeen different station platforms where he attempted this act.

VOYEURISM. This is commonly designated as the act of "Peeping Toms" who seek sexual gratification from witnessing a woman disrobe or other people in sexual play. Masturbation may accompany the scene. It is a form of deviation which is most common among youths and younger men. Voyeurism does not refer to the occasional visit to a burlesque theater where a striptease will take place; of itself, this would not be considered a pathological condition. It is the compulsivity and substitutive nature of voyeurism that constitutes its pathology. There are voyeurists who can derive sexual satisfaction only from viewing strip shows and are drawn compulsively on a regular basis to this type of performance. They usually are the same type who prowl about deriving vicarious pleasure from observing others engaging in sex acts in lovers' lanes or who visit beaches for the explicit purpose of deriving sexual gratification from observing others without being detected themselves. Many such people are incapable of becoming an active sexual participant because of a fear of interpersonal sexual relationships.

CASE: Frank, age thirty-six, has been arrested for voyeurism on the complaint of seven women in the suburban town in which he lives. A successful businessman, he is married and has one child. An interview with a social worker indicated that he has had an obsession with viewing naked women since he was a teen-ager. The whole process began with magazines picturing nudes. He graduated to burlesque shows and found complete sexual satisfaction in these visual experiences. Eventually, he realized the inadequacy of such fulfillment and married. Even in his marriage, however, he insisted that his wife disrobe frequently in his presence, during which time he would masturbate. After several years, he began the process of "walking the dog" in the evening with the hope of seeing women through open windows.

MASTURBATION. Since masturbation so often accompanies many of the sexual deviations, its consideration here is not out of place. In itself, it is a most common problem and one which constitutes for many a definite source of inner conflict and mental anguish.[9]

Viewed developmentally, masturbation is a normal part of

the entire psychosexual maturation process. In the very young, it is the result of natural self-exploration and self-discovery. This is usually the case in infantile and childhood masturbation. It is simply a somatic self-interest in a particular part of the body with little if any significant difference from a preoccupation with some other part of the body. At times, this practice in children stems from boredom or the need of self-reassurance. It has nothing in common with adult masturbation and is indulged in by children with little or no awareness that it is taking place. It requires several years for the proper nerve endings to grow and mature in the genital area and it also requires pubertal hormonal secretions to make such manipulations assume sexual significance. It is the misinformed and overly anxious adult's concern about such behavior that invests it with sexual significance. Even curiosity and comparisons with the genitals of other children is simply an awakening and normal aspect of the growing awareness of the differences that exist between boys and girls.

It is only at the time when orgasm occurs that the practice becomes a truly important issue. At this time sexual fantasies most frequently begin to precede or accompany the masturbatory act and with this it assumes proportions of adult sexuality. During the teens, however, the practice, within limits, does not imply any abnormality. It may be merely the result of the initial impact of the pleasure of orgasm accidently experienced and its continuance may be due to some emotional need stemming from adolescent insecurity and hostility. In our society its occurrence represents the only sexual expression available to the youngster at a time when the sexual drive is both extremely novel and intense. The drive for sexual congress with the concomitant experience of pleasure is a normal human phenomenon. The appearance of masturbation among teen-agers is a primitive move toward this human goal. It usually is replaced when the marital status is achieved. Even when it occurs in adulthood when no appropriate sexual partner is available it may be simply an outward expression and release for internal and external sexual tensions that are too strong to reject.

In itself, then, masturbation should never be regarded as an abnormality. It must not, however, be concluded that the practice of masturbation is a sine qua non condition for the attainment of psychosexual maturity. Psychosexual maturity is precisely psychic. It is sexuality manifesting itself mentally and characterized by proper heterosexual interest and purpose and the emotional stability to assume and fulfill the responsibilities associated with such involvement. It is a quality of maturity that is not gained by a somatic experience, even a somatic experience as intense as orgasm.

Statisticians report an extremely high incidence of masturbation within the population at large. Kinsey's figures indicating that 92 percent of American males have engaged in masturbation to some degree appears to be consonant with other competent surveys that have been conducted both in the United States and abroad. There are, of course, other less conservative estimates that could lead one to put credence in the familiar view that 99 percent of the population have indulged in the practice at some time and that the other 1 percent lie about it.[10]

It is obvious from these findings that if the practice of masturbation, as such, was associated with abnormality or physical or emotional harm the human race would be quite seriously crippled. In the past, physical and emotional ills such as brain damage, acne, weak eyes, stooped shoulders, loss of masculine vigor, impotence, sterility, feeblemindedness and a host of other disorders including insanity were attributed to the practice. Such erroneous ideas brought into existence more psychic disturbance than the practice itself ever could cause. Fortunately, most of these misconceptions have been discarded. Some remnants, which seem to stem from ill-informed, unthinking and personally anxious authority figures who employ them in an attempt to frighten a person out of the practice, remain. This approach certainly frightens but surely fails in stopping anyone for long.

The severity of this original taboo seems to have shifted to other areas. Feelings of shame, fear and guilt now surround such aspects of the problem as its frequency, solitariness and persistence beyond a certain point in life. These same psychic experiences are now related to the fantasy components that are regarded as "sick," "dirty" and "impure." It is reactions such as these that cause most of the depression and emotional anguish that surround the practice.

With due regard for moral implications, it is important to appreciate the psychological and dynamic significance of the act of masturbation. Ordinarily, masturbation is employed to relieve builtup sexual tension in the absence of a legitimate sexual partner. In such circumstances it is the lesser of two evils. It is better to masturbate alone than to involve someone else or to get involved with another. From the psychological point of view the act of masturbation, under such circumstances of deprivation, is not considered an abnormal phenomenon when it is employed sporadically as a relief from sexual tension that arises from hormonal secretions and/or external exciting factors.

When, however, masturbation assumes the frequency and uniformity proper to a habit and/or continues well into adulthood, it must be looked upon as a sign of immaturity. When it is characterized by compulsivity and deficient or distorted fantasies and is preferred to heterosexual intercourse, abnormality is indicated.

Sexual satisfaction is, of course, a natural and extremely attractive good. The mature person, however, is capable of postponing immediate gratification and is able to tolerate its deprivation within reasonable limits. He also is able to channel his energies into satisfying and constructive sublimations. When pushed beyond the limit of endurance by sexual tension, the healthy person will automatically be overtaken by heterosexual fantasies and will always be preferentially geared toward orgastic completion in heterosexual congress.

As practiced by the disturbed personality, however, masturbation presents an obviously different picture. Whenever the practice is characterized by any of the following signs, it must be judged to be abnormal:

1. When the act cannot be postponed or diminished in frequency without severe anxiety and depression and is exploited as either a remedy or to prevent such psychic pains

2. When the act is compulsively indulged in with no sexual tension present

3. When it is performed compulsively under any kind of minimal tension

4. When sexual tension is present but the person continues to masturbate after the stimulus has been removed and satisfied

5. When repeated ejaculations occur in an adult without manipulation. In adolescents this may occur while in the presence of highly sexually stimulating circumstances without abnormality.

6. When abnormal fantasies habitually accompany the act, e.g., males with males, with animals, being whipped or beaten

7. When full knowledge of intercourse is had and the person repeatedly prefers thoughts of other acts of sex to complete the satisfaction, e.g., fellatio, sodomy

8. When intercourse is available and solitary orgastic actions are preferred

9. When foreplay is indulged in, and then orgasm through masturbation is attained and preferred to its occurence in sexual intercourse

10. When masturbation is performed publicly. In adults, even in the absence of other serious symptoms, this practice is always highly suggestive of psychosis; when it occurs this way in small children who are otherwise well adjusted, it might simply be an attention-getting device. Even here, however, the possibility of maladjustment remains.

The following examples provide some practical illustrations:

John is sixteen and a high school junior. He enjoys athletics, attends school activities, "gets along good" with his peers, both boys and girls, and has a part-time job in an electrical supply store. John masturbates approximately two or three times a week. He started the practice when he was fifteen. It usually occurs at night but sometimes at the beach or movies or when he sees pictures of girls in magazines that are passed around at work and at school. He is disappointed in his lack of "better sense" and "control."

Andy is a classmate of John's and a year older. He is not as outgoing as John but gets along with others. He is more interested in books. Andy does not masturbate, although he admits of desires to do so since "all the guys talk about it." He also admits that it has happened a few times, but "nothing to talk about—maybe five times in all, I guess. I just don't want to start it. I don't think it's the right thing. I don't think I'd feel good about it."

From the descriptions alone, neither John nor Andy present any serious behavioral problem. John, however, could benefit from some counseling aimed at discovering the source of the inadequacy leading to the practice and building his ego-strength. Andy should be reassured of his mature position without pushing him in either direction.

George is twenty-one years old. He works during the day and attends classes at night. He is deferred from the service because of a chronic asthmatic condition. George is subject to anxiety and when under pressure finds his only relief in masturbation. On a busy day at the office he "must go to the men's room several times and relieve myself." At other times, he can't get thoughts of women out of his mind. His only relief comes from masturbation, which has to be repeated "for some crazy reason." The woman who lives next door arouses him. When he sees her he cannot resist his thoughts. At times, when he sees her from his bedroom window, he can't turn away. If he does he must return and then has to start masturbating. At night he frequently "just can't get to sleep. I just have to imagine being with her. Sometimes I use pictures of nudes. When I get this way the only relief is to masturbate; sometimes I have to do it three times a night."

Obviously, George's practice of masturbation is abnormal. It is symptomatic of an underlying obsessive-compulsive neurosis. Psychotherapy should be strongly urged.

Chris is thirty-two years old. He is separated from his wife and lives alone. The marriage broke up because "my wife turned out to be sexless with me and she didn't arouse me. She was a waitress and I knew the boys were having their time with her—that's for sure. I never caught her but I was certain of it and still am." Chris does not need her now because he masturbates. He claims that he does not want to do it, but women cause him to. For instance, there are two young women living in the same apartment house whose rooms are directly across the courtyard from his. "Every night one or the other comes to the window to draw the blinds. Then, from behind the closed blinds, they begin to tempt me, to seduce me. They are fiends. They get control of my body—my muscles, arms and hands. They make me masturbate before them at the open window, then they laugh at me."

The behavior of Chris, like that of George, is abnormal and compulsive, but Chris's underlying process is psychotic. The delusional elements of unreality and personalization are central to his problem. He requires immediate psychiatric attention.

General Advice

When he is approached for advice and help on a problem involving the most personal area of sex, there are certain considerations a clergyman must keep in the forefront of his mind if the relationship is to be meaningful and productive.

Initially, there is the defensive position of the patient and his natural reluctance to disclose failures in this almost sacred part of his life. A genuine person-to-person relationship must be established and the patient must have every confidence that he is talking to someone who will be more than a professional confidant, someone who will be a friend. In the vernacular of our day, it is the responsibility of the clergyman not to "turn the patient off" by his attitude or manner. This requires a certain openness on his part, which in turn will induce the patient to be equally honest and direct.

Clergymen frequently are incapable of empathy with a person who has such a problem, but this does not excuse them from the responsibility of sympathy. An erratic, unreasoned response is more often than not a mechanism that is evoked only because the problem presented may be a threat. But that is little consolation to the patient possessed by fear and guilt. Unbounded, realistic optimism must be communicated to the patient, who must be given a firm conviction that no matter how discouraging the history of failure, success is attainable with effort and determination. This reassurance should not be attempted except within the framework of a realistic evaluation of the limitations of the past and the ego-strength of the present. A positive approach to this will require that the clergyman present a program of personal, attainable and fulfilling goals. The values that each person has must be sought out and introduced as sources of satisfaction and sublimation for the patient. This search may require a number of meetings and considerable self-evaluation, but values that can form the basis for a pattern of substitution for sexual failure or inadequacy can be found, and must be found, if successful adjustment is to be made. Attention to something else and the perceived need to live unselfishly for someone else are invaluable tools by which the whole personality structure can be remade. The clergyman should be able to explain intelligently the need for and the psychological methods of attaining phantasy control. The sources of phantasy–reading materials, TV, films—must be seen as they truly are: the bases of many actions that would not have occurred had they not been stimulated by lack of phantasy control.

The clergyman should not be hesitant about frankly and directly proposing a dependence on the supernatural source of strength, God himself. Strangely, many clergyman are hesitant, if not fearful, of proposing prayer as a means of help in our woefully pseudo-sophisticated world. If the truth were known, many patients who come for help with regard to a problem involving sex are longing for someone to speak about God, his mercy and his goodness. Who better than the clergyman should be able to do this?

Just as each individual person must be accorded the special concern and care that are proper to the uniqueness of his personality, so each specific type of sexual problem requires specialized attention. Accordingly, a list of pastoral recommendations for the particular sexual problems discussed in this chapter follows.

Recommendations Concerning Homosexuality

1. Homosexuals usually will not approach the clergyman. Embarrassment and fear of both detection and an adverse reaction are the principal reasons why recourse to his help is infrequent. When they do come, however, it is usually because of guilt and fear of "acting out" in the future. Approach is also often prompted by a panic reaction in the latent homosexual on discovering his condition.

2. Compassion, common decency and the awareness that this is a punishing ordeal for the person must constitute the psychological set of the clergyman. He must project himself into the place of the patient and ask himself "How would I feel if I were now in his situation?" Reactions of anger are unreasonable. In this specific area, as well as others dealing with sexual problems, hostile reactions are often triggered by fear, due to unresolved but unconscious personal sexual conflicts related to the objective problem at hand. The homosexual is particularly aware of this possibility.

3. Receive the patient as a human being worthy of help. Set up the possibility for him to talk freely by being genuinely friendly and interested. Your aim should not be to change him, but only to help him accept his problem and do something about it. Assure him that his problem is not an intractable or uncontrollable illness, but rather a symptom that can be cared for and managed. Assure him of your willingness to support him in this effort. This will build up his ego-strength and hope.

4. Every homosexual who is overtly involved or gives evidence of a collapse in his ego defenses should be brought to the decision to seek treatment. The signs of such collapse are anxiety, depression and obsessional thinking.

5. Homosexuals who are in control of their condition and show no signs of such collapse need not be referred. They should be encouraged to persevere and provided constant ego-building assistance.

6. Motivation is critical to both successful treatment and

management. When treatment is necessary and proper motivation is lacking, the person should be told of the success that is possible in treatment and of the certain effects of learning more about himself and of being helped to live more successfully and happily. Never, however, make any false promises.

7. Even when therapy is judged necessary, never push or demand it. It is always better merely to suggest the possibility of considering it. Anxiety over the condition is always the best motivator for seeking treatment. Consequently, when indifference prevails, it is safe to create some anxiety by saying "Do you realize that you are taking chances, that you might get caught, that you might lose your reputation or job?" Such a device, however, never should be employed in a harsh or threatening manner.

8. Never condone the person's misconduct nor give the impression that you are indifferent to its moral implications. He expects you to be concerned about his homosexuality but also about its morality. Do not, however, badger him with the fact of sin. Rather, convey to him your interest in allaying his guilt and working with him to a solution to his problem.

9. When a drinking habit accompanies the problem, strongly urge its cessation. Besides weakening defenses, alcoholism is thought by some to be a homosexual substitute. Encourage, also, the avoidance of all external stimuli that have evoked homosexual responses in the past.

10. Depression is a constant enemy of the homosexual, especially the homosexual who is unsuccessful in accepting and coping with his condition. The possibility of suicide in such depressed cases should not be taken lightly. Reassurance of continued and unfailing support is the best builder of hope and confidence.

Recommendations Concerning Pedophilia, Exhibitionism and Other Deviations

1. Fear of getting caught, self-disgust and guilt are the main reasons why these persons approach the clergyman. Medical advice and legal pressure sometimes explain their coming. Though

many of these deviations provoke violent reactions in some, the clergyman must maintain a controlled and professional attitude. The invasion of personal privacy and the violation of the rights and morals of others cannot be dismissed; but neither can the offender's unfortunate condition and personal need for help be overlooked.

2. Whenever the person is actively involved in overt deviant behavior, referral is imperative for both the offender's good and the security of society. Even when these impulses are covert and controlled treatment should be urged.

3. When they resist this suggestion remind them of the possibility of detection and arrest. These people fear this possibility but believe it will not take place. Explain the symptomatic nature of the behavior and the fact that they are not alone in their problems. Others have the same condition which can be coped with when professional help is sought.

4. Assure them of your confidence. Never threaten to reveal them for this will only frighten them away and end their search for help.

5. When their behavior constitutes a social threat, as it usually does, appeal to the fact that the rights and morals of innocent people are unjustly threatened and violated by such deviant behavior.

6. Explain to them that their condition is a developmental fault that started early in life, but also insist that they have no choice except to control their antisocial impulses. Assure them of your continued help but emphasize therapy as the key to success. If necessary, offer to initiate psychiatric arrangements.

Recommendations Concerning Masturbation

1. Whenever the practice is symptomatic of neurosis or psychosis referral must be the goal. When the practice is not symptomatic, but nevertheless persistent and accompanied by noticeable tension, special counseling should be suggested. This is especially so when it continues well into adulthood. All such suggestions

should be made with due regard for the person's sensitivities and should never be pushed, except in those cases where mental illness is evident or suspected.

2. Lecturing and punishing should in general be avoided. These will only intensify feelings of shame and guilt and lead to hostility and depression which will perpetuate the practice.

3. Do not overemphasize moral implications. If the person is guilty, such emphasis will satisfy his need for punishment, which, in turn, may perpetuate a vicious circle and reduce motivation for recovery. If he is not guilty, moralizing is like talking Chinese to a Russian. You simply will not reach him.

4. Always remove depression which results partially from the highly emotional character of the act and partially from conflict between such acts and one's ideals. Depression always leads to a repetition of the act.

5. Inform the person that these acts are not limited to abnormal persons. Normal persons incur the habit but overcome it. Be sure to remove any misconceptions about adverse physical and mental effects.

6. Eventual cessation is necessary. With the abnormal practice, removal should be left to the professional. Encouragement and reduction of shame and guilt are the principal contributions of the clergyman. In other cases the person may be helped to stop through any method that works. The person should be told that control of instinctual urges is always salutary and leads to worthwhile formation of character.

7. Never insist that the person "stop it" or "never do it again." For the deeply problemed, this is useless and harmful. The compulsive individual cannot stop unless the thing that causes the practice is remedied through an approach to the real problem. For others, such promises can only lead to guilt on the occasion of remission and can perpetuate the practice.

8. Offer the perspective that any habit system is only one aspect of the entire personality. The practice may assume excessive proportions and become identified with the self-image. This

possibility is especially dangerous when disgust and guilt over the act are extreme.

9. Assure the person that it takes time to overcome a habit associated with an urge as strong as sex. When the practice is deeply rooted expect a tapering off rather than immediate cessation.

10. Urge participation in social activities. Studies reveal that the practice often occurs when people are lonesome and blue. Encourage dissipation of energy through physical activities. Exploit and reinforce talents and interests. These, however, must always be satisfying and tension-reducing.

11. Finally, always capitalize on the basic personality. Get the social-minded out, the athlete into sports and the intellectual involved in books.

Conclusion

Although we can and must understand the personal element in everyone who seeks alleviation from the pain of failure, there are certain elements that are common and form the basis of the role the clergyman is to play as a source of strength and hope.

The weakness of human nature, the force of the sexual drive and, most emphatically, the influence of the time in which we live all should provide a point of departure for constantly developing and emphatically demonstrating the qualities of divine mercy which the clergyman should represent to the victims of the world's limitations. The application of sympathy without compromise and understanding without weakness is not easy to achieve but is essential if he is to be worthy of the confidence that his people place in him. He must have an open mind and realize the contributions that have been made in a variety of other disciplines. Those contributions rule out a scrupulous adherence to the "old" when newer and wiser solutions can make life fuller and more meaningful for people.

Above all, the clergyman must be capable of an objective evaluation of himself. He should be ready to admit that there are many whom he will not be able to help for the simple reason that he cannot bring to certain situations the degree of personal involvement that is essential for success. When this becomes evident, he should be prepared to refer the case to another rather than make matters worse.

With a realization of his own natural deficiencies and a recognition of the failures of those who come, accompanied by a thorough knowledge of what makes them fail, the clergyman can actualize the great potential that is his by grace, nature and vocation.

For Further Reference

Bergler, Edmund. *One Thousand Homosexuals*. New York: Cooper Square, 1959.

Bieber, Irving, et al. *Homosexuality*. New York: Basic Books, 1962.

Bier, William C., ed. *Personality and Sexual Problems*. New York: Fordham University Press, 1964.

Ellis, Albert. *Homosexuality: Its Causes and Cure*. New York: Lyle Stuart, 1965.

Marmor, Judd, ed. *Sexual Inversion: The Multiple Roots of Homosexuality*. New York: Basic Books, 1965.

Von Gagern, F. *The Problem of Onanism*. Westminster, Md.: Newman Press, 1955.

11 The Sexual Revolution

There was a time not so many years ago when the word *revolution* had a rather particularized meaning which invariably referred to change effected by force and the alteration of structure influenced by reaction against a position no longer tenable. The notions of sudden change and forceful causation have some relation to what is known as the "sex revolution" of today. The most emphatic aspect of this reaction, however, is that it brings into focus the limited and completely inadequate view of sex that preceded it and which it now attempts to supercede.

The former unnatural approach to this very human function of life which made it appear as something unwholesome and dehumanizing has given way to the opposite and the emphasis sometimes seems almost ludicrous as the mass media of communication vie with each other in an effort to reach newer and more complete insights into a bodily function as old as man himself. Just as this effort very well may be the facade for hidden and deep-seated emotional problems, so also the restrictive and unreasoned approach to sex equally might have been a mechanism attempting ever so righteously to defend against neurotic fears and aggressions. Although the question of the sexual revolution is considered by many to be fundamentally a topic of moral theology, its psychological aspects warrant consideration.

This revolutionary aspect of the present sociological phenomenon is not per se a symptom of sickness. Quite the contrary. It very well might be a healthy reaction to the limitations of the puritanical and unhappy acceptance of God's gift of sex to man that preceded it. But the extent to which it has manifested itself suggests the real possibility of a gross immaturity, to say the least, on the part of those who insist on such extremes in their effort to reach a happy medium. The present flaunting and exploitation of sex very well may reflect the presence of individuals who have been masking hostility, aggression and fears while waving the banner of human freedom and responsibility. The "anything goes" attitude so prevalent today is not simply a reaction to the lack of reality in Victorian manners and morals. Conversely, those who oppose any open acceptance of sex as an indisputable fact of life and wish to ignore its influential presence are often revealing their own insecurities. Unfortunately, both attitudes may be communicated to others—particularly the young—and the result very well may be the extension of reactions that can cause or exacerbate mental illness.

Accordingly, this discussion will center around the following: (*a*) the fact of the revolution and its interpretation, (*b*) those aspects of the revolution that involve the possibility of mental illness, (*c*) conscience as a source of emotional conflict and (*d*) the necessity of law as a restrictive influence which, however, makes clear provision for individual differences.

The homosexual and his "gay" world, the Peeping Tom hopping backyard fences and the exhibitionist in compulsive search of an innocent female to shock constitute only a small part—possibly a superficial part—of the overall contemporary sexual scene. Such problems have been around for a long time. They have been studied scientifically and, in a sense, the general population has accepted them as part of the drama of human living. But something else has occurred within the sexual sphere which has caused responses ranging from "how sweet it is" through semi-panic to outright condemnation of its "filth." The "New Morality," the "legitimization of pleasure," the "new hedonism"—call it what you will—is spreading like wildfire throughout Western civilization.

Like everything else in our contemporary world, the whole question of human sexuality seems wide open to discussion. It is an area in which everybody appears to be an expert, where there seem to be as many pros as cons for every position. Every apparently reasoned opinion is certain to be opposed by contradiction. To imagine, however, that the surface manifestations of sex constitute the essence of the sexual revolution would be to miss the point completely. It is not just more of the same. It is an entirely new attitude toward the whole fact of sex. It represents not just an accumulation of startling statistics; it states unequivocally that the elimination of value systems must be respected and that the dangers of unrestricted freedom must be chanced if man is to be truly human. What we are witnessing is a new humanism which is prepared in its own defense to eliminate the traditional concepts of morality. The objectivity and universality of immutable principles seem completely at variance with the new personalism which now dictates right and wrong. It is not surprising that this whole philosophy of life should find its first expression in an area that touches the human pleasure principle so closely. If there are no permanent and fixed rules then men naturally will abandon earlier standards in that segment of life which involves a fundamental area of pleasure and appears, at least superficially, to offer opportunities for expression and acceptance. This is evident today among the younger generation who have few inhibitions regarding the externalization of sexuality. The influence of taboos, mores, commandments—whatever one wishes to call them—has to be reduced to the minimal when everyone is encouraged to "do his thing" with total freedom from the limitations of objective moral values.

The obvious breakdown in morality that has occurred did not happen overnight. It represents a gradual erosion over many years. There is perhaps no place where this is more manifest than in certain of our entertainment media. We can readily recognize the drastic changes in the subject matter and manner of presentation that have taken place in the film industry. The days of Andy

Hardy, thirty-five years ago, seem centuries removed from the homosexual and Lesbian themes that many of today's producers appear to revel in presenting to the public. Camera angles and stages of undress that were completely prohibited a relatively short time ago are now accepted procedure. The "reflection of life" has moved with unparalleled speed from one level to another until there seems nothing left to do or dare. When film producers feel no hesitancy about filming unnatural sex acts in meticulous detail the question must arise: Where do we go from here? Whatever the answer, one thing is certain: We have covered a great deal of territory in our efforts to picture life as it is.

The theatre, well-known for its efforts to express itself unimpaired, has made every effort to keep pace with the movies. The justification for nudity, obscenity and the presentation of moral turpitude is that it is a slice of life. The argument runs "Don't blame us. We only call them as you want to see them and that's the way it is."

Television, the greatest influence in the communications area, has had an even more devastating, if more subtle influence on the moral judgment of millions of Americans. The awareness of TV producers that they do not have the freedom of movement or expression granted to those in movies and in the theatre has caused them to resort to more sophisticated approaches. The TV industry now seeks to reflect the complete disregard for moral absolutes by irony and ridicule. The "laugh-in" holds nothing sacred. The late evening interview show gets its message across by glamorizing personalities whose hedonism is a byword and whose talent is considered a justification for license.

The fact that these mass media have assumed the role of speaking for the morals of a people is a revolution in itself and what they say must be viewed as both a cause and an effect. A cause in that attitudes are established and values abolished by a word, gesture or scene; an effect because it must be granted that they are, as faithful art forms, reflecting the standards of the society in which they exist.

But these obvious influences and/or reflections of the sexual revolution cannot be regarded as the only explanation of the changes our time has witnessed. The pansexualism of Freudian psychoanalysis, the statistical findings of the Kinsey report, the feminist movement, the plethora of literature on sexual behavior and misbehavior, the more liberal views on birth control and the concomitant availability of contraceptives and the gradual decline in influence of religious authority all reflect the scientific advances and cultural changes that have helped to effect this general modification. In addition, the justification of these changes has required a new emphasis on personal choice and freedom from the restrictions of authority. This, in turn, has caused a breakdown of discipline in the home and school, where the individual's rights seem to have superceded the common good. Moreover, the *dolce vita* that has become readily available as a by-product of the affluent society stresses the pleasure principle. For most this naturally involves sexual fulfillment as an end and justification in itself.

The current emphasis on the emotional values of personal involvements and the developing power of *love*–as compared with the ugly effects of hate, inequality and war—have laid the foundation for much of the new morality, Without doubt, however, the most potent stimulus has been the population explosion, which has lead to the de-emphasizing of woman's reproductive and maternal role. An evolution of attitude toward the human sexual function is the result and defenders of the traditional values, if only by their failure to reply, appear to be baffled and to lack consensus on acceptable standards of sexual morality.

This state of confusion is understandable. It is a normal reaction and has happened before in history whenever the traditional structure came under fire. People are naturally reluctant to give way to external pressures of change, especially when they touch upon ingrained and long-standing value preferences. Eventually, however, such conflicts of attitude must be resolved and this is particularly true in our present dilemma. Many feel that this is no ordinary swing of the pendulum between prudishness and license. Evolution seems to be its proper designation, with its effects here to stay for quite a while if not forever. Accordingly, prudent and diligent assessment must be undertaken by every humane discipline in an effort to promote those aspects that will be of ultimate value to society and to ferret out those threats that might be lurking in its depths.[1]

From a psychological standpoint, attitude is of paramount importance. Upon it hinge the all-important matters of sexual adjustment and maturity and their opposites, sexual maladjustment and immaturity. Sexual attitudes become ingrained in the personality structure and provide the basis for the all-important work of interpretation which ultimately determines the happy and healthy employment of sex or its destructive and unwholesome misuse.[2]

Human sexuality is not merely a matter of biological function, but an intricate complex of many factors. Very frequently, the dramatic physical properties of sex, with its intense quality of physical pleasure, tend to obscure the reality and significance of these other factors. Considered solely in itself, the biological drive is indifferent to healthy or unhealthy functioning. The determinants that turn this indifference into constructive or destructive channels are decidedly psychic in nature. Environmental, social, cultural and religious influences all coalesce to form an inner mental construct or attitude that determines, for better or for worse, the individual's reaction to sexuality.

Among the more harmful of these possible attitudes, fear of sex is by far the most crippling to the personality. It is the most insidious because it is practically always incorporated into the personality unconsciously and remains active without the person being aware of its presence. And, since sex is so commonly identified with virility and femininity, the natural tendency is to avoid any admission of even the possibility of sexual fear. As a result, it is always forced more deeply into the unconscious. There, it continues to exert its negative influence.

Sexual fear can become attached or related to almost any aspect of man's sexual life. The sexual organs, fantasies, unpremeditated pleasure, orgasm and copulation all can become frightening aspects of an individual's life. Some may be fearful of the size and formation of their sexual anatomy or of their ability to perform satisfactorally. Others fear that any involvement with the opposite sex is a stepping-stone to the loss or abdication of their own sexual identity.

The most common sexual fear and the one most often responsible for serious sexual conflict and maladjustment is the fear that sex is something "dirty" and disgusting, something shameful and degrading. In a sense, there is something of this attitude in everyone. It apparently has been there ever since Adam took the fateful bite. Such descriptions as "He has a dirty mind," "That picture was filthy" and "That novel was disgusting" are commonly employed. It is also quite customary to refer to the male emission as a "pollution" and to designate certain sexual thoughts and acts as "impure." It even has been suggested that the moment man learns of sex he simultaneously learns of shame and guilt.

Because of the universality of such ideas there is a degree of unconscious sexual repression in everyone. Normally, however, the tensions that accrue from these attitudes are drained off through a number of unconscious but healthy mechanisms. Sublimation and identification are perhaps the most commonly employed. Telling and listening to risque jokes, participation in dancing and innocent flirting, interest in certain forms of art and literature and many scientific and professional pursuits may serve as sublimatory releases of inhibited sexual tensions and desires. Following avidly the accounts of illicit love affairs in newspapers and magazines may offer the opportunity to identify unconsciously with the characters involved. A few chuckles or frowns of disapproval exonerate us most conveniently and re-assert our own self-righteousness.

When such negative attitudes dominate the unconscious mind they constitute a barrier to normal sexual adjustment. Working as repressing forces, these attitudes of shame and guilt prevent an integration of sex into the conscious life of the individual. When this happens, the possibility of a total breakthrough and encounter with sexuality demands a neurotic reinforcement of the basic repression. Under these circumstances, almost any type of neurotic reaction may occur. The most typical pattern is the formation of obsessional and compulsive controls. The case that follows exemplifies this maneuver.

Ray, a twenty-year-old college junior, applied for assistance at a community mental health clinic during a summer vacation. His academic record had deteriorated greatly during the previous school year and he felt that he had no alternative except to get to the bottom of his problem. He revealed that he had been suffering recently from insomnia and was constantly tortured with sexual temptations and moral scruples. "I have been troubled this way as long as I can remember, even when I was in grammar school. During high school I used to run to confession regularly. Now, I'm half out of my mind. I'm continually fighting temptations and I can't stop examining my conscience. This past school year I even spent class time going over in my mind things in the past to make sure I did not consent. I even stayed up at night walking around my room worrying. I'm afraid I'm going to have a nervous breakdown."

Interviews revealed, among other things, that Ray came from a very strict family. His mother, in particular, was overly religious, frightening and superstitious. He recalled that he never saw any physical affection between his parents. As long as he could remember they slept in separate rooms. He recounted: "I remember when I was little being punished and frightened by my mother because she said she saw me playing with myself under the covers." Ray also revealed that he had never received any sex instructions from his parents. "I was always curious but I was always afraid." The patient referred to his first erection: "I was frightened and thought something bad was happening to me." He further revealed that once he went to the beach with his friends and met a girl whom he liked but that he felt so guilty that he had to tell his mother about his feelings. He admitted to occasional masturbation which he always tried to fight off. Whenever it occurred he couldn't stop worrying about it.

In contrast to this type of compromise, an inverse pattern of behavior may be adopted in which the tyrannical influence of fear is entirely dissociated from consciousness and repudiated through the compulsive and constant pursuit of sexual intimacies. This neurotic defense is typified in the following excerpts from a case history:

Florence is a nymphomaniac. "I feel now that I will never be married and have a family like other girls," she says. "A good man just wouldn't have me, and I guess they're right. Who could trust me as a wife? Every man I've known I've frightened off by my stupidity or else I've landed in bed with him. What man wants a wife like that? God only knows how many times this has happened, and strange, I've never enjoyed a moment of it. I don't even know yet what an orgasm is like. Could you believe that with my history? Once I was scrupulous—that's a joke too—I even thought of becoming a nun. Thank God a priest steered me straight on that. But I really was scrupulous once. I know it was my mother: she was scared herself. She always held me down. She'd tell me to come right home after school and not to hang around with other kids. I was never allowed to do the things that other girls did. My mother always drilled it into me to stay away from boys. Boys were supposed to get you in trouble. On my first job I worked in the office of an engineering concern. One of the girls was a braggart and used to tell about the 'times' she had on weekends. I couldn't get the idea out of my head that I'd like to find out what it was all about. But I was scared and felt guilty about such thoughts. I went out to dinner with the girls around the Christmas holidays and some of the men from the office were at another table. I really don't know what got into to me but after we broke up I went back into the cocktail lounge and sat at the bar. I was scared, especially when one of the men came over to me and sat down. I did get away and felt awful. Well, that started me off on being a 'loner.' I did this a few times. I was always frightened but I wanted to prove something to myself, I guess. Eventually, I got picked up and landed in a parked car. That started something off and I've never been the same. Now I can't stop. I signal every man that I'm available. I've had to change jobs constantly and in every place it's the same story. I've had one affair after another. It's the story of my life now and I hate it all."

These cases illustrate predominantly psychic compromises with sexual conflict but in inverse directions. It also can happen, however, that such sexual conflicts are translated into decidedly somatic symptoms and appear under the guise of frigidity and its various forms in the female and in impotence in the male. As a consequence of such disorders the woman, at the time of sexual excitation, may experience no sexual pleasure whatsoever and, at times, may even experience physical pain. In dyspereunia, for example, lubricatory fluids are inhibited and intercourse is rendered painful; in the physical condition of vaginismus, vaginal and pelvic contractions may make sexual congress impossible. Impotence renders the male incapable of copulation or its completion. Erection is not usually attainable or, if it is, it cannot be maintained. At other times, orgastic emission is wanting, or if it occurs, takes place suddenly and prematurely.

At times, this type of somatic symptomatology may be caused by purely organic factors. When this is not the case, the negative emotional disposition toward sex disrupts the neurological bases of the physical sexual response. This physical response operates fundamentally according to a simple reflex arc pattern. Stimulation sets up an immediate and direct physical reaction. For effective and continued response, however, higher centers in the nervous system must be simultaneously stimulated by erotic imagery. Whenever sexual involvement is perceived as disgusting, shameful, fearful or in any other way repelling, the necessary pattern of erotic fantasy becomes distorted with adverse and hampering effects upon the physical components of sexual expression.[3] In this way, unconsciously harbored and adverse sexual attitudes may totally disrupt an otherwise happy life or marital union.

The neurotic sexual fear may terminate in almost any type of abnormal behavior. Experts on the matter even suggest the possibility of a generalized or collective sexual neurosis. Albert Ellis, for example, considers much of the current overplaying of sex on the part of our mass communication media to be a reflection of a wider and more generalized sexual repression.[4] If this is true, it would seem that the current effort is intended to maintain this breakthrough by overemphasizing it and thereby making doubly sure that a reversion to former taboos will be virtually impossible. In this light, the feverish treatments of sex in the movies and popular press, the inundation of pornographic materials, the increase in sexual themes in advertising and the idealized moral rearmament programs and frantic pronouncements concerning the decay of civilization are all indications of a sexual neurosis in American society. Obviously, controls are necessary if personal maturity is ever to be attained and civilization preserved. But it is equally certain that neurotic controls of fear and shame should not be among them. Unfortunately, such controls have been employed too often and too widely. Although it is hard to conceive, there have been private schools in which girls have been forbidden to wear patent leather shoes for fear their reflective quality reveal the undergarments. Similarly, it is difficult to believe that in some boarding schools children have been instructed to wear their underclothing while taking a bath and to get into their nightclothes only when under the blankets. Even more absurd is the advice given to young ladies attending private academies to sprinkle talcum powder over the water they have drawn before taking a bath. Although such regulations sound too bizarre to be true, they have indeed held sway and apparently still do in some restricted quarters.

The home, however, is the principal source of sexual fears. Despite our age of sexual sophistication, many parents, still assume an ostrich-like approach to their obligation of teaching their children the facts of life. Because of their own anxieties they rationalize their sin of omission by convincing themselves that such a dialogue will only trigger erotic cravings in the child's mind. Actually, such tactics only drive the youngsters to the wrong sources for his information. More important, parental silence in this sphere leads the child to the unconscious belief that sex is something highly secretive, something to be hidden and, therefore, something evil. When this unconscious attitude is reinforced, as usually happens in environments where only the dangers of sex are stressed, the stage is set for repression and eventual sexual maladjustment. Repeated warnings to "Stay away from girls" or "Be careful around boys, they'll get you in trouble" are ineffectual and often damaging, no matter how well-intentioned.

Parents also can transfer their personal sexual fears and anxieties in much more subtle ways and as early as the first years of the child's life. Authorities say, for example, that a parent's habitual over-concern for an infant's genitalia while bathing may evoke in the child an unhealthy regard for this part of his body. Unreasonable punitive measures at the time of toilet training may bring forth in a small child the unconscious belief that the sexual organs themselves are inherently evil. Forbidding a small child to be present when a younger brother or sister is being bathed or changed, chastising him when he is discovered handling his genitals due to the normal events of self-discovery or registering horror over his natural and healthy curiosity over the anatomical differences between boys and girls are all possible sources of eventual sexual conflict. There is a particular kind of parent who makes it almost a career to frighten his children away from normal and healthy heterosexual adjustment. The domineering and fear-instilling behavior of the matriarchal mother may generate in her son a generalized and unconscious image of womanhood in which all women are perceived as castrating and emasculating agents. A cruel, indifferent or rejecting father may create in a girl's unconscious mind a totally distorted image of manhood and man's attitude toward women. In either situation an unconscious fear of intimate involvement with the opposite sex may eventuate.

But prudish education and unfavorable home conditions are not the only sources of sexual fear and anxiety. Among cultural influences, the negative and threatening sexual message that has been dealt out by certain religious bodies is accountable for a great amount of unnecessary fear and suffering. Most often it has been the manner in which these religious expectations and sanctions have been imparted to the people and exacted from them that has caused an unreasonable amount of suffering and guilt.

In his study of human sexuality, J. L. McCary observes that there are few professionals who have worked in the field of sexology who would not agree that the greatest detriment to the sexual good health of mankind has probably been certain unbending, puritanical and guilt-instilling religions.[5] It has been unreasonable and inhuman, for instance, to label natural sexual thoughts, images and urges as unqualifiedly "impure," "morally sinful" and punishable by "hell fire." By overemphasizing a "Thou shalt not" attitude toward sexuality and continually stressing only God's retaliation for noncompliance, some religions have implicitly fostered guilt and endorsed fear as the only effective means of control over the sexual instinct. Such a threatening and punitive approach has too often eventuated in the erroneous judgment that sexual imperfections are the basest of sins and "purity" the pinnacle of spiritual excellence and holiness. The roots of this kind of thinking are deeply embedded in the traditions of many religions, in many biblical prohibitions and condemnations, in the severities of the long-enduring Augustinian morality and in the pervasive prudery of the Victorian era. On the other hand, it is interesting to note that the God-Man, Christ, insisted on the necessity of holiness of life but always exercised an extreme kindness and understanding and constructive approach toward this segment of human existence. It very well may be that the loss of influence that religion has suffered can be traced to its own doorstep because of a lopsided negative and punitive approach to this most natural part of life.

Obviously, this sway of fear, shame and guilt must give way to more positive and constructive attitudes. If the sexual revolution of our time accomplishes this it has served mankind well. But the whole movement cannot be permitted to become a double-edged sword. The current tendency in many circles to extol simply the physical side of sex, to emphasize technique at the expense of love's spontaneity and to propagate license and anarchy under the name of freedom can only turn its potential value into chaos and ruin.

The current craze to flaunt the physical and mechanical aspects of human sexuality strips it of its basic dignity. This trend, which appears in so many movies, in many paperbacks and, to a degree, in modern advertising, renders a disservice to society. It suggests that the sexual superman or proficient sexual machine is the apex of human achievement. Our adolescents are the ones who suffer the most. Vexed with the natural emotional insecurities of their teen years and confronted with a long period of self-control at the very time when their sexual inclinations are in the ascendancy, young people easily may be duped by such representations and come to employ them as instruments of defense against their own immaturity. In an effort to be popular, independent and accepted by others as masculine and feminine, they may use "sexiness" as their badge of maturity. What is most serious, however, is the possible tragedy of their identifying sexual performance with love and making skill more important than affection and devotion.

This constant bombardment of what might be called physicism and mechanization may also inflict a psychological wound on society in general. Environment is, of its very nature, contagious. When it becomes inundated with a partial view of any human value that value must suffer the loss of its full meaning. Among other things, psychological maturity involves the capacity to love and to be loved—but in a manner that is truly human and, therefore, in a manner that is more than merely physical. Consequently, sexual maturity must involve an authentic intimacy that possesses a core-relatedness and not simply a fashionable physical or pseudo-intimacy. It consists of a relationship between two people that is radically central, interior or spiritual. From this point it radiates and becomes a gift of value to the other. This type of maturity cannot take hold when only a lopsided extolling of "sex appeal" prevails. Nor can it be attained as long as a philosophy that propagandizes "sexual anarchy" is permitted to spread. A philosophy that grants unrestrained license to the individual's needs and urges and considers sex to be a free game of fun can offer human society only the surrender of its humanity.

In its most extreme form, sexual license becomes promiscuity. Promiscuity is usually defined as any intimate sexual behavior or participation in coitus with a number of different people on a more or less casual basis. Because of the extent that the modern sexual liberation movement has assumed in certain circles and the possible misintepretations that can ensue as a result of this influence, it is imperative to keep in mind that within competent psychological circles promiscuity is always looked upon as a symptom of underlying emotional difficulties. It is almost always indicative of an individual's inability to enter into an enduring relationship with a member of the opposite sex. Basically, the promiscuous person fears being trapped in such a relationship because of feelings of inadequacy toward the responsibilities that such a commitment entails. By his liberal attitude the promiscuous individual attempts to mock marital commitment and by his endless sexual involvements he tries to prove to himself and to the world how brave and indifferent he is toward intimacy with the opposite sex.

On other occasions, promiscuous behavior is a defense against unconsciously harbored doubts about one's sexual adequacy. When this is the case the number of intimate heterosexual relationships assures the individual of his sexual ability and appeal. It is as though the subject were telling himself that it cannot be true that he is inadequate sexually since the opposite sex goes wild over him. At other times, promiscuity may serve as a massive protection against the breakthrough of repressed homosexual tendencies. In such circumstances, the meaning of the overt behavior may be: "As long as I am involved with one female after another I will have no time for men." Or, "It cannot be true that I am homosexual. How can it be when I am such a tremendous lover of women?" Promiscuity also can be employed as a weapon of hostility. The "love them and leave them" behavior really says "Get the opposite sex to submit, to fall in love, and then drop them. Let them suffer with loneliness and guilt."

Rather than being an expression of sexual freedom, then, promiscuity is a form of personal immaturity and sexual maladjustment. And, in any form, sexual permissiveness may constitute a threat to mental health by eventually exacting a delayed but exhorbitant price in the form of guilt. A poorly developed and unsocialized conscience will spare many sexual liberals from this adverse effect. Unfortunately, however, the behavior of an enterprising minority can be adopted by many who really do not belong but who join the ranks either out of fear of the crowd or because it is considered the "in" thing to do. In such instances, even a puritanical conscience may be temporarily repressed by a dissociative process and ethical standards rationalized away by the appeal of "freedom" or "fulfillment." Later in life, remembrance of these erotic relationships may prove intolerable to the reinstated conscience. The case of Terry provides a good illustration.

Terry is thirty years old, married and the mother of three daughters. Her husband, who is two years older, holds a master's degree in business administration and is successfully employed. Terry's main complaints, which started shortly after her marriage and have grown steadily since that time, are excessive scruples, compulsive cleansing rituals and attacks of depression. She came for help because of the symptoms but also because she feared that she was scandalizing her young daughters by never receiving Holy Communion. Her clinical progress report contains the following: "I sometimes wash my hands thirty to forty times a day." "I don't go to Confession anymore; it's too much of a torture for me." "I go to church but can't go up to receive Communion. At Communion time I get up and try to get lost in the crowd so as to appear to my children that I have gone." Then, "My husband is good to me and we have a good sexual relationship." The clinical report observes that "obsessive sexual thoughts and urges toward members of the opposite sex are constantly experienced but vigorously controlled. These afford the patient with matter for masochistic self-condemnation over repressed guilt from the past."

These remarks are clarified by a summary of Terry's past history. She admits to what she described as "wild and heavy necking and petting" during her last year in high school and during her college days. She claims that she "seemed to have no conscience. I just went around on dates and it never bothered me. I used to confess it but only after long periods and only because I felt obliged, not really because I felt guilty. I don't know why I did so much of it except that others were doing the same thing and I guess I enjoyed it." She feels sure, however, that she cleared the whole matter up before she got married.

Perhaps the gravest threat to personal maturity and social

well-being is found in the more sophisticated and quite popular form of sexual liberalism that rejects promiscuity as at least amoral but insists upon the individual's absolute right to indulge in sexual intimacies and intercourse with a person of his choice provided it is done within the context of "love." The basic rationale is that sex is essentially a mutual manifestation of affection between two people in love, not something restricted to marriage and certainly not something restricted to the end of procreation. It forms the basis for the widespread practice of sexual intimacy between teen-agers and in its most liberal form serves as a pragmatic justification for such behavior as lovers "shacking-up" and the "housekeeping" arrangements of our "unmarried-married" subculture.[6]

According to this form of liberalism, if love exists and various reasons make marriage impractical, sex should be permitted in order to make this love as complete and fulfilling as a love relationship can be. It is argued that sex is an integral part of the overall sharing, of the give and take of such a partnership, and that if individuals are permitted to do everything else together sex should not be excluded. They discuss things together and do things together; there is intellectual intercourse and social intercourse. But if the total relationship is to be as complete as a human being can achieve, sex should be included. Such a philosophy, it is argued, is a safeguard against many of the sexual hazards prevalent in our society. If they express themselves sexually with only the one they love, they are less likely to contract a venereal disease. What they consider a safe and effective "pill" that removes the hazard of extramarital pregnancy is accessible to every girl. In addition to the reduction of these health and social threats, it is also argued that such a relationship will reduce the rate of promiscuity. Among the statistics cited are the fact that 50 percent of the girls who engage in premarital intercourse do so only with a partner whom they eventually marry and most of the others do so with only two or three partners. To the suggestion that this practice very possibly may be morally wrong, they simply reply "Why?" If one responds that sexual intercourse is for reproducing and that they are not married, they invariably respond: "No, it is not just for reproduction. Married people want to have sex because they love each other and not just to have children. Sometimes, they hope to have a child, but they do it mostly because they love each other and enjoy each other's body. We love each other, too, and enjoy the same warmth and closeness. So we have this type of intercourse in addition to all the other kinds of intercourse." If one presses the issue by saying "but God doesn't want it this way," they refuse to accept it. They respond emphatically that God wants them to love each other and that this is their expression of love.[7]

The question that immediately arises is whether such a philosophy is constructive or damaging in its effects upon personal maturity and mental health. Theoretically, when such a view is embraced as genuinely and personally justifiable no adverse psychological effects on mental health should ensue. But the question of personal maturity and its growth is not that easily resolved. The entire philosophy and the reasons presented for it do not provide the best climate for either personal or social betterment. Personal maturity always suffers when the defensive maneuver of rationalization is overemployed. It is difficult to conceive how such is not the case in this instance. Among other things, maturity involves the ability and willingness to postpone gratification of immediate needs for the sake of more ultimate and more lasting values. Mature psychosexual living involves more than the solitary capacity to enjoy the pleasures of heterosexual involvement and the many consolations of such companionship. It also is measured by the willingness to share the burdens and sacrifices involved in the mutual attainment of life's goals. Mature adults can easily detect the process of rationalization that forms the basis of this concept of "unmarried-married" living. What this subculture neglects is primarily their social obligation to their own peers and to the younger members of our society. In spite of their plea for the fulfilling benefits of love, they fail to present a philosophy of interpersonal love that is free of self-centeredness and genuinely aimed at the attainment of objective human values.

These features of the sex revolution have left many thoughtful people, clergymen included, in a state of wonderment and sometimes confusion as to what the precise limits of sexual activity should be. In the past, inner controls of conscience were quite well stabilized by the existence of reasonably clear-cut and universally approved norms of sexual behavior. Today, many of these external controls have diminished greatly in their stability and influence. Perhaps the most noticeable instance of this is the case of religion, which only a short time ago occupied the prime position among these external controls. Obviously the promulgation of moral prohibitions and the threat of religious sanctions and rejection no longer carry the weight they formerly did. Controversy within religious circles and disagreement among religious groups and among clergyman on basic moral issues have climaxed in an obvious lack of unanimity on the part of religious leaders and an understandable loss of confidence on the part of society in the church's teaching authority.

More to the point, however, is the constant complaint that religion, in general, is lamentably irrelevant to the world of today and its moral prescriptions coldly indifferent to man's concrete encounter with the hard facts of life. Without embarking on an assessment of such a criticism, it seems imperative to note the significant individual differences in the sexual segment of life. The apparent disregard for this human individuality and uniqueness in the formulation and exactment of moral laws has led many to abandon, and even denounce such laws as instances of a certain "moral facism."[8]

The problem is an ancient one and echoes the long-debated philosophical problem of the universal versus the particular. By their very nature, laws are universal and abstract. Moral laws are themselves grounded in universal and abstract concepts or ideas. The traditional procedure employed in the formulation of such universally binding moral laws has consisted of an analysis of the concept of human nature and its various powers. It is almost as though the law were twice-removed from the concrete individual person. By such a method, a kind of Platonism or Idealism sets in which is quite out of step with today's stress on existentialism and personalism. This modern emphasis on the value of each human person as an individual possessing unparalleled uniqueness has made the universal character of moral laws and prohibitions appear obsolete and devoid of human understanding.

From the practical point of view it is impossible to speak of the "average" human being's sexual drive. Constitutional, emotional, cultural and environmental realities always coalesce with the biological substratum to constitute a unique pattern of sexuality for each human being. Variations in glandular functioning can render one person sexually sluggish and another person sexually hyperactive. Because of emotional factors, sex not only can mean different things for different persons, but also can vary from person to person in the intensity of their need. One may regard it with indifference, while another may experience it as a constant and compulsive urge. It may signify love, tenderness and relatedness for one individual and serve as an instrument of hate, submission and conquest for another. It may be employed unconsciously to disprove or counteract feelings of ego-inferiority or to protect oneself against the breakthrough into consciousness of ego-alien perverse desires. A history of personal rejection, whether real or imagined, may move one person away from the intimacy involved in sexual activity and drive another into constant need for such intimacy as an assurance that he is worthy of acceptance. Age, degree of maturity, ego strength, the quality of personal defenses, previous sexual experience, habit, cultural emphasis of sex, environmental stimuli and exposure to sex, and a host of other factors contribute to forming a unique pattern of psychosexual life for each individual.

None of this erases the real possibility and value of considering the sexual segment of life from a conceptual and universal point of view. As every science ultimately is founded upon the reality of the universal, so man's behavior in general, and his sexuality in particular, also can be idealized in formulae and principles of morality. The theoretical or ideal order obviously should not deny the individual facts or circumstances of life as unreal or bypass them as insignificant; but neither should individual difficulty or the attractiveness of appeal become valid ground for discarding the bases upon which traditional and objective moral ideals are built. Unqualified permissiveness can be the fatal step in the direction of a generalized collapse of human values. Significantly, Freud himself, in spite of his emphasis on the dynamic character of the sexual drive, insisted upon the need for effective systems of repression to ensure civilization's survival. In view of the general permissiveness of our day it is imperative to insist upon the maintenance of moral ideals and principles—not as invaders of personal privacy but as safeguards of the common good.

It is equally necessary always to take into consideration the individual personality and his concrete human situation. It cannot be overlooked that universal laws create deep and painful conflicts of conscience for many. In the midst of today's sexual freedom, this obviously is true of those who continue to adhere closely to Judaeo-Christian traditions, especially those who find themselves bound by the strict rules of the Catholic Church concerning artificial birth control or clerical celibacy and, in common with other religions, the indissolubility of the marriage bond.

When sexual conflicts afflict these people, understanding assistance and support is in order. The very existence of their conflict reflects their essential goodness and sincerity. The following suggestions are offered as practical guidelines for those who are in a position to help:

1. Genuine respect for the individual personality with a sexual problem must be extended at all times. Meetings with them will naturally involve the person's painful admission of failure in this sensitive area of life. Preaching and antiquated blood-and-thunder techniques, sarcasm and all other humiliating approaches are valueless and very frequently prove harmful. Such methods often reveal unconsciously harbored attitudes of hostility regarding this segment of life.

2. Open-mindedness toward the individual problem and its concrete circumstances must prevail over personal and emotional prejudices on the subject. Otherwise, the person never will be able to grasp his own problem and work out a personally satisfying

and integrated program of adjustment. Individuals must be given the opportunity to express and discover their own ways and means to a solution. Whenever the conscience and emotions of the counselor interfere with affording the person this opportunity he should advise recourse to another advisor.

3. This is not to suggest a position of passivity or a surrender of principle on the part of the clergyman. Norms of behavior should be discussed for the good of the client and not for the satisfaction of the counselor. Explaining norms in terms of their basic rationale and ultimate personal value is always a far more constructive procedure than merely imposing them or demanding compliance with them.

4. It must be realized that self-recovery and construction requires time. Since sexual involvements usually are highly emotional and personally meaningful immediate solutions cannot be expected or demanded. Such demands only foster discouragement in the face of impossibility and lead to the eventual perpetuation of the problem.

5. Guidance must consist in discovering with the patient some personally significant motive. This could be the freedom from the dissatisfying and painful aftermath of misconduct or the satisfaction that will be derived in the attainment of higher ideals and values. Unless the person finds such a motive his chance of ultimate success will remain slim.

6. In those cases where the attainment of control is remote or borders on the impossible, simple assurance of God's understanding and your own continued support is usually the best course to maintain the individual's self-confidence and peace of mind. Where worry and discouragement are obvious, stressing and pushing toward any immediate solution may turn the tide in an unhealthy direction.

7. Suggestion is usually the best instrument in the guidance procedure. Even when the person is missing the real issue or rationalizing, this approach is the best. It maintains self-esteem and eventually leads the person to his own solution.

8. Whenever the individual's conscience is severely punitive, direct efforts must be made to break down its tryannically deleterious effects. When conscience is lax or weak, it should be built up as a source of control through appropriate but kindly presented deterrents.

9. Ego-building, through encouragement and stressing the positive qualities of the individual's personality and goodness, is always the most effective means of solution. The person must be assured repeatedly that he is basically good and capable of meeting his problem even though he feels it is insurmountable.

10. Be on guard that the person does not make the error of identifying this one problem with the meaning of his entire personality. The sexual sphere is microscopic in comparison with the total personality. Inability to cope with and guilt over a sexual involvement often miscolors the person's entire view of himself and leads to a breakdown of ego-evaluation and strength.

11. Always stress the periods of success and de-emphasize the occasions of failure. Hours, days and sometimes weeks of successful struggle often are overlooked to the detriment of the individual because of relatively brief relapses. The inherent goodness of the person's life is ignored to the discouragement of the person.

12. Simple control for the sake of control or "trying" to avoid a recurrence of failure are far too negative for constructive living. By such methods the self is turned against itself. The person must be taught to accept himself and these emotions and sublimate his energies. Trying should be in the positive direction of healthy "extracurricular" activity.

13. The "never, never again" or "promise me" approach is usually ineffective, sometimes harmful and rarely ever truly building. Sexual energy must be dealt with realistically and not forcefully repressed. The demand of blind obedience will usually only create anxiety and eventually bring depression and a breakdown of ego defense. Instead of helping the person, such authoritarian demands frequently feed the problem.

14. When the person is obviously malicious, is exploiting and harming innocent parties or knowingly and continuously violating the rights of a third party he must be told of his obligation to desist. Such sexual involvements are frequently manifestations of aggression and hostility and may be indicative of pathology.

15. Other indications that the conflict is at least veering in a pathological direction would be: disproportionate guilt, depression and loss of self-esteem, excessive worry and problem-solving, obsessions, exaggerated fears of punishment and similar anxieties. The best remedy is to build up ego defenses through reassurance techniques.

16. Obviously, recourse to God's assistance through prayer and the sacraments should always be advised and his mercy never should be withheld when requested. Assurance of his abiding love and grace is always the highest source of consolation, the best remedy for discouragement and the surest guarantee of victory.

Conclusion

The value of sex as an outward expression of an interior act of love that is genuinely concerned for and oriented toward the personal goodness and dignity of the other is an ideal worthy of our humanity. The degree to which this ideal is realized within a society, however, always will be directly proportionate to the level of maturity that has been achieved by the adults who populate that society. The burden certainly does not rest with our youth. The responsibility rests with our leaders: with our clergymen, physicians, philosophers, sociologists, educators, parents—with the adults who shape the world and influence its course. Great stress currently is placed on sex education, but the cardinal thing for our modern civilization to learn is what love really is. If man does not know at least this much he is doomed to remain alienated from his own inner life and from all the other good things in this life of which sex is surely one.

For Further Reference

Group for the Advancement of Psychiatry. *Sex and the College Student*. New York: Mental Health Materials Center, 1965.

McCary, James L. *Human Sexuality*. Princeton: D. Van Nostrand Co., 1967.

Masters, R. E. L. *The Homosexual Revolution*. New York: Belmont Books, 1964.

Schur, Edwin M., ed. *The Family and the Sexual Revolution*. Bloomington, Ind.: Indiana University Press, 1964.

Trimbos, C. J. *Healthy Attitudes Towards Love and Sex*. New York: P. J. Kenedy & Sons, 1964.

12 Violence

The headlines in our daily newspapers leave little to the imagination regarding the fact and manner of aggression and violence in the world. Although it can be argued that unbridled aggressive behavior and hostility reached equal proportions in many different cultures and at many different times, this is small consolation to the woman who fears to walk the streets, to the police officer who seeks to bring order out of chaos or to the shopkeeper who hesitates to open his store too early or close it too late. A pervasive sense of fear has gripped our people which is outdone only by a general weariness with it all. "What kind of people are we?" "Is violence and hate the American way of life?" "Are we a sick society?" These are the questions virtually everybody asks himself today.

But what are the facts? The brutal savagery of our times seems to simmer everywhere: in Vietnam, on city streets, in suburbia, in parks, in ghettos, in subway underpasses and in the home. On college campuses, student activists physically defy National Guard units and police barricades. Whole centers of learning are put out of commission by young insurgents who forcefully usurp the chairs of deans and disrupt classroom routines.

We read of a nation of frightened women. Neither old age nor youth is a safeguard. Whether they are in the home or on public streets, pushing baby carriages or walking a pet poodle, coming home from church or from work, American women are raped, have their throats slashed and are savagely beaten. In the handbags of many women can be found the "Invento Alarm," the "Rebuff," the "pen gun" or one of a host of other weapons.

New York City alone estimates that at least two persons are murdered within her precincts each day; at least four women are raped daily and a major crime is perpetrated every three minutes. On a national scale, conservative estimates place the number of privately owned guns in America at fifty million. Others estimate the number of the private arsenal at a fantastic two hundred million. Since 1900, more people have been killed by privately owned guns in the United States than have been lost in all the wars we have fought.

We read about the "battered child." Although there are no accurate figures it has been estimated by Dr. E. Helfer of the University of Colorado that at least 60,000 little children are willfully burned, beaten, starved or smothered in the United States every year. Other reports indicate that the combined ravages of tuberculosis, polio, rheumatic fever, measles, whooping cough, diabetes and appendicitis take a lesser annual toll of children under five years of age than do injuries inflicted upon them by parents and guardians.

Studies have shown that when the murder rate is up the suicide rate is down and vice versa. This fact is interpreted as indicating that hostility seeks expression internally or externally. At the present time, however, the United States is the only country in the world where both the rate of murder and the rate of suicide are on the increase. H. Rap Brown summed it up by saying "Violence is as American as apple pie." Noted authorities agree, concurring in the conclusion that in comparison with other nations America is a very violent society. Whether it be by nature, structure, tradition or habit, this is the way it is.[1]

We may explain these facts away by suggesting that new methods of reporting crime and acts of hostility are making it appear that there is an increase of both. We may argue that more efficient methods of detecting and circulating news concerning these manifestations of hostility have made us more aware of a problem that has always existed in different forms but proportionately to the same degree. While such arguments have some validity and sensationalism in reporting has become a hallmark of our times, it is evident to even the casual observer that the outward appearance of our society leaves much to be desired. It is of little account whether numerically there are more crimes, or even more vicious crimes. Everyone will agree that there are far too many and that they give strong evidence of a sickness our present structure of life cannot survive.

It is no longer a question of the occasional feud or family disagreement which leads the police inevitably to the perpetrator. It is now race against race, ethnic group against ethnic group, with an apparent return to the fundamental law of survival of the fittest. The attempt at sick humor illustrated in the slogan "Do unto your neighbor before he does to you" has taken on a macabre realism which each of us recognizes as a threat to his own personal security and to the beliefs he considers necessary for a modicum of balance and happiness.

The statistics on the question are in one sense meaningless. They change drastically before they can be printed. The sociologists' surveys, studies and analyses and our own powers of observation all lead to the inevitable conclusion that the lion is in the streets seeking whom he may devour and that we all had a hand in putting him there. One is reminded of Macbeth's ominous warning: "That we but teach bloody instructions, which being taught, return to plague the inventor."

By any standards, the violent results of what is described by some as "a perfectly natural tendency of aggressivity" are out of all proportion to a natural tendency.[2] And yet we know that this explanation has merit and must be considered if we hope to have some understanding of one of the most obvious ills of our society, one which threatens its very existence if not its immediate future.

There is a definite natural "assertiveness" in the newborn

infant. Certain limited elements of hostility and aggressivity which are not only natural manifestations of health and adjustment but absolutely essential if the child is to make any progress in growth, health and efforts at survival gradually appear. The energy called life impels the infant to assert his inherent biological and psychological needs. To gain security and satisfaction, he cries and screams, reaches out, points and crawls. Through these infantile and fumbling efforts at self-assertion, the infant gradually experiences differentiation and his own self-identity. Through the gratification afforded by action, there is a progressive stimulation to further satisfaction of new and constantly emerging energies and he grows neuromuscularly and emotionally. But since he always interacts with external social forces, he inevitably encounters frustrations. Under these tensions his native assertiveness is channeled into the more forceful behaviors of rage, hostility and aggression. He reacts with some degree of hostility when he discovers for the first time that he cannot live in his world of "illusionary omnipotence" but must comport himself in accordance with norms and standards that he did not create. His initial encounter with a parent who indicates forcefully that he must be properly toilet-trained, that he must develop proper habits of eating and that he must be prepared gradually to submit to the demands of cleanliness and health can provide painful experiences and will engender some antipathy against the source of authority which restricts his freedom in behalf of the common good. This type of forceful reaction is both healthy and helpful in establishing those patterns of interest in his environment and responses to it that will enable him to enter the arena of struggle for survival and assert himself against those forces of nature that might jeopardize his capacity to evoke reactions to the stimuli of the living process. If a child were to remain completely passive his whole being would become atrophied and he would be unable to survive either physically or psychologically.

As the child grows older he becomes aware of the need for competition as a prerequisite for achievement. The challenges that he meets provide a stimulus to his natural assertiveness. Whether it be sibling rivalry at home or academic or athletic competition at school, he is always engaged in preparation for a goal-oriented existence. He has overcome some of his natural antipathy to the restrictive influence of society as represented in the seemingly unreasoned demands of his parents regarding fundamental life processes because he comes to know their value and necessity. As his teen years approach he must submit to further limitations of his natural inclinations. The experience of his parents, teachers and surrogate images is matched against his own judgments which are now attempting to assert themselves. He wants to do his own thing despite the warnings and counsel of those who watch nervously as he takes his first faltering steps into the world of adulthood. This aggressiveness is not necessarily evil or undesirable. It is a reflection of the central phenomenon of adolescence, which is the establishment of the ego. As a child he was more or less a part of his total environment. So many things were done for him that there was little need for him to plunge out on his own. Dependence was his characteristic trait. With childhood a matter of the past and the challenge of adulthood the goal of the future, he must become accustomed to standing on his own feet, making his own decisions, bearing his own responsibilities. A new world view is awakening for him and he perceives himself as part of it, but as an independent individual with powers of self-direction, choice and decision. These experiences bring to life his basic wish to be totally on his own and so he begins to assert himself more vigorously as this particular human being. Testing of reality and of himself in the real world of adults instead of the make-believe world of games and toys is absolutely necessary if he is ever to acquire the independence and autonomy which are the hallmarks of maturity.[3]

The absence of this naturally good aggressiveness in the adolescent makes for an overly submissive youngster who never will be able to compete unless he is afforded some obviously secure opportunity to express himself and the ideas that he has sired within the framework of his own experience and thoughts. On the other hand, the young man or woman who assumes an arrogant and disrespectful autonomy and aggressively tramples under foot time-tested truths and principles which have guided many through difficult moments is responding with defensive fear or hostility in the worst sense of the term. The problem that dominates the front pages of newspapers all over the world is a reflection of the unwillingness of many of our youth to submit to any value system other than that provided by their own ephemeral and uncertain pragmatic standards. Essentially, the youngster wishes some basis, some criterion, by which he can make a value-judgment; but he is caught in the untenable position and apparent contradiction of accepting the standards of those against whom he rebels a priori. We have all witnessed the teen-ager who hears warning after warning from an experienced, concerned parent but must "find out for himself" only to discover too late that his parent knew best. Unfortunately, there are many youngsters who cannot, or will not listen to advice because it seems to be a capitulation to do so. Such a young person's hostility toward the infringement of parental authority on his freedom requires that he strike out blindly and unreasonably against wisdom and experience because he would rather "do it himself."

For a parent to know when passivity is to be discouraged and when ingenuity, assertiveness or hostility against the system has gone too far is indeed a difficult task and one which parents today obviously are not accomplishing with notable success. Constant reference to the generation gap, daily departures by children who no longer can abide the presence of parents who don't understand and regular recourse to faulty escape mechanisms which lead to disaster have become part of a growing number of our young people's way of life. In New York City, for example, which reflects the pattern across the nation, 85 percent of the missing persons reported to the police are teen-agers whose peak age is about fifteen, with girls sometimes outnumbering boys. Daily, scores of these youngsters arrive in the big cities as runaways, dropouts, all seeking the anonymity of the city rather than be identified with a structure of authority and with parents who represent it. In recent years technological advances have made available to children complete contradictions of the value systems, principles and norms which once were accepted even by the most aggressive of young people. Today all a youngster needs to do is turn a television dial or a page in a magazine or book, enter a classroom and listen or tune in his transistor radio and he can hear a hundred compelling reasons why the old standards and the voice of experience are completely wrong. This was not remotely possible a generation ago and it is one of the sad commentaries on social and psychological research that it has not provided an awareness of this tremendous influence on our society nor given direction to those who perceive in it a foreshadowing of disaster.[4]

There are also more subtle forces at work which explain some of the teen-age hostility toward "the system." The young person is moving toward emancipation. In his march away from dependence he must seek his own fortune because he is becoming more aware of himself as a particular individual who must represent his identity properly to a world which waits to see what he has to contribute. This is part of his ego development. As he establishes new relationships outside the family, they will color his judgments, determine his choices and affect his responses to the stimuli of life. This natural development will involve assertiveness and some degree of hostility toward judgments that are opposed to his own. Ordinarily, he will respond to understanding and the rational presentation of positions he has not yet accepted or rejected. It does happen, however, and much too often in our day, that hostile rejection of time-honored positions is the adolescent course of action and that there is no remorse or shame for overreacting. Such militancy in manner of speaking and deportment most often represents a tardiness in psychic maturation if not a more basic disorder in ego or superego functioning. It very well may be, however, that the hostility that the individual had as an infant has yet to be allayed, overcome or dissipated by the acceptance of the demands of rational living. This is frequently the case with youngsters who cannot accept "life with father" and the root cause why many descend daily upon the big cities in search of identity in anonymity. In such instances, professional skill may be the only way to discover those factors in the child's life that never have been properly understood or justly considered, much less adequately dealt with.

It would be foolhardy indeed to imagine that hostility or

aggression are completely dissipated in the frustrations of youth and that once adulthood is reached there is an automatic adjustment and the capacity to live with one's own limitations as well as with those of others. Anyone who has grown to adulthood knows well that this is not the way it is. A competitive world calls into play a more than ordinary assertiveness if survival is to be realized. The hectic pace of modern living demands that everyone be aggressively on his toes and on the move, not in order to get ahead, merely in order to keep up. Whether it is business prospects, bargain sales, hotel reservations or getting a seat by the window, someone is sure to have gotten the jump on someone else. The result is an adult society in which patience and common courtesy are rarities and quick tempers and short fuses are in abundance.

All this is a reasonably normal expression of the natural assertive quality of the adult personality to have his place in this world. Adult assertiveness is necessary if families are to prosper, if contributions are to be made, if rights and human values are to be preserved, if civilization is to continue. It is a mark of immaturity, however, and an unfair disruption of everyone's right to peaceful accomplishment and living to go around with "a chip on the shoulder," to be constantly causing dissension and to be angry at the world because of being angry at oneself. This kind of hostility has caused our divorce courts to be jammed. Margaret Mead laments that fifty years ago our children had no guarantee that they would not witness the death of one of their parents during their childhood. Now, she claims, an equal number of children cannot be sure that their homes will not be broken by divorce. Marital fighting, nagging and bickering, slamming doors, punching holes in the wall and outright assault are all indices of self-assertiveness turned toward destruction. It is equally present in the more cowardly measure of the "silent treatment," in the negativism of always thinking and doing just the opposite, in habitual pouting and sullenness, in racing and taking corners at top speed while the rest of the family sits frightened and helpless.[5]

Such expressions of unreasonable aggression within the precincts of the home account in large measure for both the causation and the continuance of hostility in the public and civic areas of life. Both the instigation and the reasonable control of hostile impulses have their ground in the interpersonal dynamics of the family nucleus. Research studies reveal that the failure of this socializing function of the family is a major cause of much of our contemporary delinquency, crime and violence.[6]

Apart from these schematic and descriptive aspects, aggression also involves clinical and dynamic considerations. A variety of theories have been proposed, among which Freud's "Mortido" concept has been given wide publicity. Toward the end of his career, Freud postulated a general destructive instinct in man—the "Thanatos" or "death wish"—which existed side-by-side with the constructive impulse–"Eros" or life.[7] Influenced by Gustav Fechner's "principle of constancy," which taught the reversion of all living matter to the stability of the inorganic world from which it evolved, and deeply moved by the brutality of World War I, Freud conceived of this inborn tendency within man to return to his prior state of quietude which he had lost in the evolutionary process. This Thanatos or "death trend" was the psychic counterpart of the constancy principle. On the one hand, therefore, man is ever striving toward the pleasurable reduction of those tensions and energies that are constantly emerging from his organ systems. This preserving and constructive trend is subsumed under the general work load of Eros. But all this positive tending is counteracted by Thanatos, which turns life into a roundabout journey toward death or absolute zero. For Freud, aggression and hate were direct derivatives of this instinctual drive toward the grave. These two forces—Eros and Thanatos—should balance, however, and neutralize each other. When this fusing process fails, Thanatos remains in its crude and unmodified form and either may remain internally directed against the self to its final annihilation or be externally expressed against substitute objects in acts of hate, aggression and violence.

Modern Freudians maintain the concept of Thanatos but also see in it constructive elements. Its destructive characteristics appear as early as infancy, in the pleasurable biting tendencies of the nursing child. Later in life, these oral-sadistic remnants of

Thanatos break through in the neurotic-compulsive eater who bites and chews away almost incessantly and, more symbollically, in the hostile personality who is given to "biting" remarks and habitually is "chewing" someone else out. The important point, however, is that according to this line of thought aggression and all its derivatives are inborn instincts and not merely an emotional response or the by-product of thwarted needs.

This instinctual point of view is mirrored in many modern evolutionary theories. It is an amazing fact that practically all carnivores have built-in inhibitions against exercising this native destructiveness against their own kind. Konrad Lorenz theorizes that this is all part of nature's design to preserve and safeguard the species against its own lethal endowments. Man, however, not being equipped with claws and razor-like teeth, had no inherent need for such inborn controls. Consequently, he finds himself at the mercy of his own violent tendencies and, paradoxically, in constant fear of the very instruments he has devised in the interest of his own defense and survival.

Recent comparative studies with animals and neurophysiological experiments with humans have given rise to a psychobiological movement toward an answer to aggression and violence. They stress the existence of precise loci of aggression in the primitive brain. Through the lessons of evolution and the socializing process, however, the higher structures of the cerebral cortex can acquire effective "impulse control." Environmental conditioning, therefore, is radical to their doctrine. Within the limits of their research, however, they teach quite emphatically that actively aggressive and violent people suffer some organic impairment of these ancient brain centers. These defects cause a disorganization and scrambling of electrical discharges which, in turn, trigger irrational outbursts of rage and violence. Without doubt, brain damage, brain tumors and idiopathic epilepsy do contribute proportionately to abnormal aggressive behavior.[8] But, outside of extreme organicity, poor impulse control is generally regarded as a psychic deficiency which is woven out of early and unfavorable environmental circumstances.

This socio-cultural theme is the main emphasis of the so-called reactive theories of aggression. Here, the move is away from the instinctual and toward a psychologically instigated presence of tension due to the thwarting of fundamental needs. In this framework, aggression is looked upon as a normal, positive and constructive element in personality, which, in this sense, is best referred to as simple assertiveness. It fulfills the needs of love, hunger, achievement and survival and is not necessarily related to hostility. In the search for satisfaction, the individual does not remain passive but openly asserts and expresses his want to live and to love. When, however, these needs are blocked and satisfaction is lacking, hostile feelings are aroused and the organism marshals its native energies of assertiveness into more forceful expressions of aggression. Depending upon the nature, extent and intensity of the frustration, there will be a corresponding emergence of hostility and a proportionate discharge of energy expended in the aggressive effort to remove the obstacle to goal satisfaction. Out of this set of circumstances an altogether negative and destructive response which is expressed in the emotion of rage and externalized in an act of violence may arise.

Regardless of what theoretical construct is proposed or espoused, the goal of mature living is always envisioned to consist in the constructive employment of life's assertive tendencies and the intelligent management of hostile and destructive impulses. In the mature personality the ego is the central and controlling agency of the entire personality. In other words, a balance and integration of id impulses and superego dictates has been achieved in which these two functional aspects of the personality are recognized for what they are and brought into the service of the ego's needs and adaptations to the external circumstances of concrete living. Present surgings of hostility and aggression and their earlier repression can be faced and resolved in an intelligent and satisfying fashion. Repressions of an infantile type is no longer necessary. Whenever any measure similar to it is employed it is only in the sense of freely and deliberately forgetting the entire frustrating situation after it has been intelligently assessed and satisfactorily resolved. Frustrations are met with reactions that are of a problem-solving nature rather than by either open and hostile attack or neurotic escape. The mature person discusses with himself and with involved parties the conditions that are potential stimuli for aggressive displays. Though he cannot resolve consciously all his frustrations and their hostile accompaniments, he controls his emotional impulses and dissipates their eneriges by reasonable defensive activities. Under such stress, the mature person may simply retreat and afford himself a "cooling-off" period during which more stable patterns of personality regain ascendency. At other times, he may physically work off the energies of frustration by engaging in activities, recreations and hobbies that permit a successful displacement of his hostilities and also provide a healthy fatigue and distraction.[9] The same draining-off is achieved through spectator participation in sports events, where pent-up hostile tensions are relieved through identification with the athletes and expended in the excitement of rooting the home team on to victory.

This, however, does not imply that the mature person is passive when his rights are threatened or that he is submissively tolerant of an undue amount of injustice. Quite the contrary. He asserts himself intelligently and according to the real demands of the situation. Objectively real stimuli beget appropriate and conscious appraisal of his own imperiled needs and the situation objectively at hand and are always in step in terms of duration and intensity with the real and unreasonable stimulus-threat. His assertiveness and aggressivity is positive and ultimately constructive. If his survival is threatened unjustly and physical aggression is his only line of self-defense he will act accordingly. He will not, however, employ aggressive tactics to compensate for weakness or to substitute for his inability or unwillingness to bear the pain of self-construction. His "will to power" is governed by an honest assessment of himself and its purpose and, consequently, is employed for his own construction and that of the community of which he is a part.

The immature personality, on the other hand, lacks the ability and ego-strength to deal intelligently with frustrations and their hostile and aggressive components. His interior psychic world is structurally out of balance and nonintegrated. Inner controls of conscience are either overly demanding and inhibiting or woefully deficient and in some cases nonexistent. As a consequence, id impulses to rage and violence are never assessed and dealt with in a reasonable fashion. In the absence of effective superego functioning, these impulses are either unleashed in an infantile and primitive manner or are totally denied through a tyrannical and massive program of repression. Due to early environmental deficiencies, the ego of the hostile personality emerges as an inadequate executive agency. In its undeveloped state, it remains at the mercy of a tyrannical superego or at the beck and call of uncivilized id emotions. Depending upon the severity of this inner psychic imbalance, there will arise in the immature personality varying degrees of hostile and aggressive abnormalcy. A continuum of intensity may be imagined, therefore, which ranges from a rather heavy reliance on ordinarily employed defense mechanisms through a series of pathological personality disorders to neurotic and psychotic symptomatology.

Within the child's world displays of open aggressivity toward parents, siblings and playmates are always met with social opposition or the withdrawal of love. In spite of numerous frustrating stimuli, these socializing techniques require the child to learn the lesson of repression toward his hostile and aggressive inclinations. If this controlling lesson is presented and executed fairly, the child does not come to experience his world as hostile and frustrating. If he is afforded the opportunity to gratify his legitimate needs for pleasure, self-assertion and achievement, then the outlook for the development of a mature regard and control of such inclinations is favorable.[10] In such an atmosphere the ego can experience independent and satisfying self-expression and learn, under a balanced and wise interplay of external controls and permissions, how to cope with the experience of frustration. When this balance is lacking and external controls are characterized by extremes of discipline—either too much or too little—both ego and superego development suffers. Under these circumstances various reactions and habits may set in. The simplest possibility is that the undeveloped ego decides to side completely with authority and deny all awareness of hostile and aggressive impulses. Through the incorporation of a stern system of controls, the person may resort to a reaction formation type of defense and assume an overly passive, excessively mild and extremely compromising demeanor. Beneath this facade of peace and love, however, rage and hostility may ferment. Often, such persons manifest a variety of physically distressing symptoms without organic reason. These physical symptoms, which can range from hypertension and migraine headaches to gastritis and peptic ulcers, are reflections of the inner tensions of repression and result from the various organ systems being in a constant state of readiness to fight the repressed enemy within or the hostile world without.[11]

At other times, when this combination of a weak ego and an overly idealistic superego is coupled with intense feelings of hostility and aggression, neurotic symptoms may be called upon to maintain repression. Either the anxiety of these impulses breaking through the repression or the anxiety of guilt over their presence in the personality demands the assumption of this kind of defense. Phobias of knives, scissors, guns and high places can be protective measures to ward off an attack of violence. Habitual neurotic depression can serve as a punishment for unconsciously harbored hostile feelings or as a safety device against acting these impulses out. The individual is so psychologically lethargic and physically retarded that he does not have the energies required for an aggressive attack. Obsessions of a sadistic and destructive nature, compulsive tendencies to inflict injury on oneself or others and painfully blasphemous and sexual thoughts about God all can be indices of repressed rage and hatred.[12]

Hostility and violent tendencies, therefore, are not always overtly evident. Even when aggressive behavior is in evidence, it need not always be rooted in hatred. It may be a defensive measure against ego weakness, insecurity and fear. A low intelligence, for example, or a generally weak constitution and appearance may call forth unconscious compensatory reactions in the form of over-aggressivity. In such cases, the best means of preserving self-esteem and warding off an unmanageable attack from others seems to be to strike first and, therefore, keep everybody on the defensive and at arm's length. The real or fantasied constitutional inadequacies engender feelings of hostility which are ventilated in aggressive ways; but when the person's bluff is called, his radical insecurity and fear practically always break through and cause an ego collapse.

Whenever aggressive behavior, whether it be rooted in hostility or fear, becomes inconsistent with the stimulus situation, it must be categorized as an abnormal reaction. Unlike the normal response to frustration, the stimulus that provokes an abnormal response may be totally subjective or imagined. Whether it be objectively real or only fantasied, the abnormal aggressive reaction is always out of step in both intensity and duration with the concrete objective facts. The whole situation is unrealistically perceived and erroneously assessed. As a consequence, the reaction is disproportionate and unreasonable. The more reality is distorted and lost the more abnormal the response becomes.

Abnormal hostility and aggressivity is most pronounced in a number of clinically designated personality disorders and psychotic conditions. It is in evidence, for example, in the "explosive" personality and in the "passive-aggressive" personality. In the former, a general excitability and over-responsiveness to environmental pressures is characteristic. Sudden and intense outbursts of rage and destructive aggressivity occur before which the individual's ego is totally helpless. During such breakthroughs, the individual may become grossly abusive, both verbally and physically, throw objects about and even commit murder. In such persons, frustration tolerance is low, egocentricity is high and ego development retarded.

The "passive-aggressive" personality, on the other hand, seethes with hostility but releases it through passive measures. Stubbornness, uncooperativeness and obstructionism are characteristic personality traits. This individual is a master at the art of punishing another through the "silent treatment." He frequently is found on the scene of public violence in the contemporary passive resistance movement. Most frequently, the early environments of such people were hostile. Because of this and their own dependency needs, hostility reactions were repressed as realistically ineffective, but also as subject to retaliation in the form of punishment and the loss of love. This hostile climate breeds a personality marked by insecurity, resentment and hate. Such harbored hostility eventually is measured out slowly and subtly on some surrogate victim who becomes identified with the real object of hate. Still dependent and inadequate in ego structure and possessing a rather strong superego, the passive-aggressive person fears retaliation if he puts forward any positive expression of his hostility. Consequently, he displaces his hostile feelings. He punishes some other person and "gets even" by making this innocent party share his own former sufferings. Passive-aggressive people are totally unconscious of the real cause and object of their hostility. It is invariably, however, a parent and one whom the hostile person keeps forever on a pedestal. They also are characteristically unaware of their resentment over their present inability to find satisfaction in an institution or relationship, which only compounds their internal world of hostile living.

Two other personality disorders that somewhat parallel these are the antisocial or sociopathic personality and the paranoid personality. The sociopath is basically unsocialized, impulsive and irresponsible. His continually hostile attitude toward authority brings him repeatedly into conflict with society. His superego is so deficient that he suffers an ethical blunting and, consequently, never experiences guilt over his offenses nor learns from his past antisocial behavior. The sociopath has been referred to as a "moral imbecile" and his offenses against persons and property cover the entire spectrum of crime from vandalism and theft to sex attacks and violent murders.

This individual's early environment was such that superego controls simply were not incorporated into the personality structure. Extremes of discipline—either excessive rigidity or its total absence—cause this failure in the socializing process. In the former instance, there is a hostile rejection by the child of the excessive demands of the parents; in the latter case, there simply are no standards with which to identify. It sometimes happens that reasonable controls are presented; but when only reprimands are given for noncompliance and no rewards for obedience, the child concludes in his frustration that there is no benefit in accepting and complying with the rules of social living. He feels that he has been maltreated; he becomes hostile and, as time goes by, in the absence of a personal system of values, he simply acts out without any remorse his inner hostile and aggressive tendencies.

The paranoid personality, on the other hand, wages a cold war with society and always in defense of himself. His oversensitivity, critical and sarcastic spirit and suspicious and envious disposition cause his interpersonal relations to be strained and antagonistic. Hampered by a basic ego inadequacy and intolerable self-evaluation, he is forced to be forever on his guard. As a result, he continually makes mountains out of molehills and goes about with a perpetual chip on his shoulder. He is argumentative, flippant and uncompromising and has little if any sense of humor.

Because of early frustrations, an image of a hostile world once again is born. The child interprets unreasonable punishments and rejections as indicative of his own worthlessness. Inadequacy feelings and a self-image of low esteem unconsciously are formed. In such a situation the child naturally overcompensates. In striving for goals beyond his reach he reinforces his bad self-image and intensifies his feelings of hostility. He becomes oversensitive and cautious. Because he cannot continue to admit to failure he commences to put the blame on others. In this way the world becomes even more hostile than it was before and he is ready to fight at the drop of a hat. This belligerent attitude begets the animosity of others and the vicious circle spirals on.

Such paranoid projections also can turn up in a psychotically prone person and may terminate in a full-blown psychosis. In the schizophrenic person, for example, such projections may lead to a total psychotic distortion of reality. In the active paranoid schizophrenic, the world becomes populated with individuals who are fantasied as following the sick person and being out to get him. For such a person, people carry secret weapons, make false accusations or burn out his brain cells with invisible lethal rays. In this deluded state, visual and auditory hallucinations of persecution may make innocent parties appear in the sick person's mind as menacing personalities. As a result, the paranoid schizophrenic can kill another person and literally believe that he is doing the only correct thing.

In these extremes of psychosis, the individual's ego has ceased to function and has been unseated by the irrational id. Even though the person may have a normal or even severe superego, it has no impact on the ego in its disorganized state. In the battle with the hostile impulses of the id, the ego has relied so heavily on the defense of projection that the superego's dictate not to kill has no significance in view of the subjectively distorted condition of the real world.

The recent political assassinations and their analyses offer a good example of how defense mechanisms can be constituted as a means of coping with severe tension-producing frustrations. In one way or another, the assassin is a child of rejection or abandonment. He spends his early days wondering: "Why did my father go away?" "I must have done something wrong." "I must be bad." This leads him to depression, low self-regard and a bitterness over not having had the opportunity to prove himself. These experiences, which generate contempt both for his own miserable state and for his father who caused it all, must be repudiated, and so the potential assassin begins to blame the world. This malevolent view of the world appeases his guilt over his own hostility. As long as the world remains bad he has a justification for being interiorly angry. A definite threat occurs, however, when a leader appears who promises world reform. Dr. E. J. Khantzian, a psychiatrist who has made a special study of this subject, suggests that this "man of hope" must be erased by the assassin for one of two reasons. If he is not killed, then the world will be reformed and the assassin's defense against his inner hatred will be obliterated. He will be turned inward and forced to face himself and his own bitterness. Moreover, this new "man of hope" reminds the assassin of the original man of hope, the father who failed. To save the world from this intolerable pain of frustration, the potential assassin convinces himself of his need to kill. In this way he adds to his projection the defense of displacement and symbolically kills his own father through his act of assassination. At other times, he compensates for his lowly position and self-dissatisfaction by perpetrating his act of "magnicide." In killing the man of hope he not only acts out his hate but also becomes the number one man in the eyes of the world.

These paranoid delusions can be found in the people with whom we rub shoulders every day. They are present in the high school student who is convinced that the school administration is discriminating against him and is bent on his dismissal, in the college student who pulls a switchblade or beats up the co-ed who rejects his sexual advances, in the gung-ho fanatic who vociferously proclaims the injustices of the establishment and who is forever espousing the widest range of movements from the most radical to the most reactionary, in the jealous husband who won't let his wife out of his sight because of her supposed adulterous intents.

Even the virtuous young mother and the middle-aged spinster can be overtaken by paranoid delusions of psychotic proportions. In the former instance, which finds one expression in the clinically designated "postpartum" psychosis, repressed hostility breaks through into consciousness under the physiological and psychological strains of childbirth. The young mother is tortured with destructive impulses toward her newborn child. She feels impelled and fears the possibility of carrying out her inclinations to drown the child, to smother, drop or strangle her baby. The newly achieved mother-child relationship has caused a surfacing of unconsciously harbored hostile feelings. In addition to representing the unwanted responsibilities and heavy burdens of motherhood, the infant may represent for the mother her own miserable and hated childhood. She may be reminded of significant personalities whom she unconsciously hates, such as her own mother, whom she perhaps always perceived as threatening and rejecting, or of her husband, who is to blame for the child in the first place. Most frequently, however, it would seem that such hostile reactions are grounded in the mother's attitude toward herself as an unwanted and worthless personality. In its most extreme psychotic manifestation, such a reaction may terminate in her deluding herself with the belief that a perfectly healthy child has an incurable disease; she can kill the baby thinking that this is the best and most humane thing to do.

During the involutional period or so-called change of life, similar delusions may occur. Under the strain of internal changes and adjustments to them, the individual's previous defenses against hostile impulses and ego dissatisfactions may prove ineffective and recourse to more extreme forms of paranoid projection may become necessary. Here, prior personality traits of suspiciousness, cynicism, obstinacy and fault-finding become pronounced in delusions of self-importance and fantasies concerning persecution.

The same defensive reactions to frustration and hostility can be seen at work on a mass level in collective violence, in the race and campus riots of our day. In his study on violence, Dr. Khantzian traces these unreasonable destructive acts to a breakthrough of long-standing but unconsciously repressed attitudes of bitterness and vengeance.

Deprivation, occasional injustice and the pain of submission are experiences that sooner or later enter everyone's life. They are especially characteristic of early childhood. In adulthood, when senseless violence occurs the memory of these former experiences and their submerged emotions rise to the surface and cause an identification on the part of nearly everyone with either the "attacker" or the "victim." The disproportionate and senseless quality of the violence, even by and upon those who are not truly involved in the issues, indicates that reason has been overthrown by a massive emotional eruption. A storehouse of locked-up hostility that objectively belongs elsewhere is released and displaced onto other persons and objects. Dr. Khantzian hypothesizes that such identification with the rioter or attacker on the part of uninvolved persons really stems from personal frustrations of another and earlier origin. Participation in head-thumping and clubbing, in burnings and generally destructive behavior, all in defense of the underprivileged, affords a rationalized release of rage and violence that could not be expressed otherwise. These unconscious dynamics are, according to Khantzian, at work whether one identifies with the attacker or with the victim. In the latter instance, even though the victim of the riot is the police or some other form of authority, the threats and violence displays of the rioter are seen as totally disproportionate and, therefore, unfair. Past and personally experienced injustices cause a surge of emotions which motivates some persons to join ranks and fight side by side with the victimized. According to this way of thinking, the senseless race and youth violence of our day is really a displacement of hostility that belongs to another period and to other people. On the other hand, those who assume an ostrich-like attitude and are reluctant to oppose such indiscriminate displays of violence may do so out of cowardice but, quite possibly, do so out of fear of guilt over their own harbored hostilities toward significant persons and events of the past.[13]

Aside from these deeper dynamic possibilities, there can be no doubt that most Americans and especially our children have become conditioned to aggression and violence and to its casual acceptance. Disregard for the value of physical integrity and human life are common themes in the movies, in novels and in newspaper headlines. Our national involvement in the destructiveness of a foreign war and the bloody riots that mar our peace at home have become a part of the American living-room scene through the medium of television. Dr. Leonard Berkowitz of the University of Wisconsin and other investigators at the University of Washington and Florida State University have shown that television and film reproduction of violence are more likely to stimulate emotions of violence than to drain them off.[14] Even toys have become suspect. A generation ago, "Cowboys and Indians" and "Cops and Robbers" were engaged in by the child but with the unconscious realization that they were all part of his own world of make-believe. Today, toys are such perfect replicas of modern instruments of destruction that the child cannot but perceive them as temporary substitutes for the real thing.

In 1965, the President created a commission to assess the magnitude of the problem of aggression and antisocial behavior in our country and to draw up recommendations for its reduction and eventual control. After two years of extensive study, this commission concluded that a nationwide program of active involvement and cooperation on the part of every American institution and citizen was the only effective way to meet the proportions of the present problem and cope with its threatening possibilities in the days ahead. The commission especially emphasized the challenge of the future and the fact that the teen-agers in our society are sharing disproportionately in the antisocial conduct of our day. They cited, for example, that although the fifteen-to-seventeen age group constituted, at the time of the survey, only about 6 percent of the total population, the same age bracket accounted for the highest arrest rate in the country. The commission regarded statistics such as this as particularly significant in view of the fact that our younger citizenry is increasing steadily, with present estimates placing approximately 25 percent of our populace at ten years and under and others predicting that within the seventies the proportion of our population that is twenty-one and younger will rise to 50 percent. Accordingly, the commission strongly advocated a revolutionary change in the American attitude toward aggression and violence. Among the recommendations was a call for all religious institutions to join in the effort to restore peaceful living to our homes, communities and the nation as a whole.[15] The following suggestions are offered to the clergyman to aid in his efforts to comply with this recommendation:

1. Early detection is always a major factor in preventing future serious problems. In young children, overaggressivity, meanness, hurting playmates, destructive tendencies, cruelty to animals, accident proneness, chronic disobedience and wandering from the home are all signs of potentially serious hostility. Temper tantrums, head-banging, marking walls, enuresis and refusing to breathe are most frequently attention-getting devises, but they also may be indices of underlying hostility. Whenever these and similar behaviors are frequent and enduring in spite of reasonable corrective procedures professional assistance should be recommended.

2. Because of natural growing pains a certain degree of aggressivity is to be expected at times of frustration. As a consequence, the line between normalcy and abnormalcy in childhood reactions is often quite difficult to define and overly tolerant

parents and other authority figures may bypass unreasonable aggressive conduct. When, however, complaints from outsiders and especially from those who work with the child are frequent and constant, special investigation is the safe course of action.

3. Common signs of adolescent hostility are disrespect for authority, lying, stealing, vandalism, destructiveness, assaultiveness, truancy and unexplained failure at school. When such behavior is chronic, uncontrollable by authority figures and constitutes interference with interpersonal adjustments, professional consultation is in order.

4. In passing judgment on childhood and adolescent behavior the youngster and his entire interpersonal milieu must be investigated. Merely listening to complaints that are chronicled unilaterally is insufficient. Aggressive behavior on the part of youngsters is sometimes a reaction of frustration to trying familiar circumstances and unfair demands. Both the youngster and his parents should be interviewed separately before any final impression is reached.

5. When it is discovered that parents are unreasonably demanding or failing in their responsibilities toward their children or are providing a family situation saturated with aggression and fighting, they must be presented with the potential damaging effects of such shortcomings. Parents must be informed that children are always affected adversely, even unconsciously, by such family strife. When a united and peaceful front is not presented, the youngster either will take on such aggressivity or become internally conflicted as a result of the dual nature of the identification process. On the other hand, when parents have fulfilled their obligations, they should always be reassured that they are not to blame when their children become involved in aggressive or antisocial misconduct.

6. Improving the quality of family life should be a prime target in both solving and preventing hostile and aggressive patterns in youngsters. Parents should be instructed in the rudimentary dynamics of interpersonal relations in the life of the developing child. The importance of parental love and acceptance, the neces-

sity of controls with prudent allowance for self-expression and the experience of independence and the need of parental understanding and adjustment to the various developmental phases of youth must be imparted to the parents. To this end, clergymen should be formally educated in the psychology of childhood and adolescence.

7. Clergymen should dedicate themselves to increasing the number and improving the quality of community youth programs. Authorities state that communities do too little too late in safeguarding many of our younger citizens from becoming delinquent. Such programs should be comprehensive and geared to the needs of the particular neighborhood and the dispositions of the participants. They must be more than merely recreational centers and should include educational facilities of a vocational nature, meaningful work opportunities, job placement agencies and counseling services for those in need of such help.

8. On the adult level, and within the marital sphere in particular, occasional quarreling, loss of temper and emotional displays are to be looked upon as normal occurrences. When, however, aggressive behavior in either its passive or active form occurs on a more than casual basis and interferes with the relationship, then confrontation with the source of discord is in order. In discussing such problems with the involved parties, neutrality must be the position assumed by the clergyman. Both parties should be interviewed independently with equal time allotted to each. This provides the therapist with the material necessary to form an initial impression. Both parties should then be seen together and invited to debate freely the entire problem. This procedure enables them to see the problem more objectively and, under the guidance of the therapist, to learn of more intelligent problem-solving techniques. When either party is obviously at fault he must be brought to face this fact squarely but always within a framework of kindness and construction. When these measures fail or when the aggressive party refuses to appear, recourse to professional counseling and advice is the only prudent course.

9. Destructiveness and violence, on any level, never can be tolerated or permitted to continue unattended. When confronted

with an actual threat of violence the best procedure is to attempt to alleviate the emotion of rage through an explicit expression of understanding for such a reaction in view of its frustrating source. This should be followed by the suggestion that the situation will best be remedied by a thorough discussion and investigation of the entire problem. Assure the individual or the group that an honest effort will be made to work out some reasonable solution to the sources of discontent and frustration. Never guarantee any specific set of changes but promise an objective and honest evaluation of the facts and possible solutions. When such efforts fail and the threat persists, security measures such as police intervention must be employed.

10. A harsh, punitive approach either before or after a destructive or violent outburst has little remedial value. In the best interest of the individual and the common good, clergymen should insist that retributive justice he honored. When punishment is deemed necessary they should uphold the position that the punishment should be tailored to fit the perpetrator's needs rather than his crime. Aim at superego development and the removal of paranoid ideation. True healing in this area will consist basically in the experience of remorse, the acknowledgment of the unsocialized nature of aggressive tactics and the assurance of acceptance and approval by others when more civilized patterns of solution are adopted.

11. In the prevention of public acts of aggression, clergymen should not hesitate to remind their people of their share in this responsibility and not leave the entire burden to the police alone. People should be told of their duty to report acts of violence, to support projects dedicated to the de-emphasis of violence in our mass communication media and to cooperate with movements supporting more rigid gun control regulations and the boycotting of toys that extol and symbolize violent behavior. In general, clergymen must work through their people toward the reinstatement of those human qualities that engender respect for both the value and the fragility of human life.

12. Finally, every clergyman should support the removal of racism, discrimination and bigotry. He must exercise leadership

governed by objectivity and acknowledge frustration and injustice regardless of where they are found if the communication gap between members of our divided society is to be narrowed. This effort at social amelioration must be more than verbal and must be aimed at extending to all both the benefits and the responsibilities of our nation's goods. Equal housing, education and employment opportunities and the willingness to fulfill the obligations correlative to these are essential prerequisites in lowering the amount of violence in our society and uniting all in the work of making our country and the world a better place to live.

For Further Reference

Berkowitz, Leonard. *Aggression.* New York: McGraw-Hill Book Co., 1962.

Erikson, Erik H., ed. *Youth: Change and Challenge.* New York: Basic Books, 1963.

President's Commission. *The Challenge of Crime in a Free Society.* Washington: United States Government Printing Office, 1967.

Storr, Anthony. *Human Aggression.* New York: Atheneum, 1968.

Toch, Hans H. *Violent Men: An Inquiry into the Psychology of Violence.* Chicago: Aldine Publishing Co., 1969.

13 Guilt

The experience of guilt is one of the most critical factors in the entire study of mental health. It also happens to be the reaction within the total spectrum of human behavior that hinges intimately on the values that underlie the clergyman's dedication and presence to the community. Every priest, rabbi or minister is a sign, living in the midst of men, reminding them of God and thereby keeping their minds awake to the facts of right and wrong, good and evil. On occasion, his presence alone is sufficient to stir guilt in the souls of people. And yet, when this matter of guilt is looked at from another angle, the clergyman is assuredly man's friend since he is the authentic dispenser of God's mercy and therefore the living answer to man's hope for pardon.

The clergyman has a grave responsiblity in this delicate area of mental health. From one point of view, he must be the builder and defender of conscience and, therefore, one who prolongs the anxiety of guilt. From another point of view, he must be the one who better than any other person in the community knows how to alleviate the pangs of guilt and convert them into the constructive forces they can be in the lives of his people. This dual responsibility demands a practical knowledge of the many faces of guilt and the talent born of God to treat them effectively.

Guilt and Anxiety

When the psychological experience of guilt is defined, it invariably is conceived as an uncomfortable mental state subsequent to the transgression of one's personal ethical values. Such a description is simple and correct. But in any attempt to arrive at an understanding of the experience of guilt its close tie to anxiety cannot be overlooked. In *The Third Revolution,* Karl Stern indicates that the problem of guilt is inextricably intertwined with that of anxiety.[1] Its very genesis is grounded in anxiety. An infant apparently does not possess a sense of guilt. He does, however, undoubtedly undergo anxiety over the frustrating demands of significant personalities in his environment and their retribution. When the young child comes to the realization that he possesses an independent personality he naturally commences to explore its possibilities. In the course of this adventure he inevitably comes into conflict with the persons he loves and depends upon. Such a dilemma, with its many anxieties, is terminated by the formation of a conscience. In most cases this occurs about the sixth year of life. When it does the child begins to experience guilt stirrings relatively similar to those of adults. From that point onward, whenever the conduct profile approved by the individual conscience is violated guilt feelings and anxieties over dangers that threaten from the frustrated conscience emerge.[2]

This close kinship between guilt and anxiety is succinctly expressed in the term *moral anxiety.*[3] In a very real sense, the "man of conscience" is called upon to spend most of his days under this kind of experience. He can never escape the struggle between such natural surgings as love, sex, domination and aggression and the many taboos of his built-in moral censor. Even if he avoids the pressures of these internalized ethical standards he cannot escape the demands imposed upon him by the human family at large. It has always been, and necessarily so, one of society's principal functions to bind many of man's natural inclinations. In this human situation, lifelong conflict is inescapable. When there is an internal clash between one's moral sense and natural strivings there is division within the personality and with this an experience that might be termed "simple moral tension or anxiety." For the most part, man can live with this kind of moral anxiety. He learns to accept it, difficult thought it may be, as part of the human condition. But when it comes to that more specific kind of moral anxiety called guilt the experience assumes a markedly different complexion.

Although everyone undergoes the discomfort of guilt at some time, the concrete existential experience is incommunicable and as individual as the person who suffers it. As such, it is an intensely personal concern. It touches the core of a person's being. It is a painful interior speech whereby one tells and reminds himself that he has been unfaithful to the kind of self he ought to be as a result of violating his standards of conduct. It is, therefore, a reaction to personal failure in the business of living. For this reason guilt is always accompanied by anxiety and depression. The anxiety that basically is due to a fear of punishment is compounded by the fact that the person who has transgressed his moral code feels the need to undergo the very punishment he fears. The depression, on the other hand, stems from the awareness of having fallen short of what one ought to be. As a result, two other aspects of guilt make their appearance. One may be looked upon as a certain "longing," since the guilty person feels that his crimes have lost for him his right to be loved. The other is "shame," which makes the person want to hide.[4]

This composite picture of guilt, drawn from a number of authoritative views, should before all else impress the clergyman with the plight of those who are troubled with guilt. When people experience guilt they need help. They invariably seek out their clergyman. Whether healthy or sick, such people instinctively know that he has the answer to their suffering. By such an action they are rendering the priest, rabbi or minister a high compliment. It is only fair that the clergyman respond with kindness toward the person and respect for his human situation. A fund of technical moral principles, an abstract knowledge of moral personality and a severe and bookish approach to the problem are cold and lifeless. Beneath every revelation of guilt, regardless of its cause and of whether it is reasonable or abnormal, the clergyman must see a person who is seeking his help and act accordingly. He should see the anxiety of guilt for what it really is: an admission of failure, but perhaps more important, a defense that is signaling the fact that this person's moral integrity is in danger. Without dismissing the fact of sin or its possibility as meaningless, the clergyman should capitalize on the guilt experience as an opportunity to bring God's loving concern to the person and, in turn, the person's humble contrition to God.

In every case of guilt, the clergyman's view must be one of construction. He should view guilt in his people as a manifestation of their basic goodness, as a potential deterrent from future misgivings and, therefore, as a springboard to a sounder and healthier moral and mental life.

The clergyman's words, tone of voice and facial expressions, in fact his whole bearing toward problems charged with guilt, are crucial in ameliorating the person's plight and building hope for the future. The so-called father image is high among the motives that prompt a guilt-ridden person to approach a clergyman. The guilty person perceives the rabbi, minister or priest as somewhat omnipotent, someone who, in lieu of his parents and ultimately of God, is imbued with the authority to sit in judgment on his unacceptable thoughts and sinful deeds. Under such circumstances, the clergyman must be keenly aware of the impact that his presence may have on a person suffering from intense guilt feelings. Guilt reactions can be constructive forces in a person's life, but when they are extreme and associated with a problem that is personally distressing in itself, they easily may be diverted by mishandling into negative channels. This is especially true when the problem that prompts the guilt touches upon the more sensitive areas of an individual's conscience and problems that he finds too painful or impossible to solve. The more obvious instances of such problems would be love relationships between persons who for some reason cannot contract marriage, marital infidelities, homosexual episodes, alcoholic relapses and cases where a person feels responsible for the downfall, failure, death or suicide of another person. Any approach that would aggravate or intensify such guilt feelings can only open the door to more depression and possibly provide the occasion for the person or persons involved to either give up the struggle or break under the strain. Every human has a breaking point. Precisely where it is and when it will occur no one knows. Most important of all is the obvious fact that "breakdowns" do occur quite frequently in the problem areas just cited. Even in less severe attacks of guilt, the first approach of the clergyman must be that of the "physician of the mind" in dealing with an upset person. He must remove as much pain and discomfort as possible, then reactivate pride and self-esteem. If this is accomplished, guilt will give way to hope and the psychological outlook for constructive measures will follow.

The constructive power of guilt may perhaps best be seen by considering what may happen when guilt is absent from a man's life. Psychopathic personalities are good examples of this condition. The psychopathic personality appears normal in many ways. His behavior and speech are not strange or affected, nor does he display any of the gross symptoms of the neurotic or psychotic. He is, in fact, quite often an attractive and charming personality. But he is sick, with his sickness residing in his character. Fundamentally, he lacks a socialized superego or conscience and possesses little or no sense of responsibility or decency. Intellectually, he knows the difference between right and wrong but in the practical order such knowledge has no emotional or motivating appeal to him. As a consequence, he is forever in trouble and repeatedly involved in antisocial and immoral behavior. Since he lacks the inner voice of conscience to pass judgments on his behavior he neither cares nor experiences guilt or remorse. External censures are equally ineffective since sociopaths are characteristically indifferent to the rights of others and care little for what others may think or say. Even punishments fail to bring about a modification of behavior. Sociopaths plunge from one misbehavior into another almost immediately after they have paid the penalty for the last.[5]

Although the presence of guilt in a human life is a constructive force and consequently a value to the person, it can at times become exaggerated and so distorted that it constitutes a stumbling block to personal perfection and even a symptom of mental illness.

Pathological guilt, however, need not always be consciously experienced. It can be submerged beneath the surface of consciousness and manifested in a variety of symptoms apparently unrelated to it but nonetheless caused by it. One such instance is found in the person who experiences unexplainable and uncontrollable anxiety over certain matters of a religious nature. For such a person prayer, attendance at religious services and even places and objects associated with religious worship may be sources of painful anxiety. These people sometimes experience such symptoms as palpitations, trembling, perspiring, claustrophobia and nausea. They do not, however, consciously experience any guilt. In such cases the circumstances, which are all related to God, become stimuli to the emergence to consciousness of unresolved and repressed guilt. This threat is met and effectively controlled by these anxiety attacks which are always painfully real. People unaware of their origin frequently simply endure and accept them as suffering. Others in the course of time rationalize the avoidance of the disturbing circumstances through the assumption of indifferent and even hostile attitudes toward God and religion.

The compulsive hand-washing rituals of many neurotics are another instance of abnormal but unconscious guilt. These cleansing routines invariably are symbolic attempts to achieve some degree of moral purity and to relieve the pressure of unresolved guilt feelings. There are also those who compulsively pick at their bodies, sometimes to the point of making themselves bleed. Unwittingly, they are laboring to undo repressed guilt feelings through self-inflicted punishment.[6] Unconscious guilt may also be at work when people suddenly fall into a severe moral problem for no intelligible or objective reason. An unwed pregnant girl with an otherwise examplary moral record may reveal a lifelong history of unexplainable guilt feelings. Here the person may simply be in search of some objective reason to offset or substantiate a habitual gnawing of unconscious fantasies of guilt.[7]

Guilt obviously makes many appearances in the lives of men. Most often, however, pathological guilt is directly experienced in consciousness and usually is manifested in one or another form of scrupulosity. Though this disorder does not appear to be as prevalent today as in former times its existence is real in the lives of many and always is indicative of pathology. The type of scrupulosity that may be termed "endogenous," and will be explained in subsequent pages, will apparently always be in existence in spite of our liberalism and freedom of conscience.

Hypothetically, it is altogether possible that the freer society becomes the more certain neurotically prone individuals will be forced into severities of conscience as a defense against their own inadequacies and fears. In any event, scrupulosity is an emotional disorder essentially related to guilt and frequently symptomatic of a serious mental illness.

Scrupulosity

Scrupulosity is a difficult and painful problem both to the one who is afflicted with it and to the one who attempts to talk or write about it. Its complexity, coupled with the extremely personal and individual significance it assumes for each of its subjects, makes it a near impossible matter to discuss in general terms. There are, however, certain features of the disorder that recur with sufficient frequency to provide a basis for a general phenomenological exposition.

The scrupulous person essentially suffers from moral insecurity. When functioning in the ethical order his practical intellect is either hampered in its administrations or brought to a complete standstill. He finds it difficult to bring himself to a final and decisive judgment about the moral quality of certain aspects of his behavior. He practically always suffers the additional handicap of being unable to submit to or follow the moral decisions offered him by another. Any person would feel distressed in such a predicament. But the average person, if he found himself in this dilemma, would intelligently accept the insoluble quality of the situation and settle the whole matter either by dropping it all as a futile cause or, if necesary, by abandoning it to the goodness of God. The scrupulous person will not and in fact cannot venture such a risk. Taking a risk always involves the possibility of failure and this is precisely what the scrupulous person fears most desperately. His exacting and perfectionist conscience forbids such a compromise.

In the face of such interior moral pressure the ego becomes obsessed with a never-ending search for a degree of moral certitude that is beyond human reach. As a result, an ethical meticulosity sets in which keeps him continually surveying the past, constantly on guard in the present and fearfully anticipating threats in the future.

Such moral overachieving practically always excludes from the lives of the scrupulous any moral content of consequence. The matters over which they worry and torture themselves are for the most part morally indifferent. Even when something does occur to provoke a genuine guilt reaction, the scrupulous person distorts its objectivity either by exaggerating its intrinsic malice or by magnifying it in terms of its accompanying circumstances. Unwittingly, scrupulous people have a certain semiawareness of this poverty of matter when they make such statements as "I know this sounds foolish, but . . . ," "Why can't I judge things as others do?" or "I don't understand why I worry about such things." In fact, it is this very paucity of objective content that explains the employment of the term *scrupulosity* in the first place. In Latin the word *scrupulum* denotes an extremely minute particle or the smallest portion of a measure of weight.

To the scrupulous person, however, such matter is overwhelming. Thoughts, images, feelings, meetings, conversations and many other behaviors and happenings which to the average person are all part of the human condition become insoluble moral problems and, at times, immobilizing experiences for the scrupulous person. This fact highlights the essential subjective character of scrupulosity. In the endogenous type of scrupulosity the ego, without conscious or deliberate intent, actually instigates the disorder. In all cases, the scrupulous person appears to have reified the whole matter. He grapples with it as with some objective and independent entity to be conquered. When he attempts to come to grips with the problem itself he wrestles with it as though it were a concrete opposing force existing apart from himself even though still within himself. The truth is that within the framework of this condition the scrupulous person has only one objectively real problem, his own subjective world of self.

This type of person cannot live without a problem, even if he must perpetuate or even create a pseudo one as painful as scruples. In this light, scruples appear to serve a purpose. They are an answer to some inner psychic need. The need in question is rarely, if ever, of the cognitive order. By personal industry and expert instruction the scrupulous person frequently is better informed about moral principles than the average citizen. It is the affective or emotional life that is at fault and in need of a solution.

This basic emotionality is practically always missed by its victims and sometimes even by those who attempt to assist them. As a consequence, effort frequently is focused on the intellectual or the logical. Total concentration on this area, however, rather than solving the problem can only aggravate it and deepen the habit. Though this emotional base escapes the consciousness of the sufferer, he nevertheless is constantly referring to it: "I *feel* so guilty and unworthy." "I know God is merciful but I do not *feel* that I have been forgiven." "I have been assured many times, but I never *feel* satisfied." This emotional base is very much in evidence when a person is approaching victory over his scruples. At this point, periods of peace invariably are accompanied by an overall apprehension that something is wrong or about to happen.

Such relentless guilt feelings naturally generate expiatory reactions. Rejection of the evil and atonement for it are natural sequels to any guilt experience. But since the evil haunting the scrupulous person is not real but only a fantasy, his efforts are always in vain. He is forever struggling to strike out that which cannot be erased simply because it does not really exist. His efforts become repetitive, obsessive and compulsive.

Narcissism is a characteristic of the scrupulous personality. He believes that he is laboring at pleasing God. In fact he is totally wrapped up in himself and in his own security. This is not a deliberate selfishness but one born of immaturity. This egocentricity, like nearly all other aspects of scrupulosity, does not entirely escape his conscious mind since he so often expresses the wish to see and enjoy the world of persons and things about him as others do. He is unable to do so and hates himself for it since he knows that, as helpless as he is, he has no one to blame but himself.

Obviously, personality growth is stunted and mental health seriously imperiled whenever one is caught in such a state of affairs. The disorder has varying degrees of severity. It can range from transitory scrupulosity with no underlying pathology through the obsessive-compulsive type, which is neurotic in character, to the symbolic and bizarre sphere of the schizophrenic psychotic.[8]

BENIGN SCRUPULOSITY. Essentially transitory in nature, this form appears at more or less defined periods in the life cycle. It may occur during adolescence, with its new and sometimes overpowering and threatening emotional experiences; old age, with its employment of the past as a defense against the loneliness and diminishing importance of the present and at critical times when major and decisive steps are to be taken which involve lifelong obligations and commitments. If the anxiety manifested is concretely related to the real situation and not unreasonably intense or prolonged, no other diagnosis is necessary. Usually, the support of repeated explanations and the assurance that these emotional upheavals are understandable and frequently experienced by others is sufficient to dispel much of the anxiety.

With some people, this benign type of scrupulosity may occur at more or less regular intervals. This usually happens when people for some reason feel compelled to reexamine their conscience from time to time. Simple ventilation on the part of the subject and reassurance on the part of the clergyman are sufficient to allay the anxiety of guilt such people suffer.

NEUROTIC SCRUPULOSITY. This is a far more devastating form and falls into the neurotic category of an obsessive-compulsive reaction. Here, the scrupulous behavior takes on the role of a symptom which contains the anxiety proper to an unresolved and repressed conflict. This latter psychic condition is the true problem.

This is the most common form of true scrupulosity. The fundamental key to its presence is obsessional thinking. The subject's focus of attention is habitually and irresistably dominated by the idea that he is always in the wrong and seriously so. The tenacity of this thought pattern is such that no amount of explaining or reassurance will dissuade him. Compulsive propitiatory acts frequently coincide with this obsessional thought pattern. These can range from simple repetition of prayers and penances to uncontrollable hand-washing. Such acts represent efforts to undo the guilt and are unconsciously phantasized as possessing a certain magical power.

Depression is an unavoidable by-product and regular companion to this type of scrupulosity, in fact its most devastating aspect. The contradiction involved in knowing that the very security-means one is driven to employ in order to procure some relief from guilt and unrest is simultaneously sabotaging one's peace and security can only terminate in feelings of despair. When this disposition begins to overtake the victim and the defensive character of the scruples fails to contain the anxiety a severe depressive reaction is almost inevitable.

PSYCHOTIC SCRUPULOSITY. Scrupulosity also may be symptomatic of an underlying schizophrenic malignancy. Though the pattern is much the same as with the neurotic, there are certain distinct features that make the behavior fall into this category. Primary clues are the bizarre nature of the preoccupations, exaggerated employment of symbolism and, perhaps most important of all, a breakdown in reality testing. As anxious and as obsessive as the neurotic may be, he never loses his grip on reality or his insight into the absurdity of his obsessions and compulsions. The neurotic continuously wrestles with his recognized subjective fears. The psychotic, on the other hand, battles with his delusions. The neurotic is tormented by his inability to control his useless preoccupations; the psychotic is totally engrossed in believing in and reacting to his own self-constructed world.

We see, for example, the proverbial Mr. Smith getting up every morning and habitually putting his right shoe on before his left shoe. We have a more or less definite pattern of dressing, whether we are aware of it or not. But Mr. Smith is an obsessive-compulsive personality and scrupulous as well. If he does not follow this routine with exactness every morning he is overtaken by anxiety which will give way only if he redoes the entire process. He fears that something terrible will befall him or his family during the day if he does not. He may even fall into the compulsion of putting on and taking off his shoes a definite number of times with the entire operation following an almost ceremonial exactness. If any deviation occurs during this ritual he is obsessed with painfully foreboding thoughts throughout the day. One day his son falls and breaks his arm. On hearing the news Mr. Smith recalls that on that particular morning he did not fulfill with perfection his self-prescribed dressing routine and he begins to worry and feel guilty. He recognizes the absurdity of it all, labors at banishing the whole matter from his mind and resolves, albeit in vain, to overcome the nonsense of his morning ritual.

Obviously, Mr. Smith is scrupulous and his scrupulosity is neurotic. But say another Mr. Smith, in the same set of tormenting circumstances, believed in his ritual and its possible consequence and, moreover, that by his failure on that particular day, he actually was responsible for his son's mishap. Such bizarre and dereistic behavior is symptomatic of psychosis.[9]

Again, take the case of a pharmacist who becomes obsessed with the unreasonable fear that if he thinks of a particular person while recording disease abbreviations like "Ca" or "TB" in his report that person will die of that particular disease. If by chance the person does become ill or actually die of that illness and the pharmacist in question becomes even more anxious but acknowledges the unreasonableness of his fears and struggles accordingly, his condition is neurotic. If, however, he deludes himself that his thoughts actually were responsible for the illness and death his scrupulosity is psychotic.

Finally, consider the neurotic who becomes scrupulous about looking at television because he fears certain programs will be a source of temptation to him. Although he knows that this is unreasonable, he habitually worries and accuses himself of moral carelessness and sin whenever he happens to see certain love scenes or dance routines. In the same circumstances the psychotic's behavior may become so bizarre and out of touch that he actually believes that the television personalities are constantly seducing him and leading him into sin.

Dynamics

How do people get themselves into such states of mind? Why do they permit themselves to make a career out of so painful a way of living? Although answers can be given to such questions, they always will remain, like the questions themselves, abstract and general. Scruples are not objective problems to be solved through the application of general formulae. They are behavioral phenomena stemming from and revealing a highly complex and extremely unique personality source. With this personal uniqueness uppermost in mind, it can be observed that certain dynamic patterns do occur with a reasonably high degree of frequency. These patterns may be classified under two wide headings of etiology, the exogenous and the endogenous.

In the exogenous type, early environment was overly legalistic. Parents and other significant figures consolidated in presenting a prudish, puritanical and excessively moralistic attitude toward life. In the process of identification, the child totally incorporated these significant figures. No differentiation between the persons and their rigorous misconceptions was made. Under pressure of the law of respect for parents and authority, which in this type of environment is usually harped upon, these severe moral attitudes became as worthy of honor as the authority figures themselves. To have cast these attitudes aside would have represented disrespect for authority.

In this way, a tyrannical superego comes into existence and becomes so entrenched that it rules the entire personality. Neither the passage of time nor the accumulation of correct moral information is capable of overriding the superego's despotic power. With this type of superego the person is forever building up, even in his earliest years, regular deposits in a personal and emotional guilt bank. Eventually, the amount of guilt that is harbored becomes so enormous that the pressure must be released in some way. It is like trying to boil water in a closed vessel. There has to be a safety valve or some kind of mechanism to let the pressure out. In much the same manner, these people must have some mechanism of release. But since their tyrannical superego is unbending there really is no way for them to discharge their pent-up guilt. Consequently and necessarily they resort to the formation of symptoms. This must be done in order to find some outlet for at least a portion of their accumulated guilt. They will either exaggerate the seriousness of real sins or make sinful things that are not sinful at all.

In the endogenous situation, the environment was wholesome in terms of moral attitudes. But, for some reason a weak and impoverished ego came into existence. An overly competitive environment, excessive sibling rivalry, a weak or passive parental model or one of a host of similar possibilities contributed to the formation of ego-inferiority. With this kind of personality structure, the fragile ego is forced to defend itself against any and every experience that might cause further deflation of the ego. Most often, feelings of hostility and sex are the materials such a person judges as too powerful to handle if they are given entrance into consciousness. A variety of different defense mechanisms may be employed as the ego constructs for its security an excessive guard in the form of scrupulous controls.

Personal inadequacy and insecurity may drive the weak ego to resort to the mechanism of reaction formation. The individual draws out of his environment those values that are strongly advocated and well presented and defends his vulnerable ego by exaggerating these moral virtues. In this way he becomes scrupulously meek and pure. By such constant and excessive concern to be meticulously charitable and chaste he harnesses the aggressive and sexual tendencies he finds impossible to face and manage. At the same time, these preoccupations may serve as a means of unconsciously gratifying the very inclinations he fears to express. This is especially obvious in scruples concerning sexuality. By a constant return and repeated scrutiny of every detail of a temptation the person, in the name of conscience, lives again and again an entire experience.

Rationalization is another technique that is employed. A young person who feels sexually inadequate and fears rejection by the opposite sex sometimes defends his ego against such a deflating insult by becoming scrupulously concerned about matters of sex: "If I get involved, I might fall into sin and displease God." This line of thinking becomes a basic premise upon which an entire system of scruples is built. This type of person is not afraid of *sex,* but afraid of offending God through *sin.* The overall sexual fear and insecurity are rationalized away.

In somewhat similar fashion, scruples may provide the means to avoid some unpleasant situation that exists in a person's life and the decision that it demands. A wife in an unhappy marriage may isolate the anxiety proper to her intolerable situation and displace it to ideas of a religious and moral nature. "If it were not for these scruples my life would be so happy," she says. Her total absorption in moral worry protects her from facing the real truth of her unhappiness and safeguards her weak ego from making a decision regarding her marital problem. If sex is the principal content of her scruples, such worry very possibly may be serving as a safety device against unconscious but repressed inclinations toward extramarital involvements.

Then there is the perfectionist for whom the most perfect is not perfect enough. He is always playing God. He cannot allow himself to make a mistake because he constantly fears the criticism of others. For him, criticism is intolerable since in his eyes it is tantamount to personal rejection and ego-reduction. He devises a scrupulous pattern of living by which he protects his fragile ego against the possibility of these subjectively conceived threats. His scruples set up such an intense guard that human error is near impossible. In this way the chance of criticism becomes far removed. The punitive character of his scruples enables him to regulate any punishment that might be due, thereby sparing his fragile self from the ego-insult of objectively imposed censure.

The involutional attack of scruples or those that occur during the so-called change of life are another instance of the endogenous brand of scrupulosity. Feelings of worthlessness and self-depreciation are part of the involutional syndrome. To justify such depressive reactions some persons draw into consciousness a rash of past sins or imagine new ones. By so doing, they avoid facing the real cause of their depression. Through their scruples they can rationalize their sadness, which most often is rooted in a repressed fear of losing female attractiveness or male virility.

It must be remembered, however, that these dynamic workings are always hidden well beneath the surface of the conscious mind and are as varied and unique as the persons in whom they are found. On paper they appear quite simple and obvious. When invested with life and concretized in flesh and blood, however, the disorder's puzzling and exasperating complexity returns to haunt both the sufferer and the one who aspires to help. The matter should never, however, be looked upon by either as a lost cause. With a close degree of cooperation among the scrupulous person, the clergyman and quite often the psychiatrist, even the most stubborn condition can be ameliorated.

Advice

The experience of guilt has always been with man and no matter how far he travels in the direction of freely deciding for himself and "doing his own thing" it always will be with him. In spite of all his rationalizations and projections of blame, human nature and its unalterable tendency to do good and avoid evil will prevail. The apparent lack of guilt in the lives of many today very well may be a massive repression of one of man's most natural and potentially constructive reactions. Guilt remains a constant topic in psychiatric literature both as a factor in the building of character and as a dynamic emotion in the etiology of many mental disorders. In the former instance, its value as a deterrent to personal and social wrongdoing and as a stimulus to self-improvement and the pursuit of higher values must never be forgotten by the clergyman or abandoned by him in the name of freedom and progress. In the latter instance, when guilt is among the instigators of an emotional illness, the clergyman must be aware of the unparalleled work he can perform in alleviating its harmful effects.

Psychiatrists, psychologists and social workers are all at a relative standstill in this dimension. No one, no matter how hard he tries, can alleviate or remove the pangs of guilt quite like the man of God. The lay therapist is the first to recognize this fact. Accordingly, the clergyman has a great service to offer the disturbed personality in coping with this aspect of his problem. He is, for example, the only one who effectively can build for the person who is chronically disturbed with guilt a new and sound image of God. Whether the guilt be covert or repressed and reflected in a variety of overt and apparently unrelated symptoms or directly experienced, as in the case of the scrupulous, this image of God as understanding and merciful is indispensible in the alleviation of the person's condition.

People with unconscious guilt need the experience of God's forgiveness and understanding as much as those who consciously experience its presence. Sometimes these people are objectively involved in a type of misconduct, very frequently sexual in nature, which they believe they have sufficiently justified. In fact, they have only rationalized their conscience away and forced it into the unconscious background of their minds where it continues to dictate disapproval and generate anxiety. At other times, their conduct in both its past and present forms is totally in accord with reasonable expectations but their conscience is overly idealistic and forever creating an intrapsychic environment of tension. But whether the guilt is grounded in reality or subjectively generated it is real and as a cause of illness requires special attention.

With the person who has repressed his conscience or "conned" himself into believing that his misbehavior is legitimate but who is suffering from a variety of other symptoms, simple willingness to hear and discuss the guilt-provoking behavior in itself often provides a release for the individual's pent-up guilt.[10] Immediate branding of the behavior as sinful or disgraceful or directly berating the person for his misconduct will result in the complete loss of constructive dialogue. Most frequently, such an unreasonable approach to the problem only contributes to the continuance of the rationalizing process and encourages the attitude that "There's no sense in talking to priests or ministers, they don't understand. Religion is unreasonable, and so are God and conscience." The anxiety-provoking defense is thus perpetuated. Genuine acceptance of the person, open-mindedness, suggesting rather than imposing insights and solutions and, above all, assuring the individual of God's acceptance of anyone who is honest and willing to discuss a problem are always the most effective procedures both in reducing the anxiety of guilt and in paving the way for an eventual and hopefully constructive solution.

This manner of deportment on the part of the clergyman invariably serves as a beneficial influence on the individual's concept of God. This improvement is even more imperative in the lives of those whose moral anxiety and pathological guilt is caused by an overly exacting or tyrannical superego. Whether this kind of perfectionist conscience results in a deposit of guilt that is hidden from the subject and expressed overtly in other forms of anxiety or in the directly experienced guilt of the scrupulous, the same need is present.

In spite of what they say, people with such frightening consciences always suffer from an impoverished image of God. Intellectually, they hold to God as kind and merciful, but unconsciously or emotionally they fear him as cruel and punishing. The mere emotional proportions of their guilt reactions prove this, but to convince them logically of this fact is virtually impossible. To speak to them in abstract and cold theological terms will never do. The only approach to follow in attempting to counteract this negative disposition is to depict objectively a vision of God as he really is, personally real but accepting and kind. The most effective instrument in this type of communication is the clergyman's personal and living conviction in God being precisely this way. The degree to which these divine perfections are reflected in his own life and conveyed through the sincerity of his words and deportment toward the person will contribute to a new and healthy image of God in the soul of his listener. As a representative of God every clergyman is an important figure in the eyes of his people. Whether he realizes it or not, his entire demeanor, his every word and deed have special significance. Only he of all the helpers of men can effect this kind of change.

Closely allied to this is the task of clarifying for the person God's benign regard for the human condition. This involves not merely the creation of a new image of God but an effort at getting the person to see himself and his world from a different point of view. He should be told frankly that God is interested in him precisely as he is—with weaknesses like everybody else but with talents also–and that God's view is definitely not absorbed as he himself is with past and present mistakes. He also should be told that God doesn't relate to him with a scorecard, magnifying glass or stick in His hand; nor is He a district attorney out to prosecute and levy penalties. A positive attitude toward God and himself and a recognition that God's concern for him far outreaches the negative aspects of sin and failure must be the aim.

The entire program of education must be geared toward overcoming negative attitudes by stressing and building up positive ones. Neurotics in general work on the negative premise that they are unloved and unlovable. This is characteristically so in the case of the pathologically guilty who continually look upon themselves as bad, unworthy and inadequate. For this reason, ego-building must be a primary objective of treatment. It is the truly critical need in the entire procedure. Whether the illness of guilt is generated by exogenous factors or because of endogenous reasons the ego always is fundamentally weak. In the exogenous type of scrupulosity the ego needs building in order to harness and eventually overrule the harsh demands of the dominant superego. In the endogenous type the ego requires strengthening in order to meet the instincts and drives it fears without recourse to the unreasonable defense of tyrannical censorship. Total concern or preoccupation with the severities of the superego is a misplacement of emphasis. Direct focusing on the ego through education, encouragement and constant assurance that the person is good and capable in spite of how he feels about himself is always a correct and effective therapeutic procedure. The ego gradually must be given an insight into the emotional nature of the disorder. If the severe superego results from an incorporation of the rigidities of an early childhood environment—information that easily can be gained from questioning the person—he should be instructed about these dynamics and the unreasonable character of his early environment. The ego must be enlightened as to a very common error in this type of scrupulosity. Invariably, these people identify their egos with impulses and urges they erroneously judge to be wrong. The clergyman must explain to the person that these impulses are spontaneous, indifferent in themselves, shared in by all humans and, above all, not identical with the ego as such. Such explanations always result in a reduction of some of the pain of guilt and gradually can lead the ego to a healthier and more acceptable image of himself.

When it is evident that the harsh superego did not evolve from a rigid environment but was devised unconsciously by the ego because of its own fear of personal inadequacy and inferiority, this too should slowly be disclosed to the patient. His self-image can gradually be improved by simple encouragement, by drawing his attention to his real strengths and assets and by assuring him that he is as good as the next person.

Because of the highly protective nature of this disorder improvement is always slow and won only after a prolonged struggle. The clergyman should never consider himself a failure in his efforts with these people and should never approach such a case with the idea or goal of total or rapid improvement. The very symptomatic nature of pathological guilt disturbances should steer him away from the goal of immediate removal of the scruples.

The following points are worth remembering:

1. Strongly and constantly stress the significant difference between natural and healthy thoughts and emotions and the deliberate translation of these into malicious activity. When dealing

with these people it is better to emphasize in general terms what sin is *not*, rather than to define specifically what constitutes various kinds of sin. The high degree of suggestibility in such persons prompts this approach. An overall working rule is to avoid all directive techniques, even by inference.

2. Avoid stern prohibitions. With minor cases a trial run at obedience sometimes works. With other cases such a procedure only creates an impossibility for the obsessive-compulsive personality and establishes the occasion for an increase in anxiety, guilt and depression.

3. Avoid arguing or explaining away each of their misconceptions. To become too meticulous is to get caught up in the person's own error. Attempts at clarifying such questions as "Did I go too far?" "Did I consent?" or "Was that wrong?" will only terminate in more confusion than existed before. When answers cannot be avoided, a categorical yes or no or the suggestion "You are able to answer that yourself" are the best responses.

4. Never permit them to take over in any area. Control the time by spacing it and setting limits. Do not permit yourself to be cornered outside these times. If this happens, simply assure them "We will talk about that the next time we meet." Do not give in except when extreme anxiety is in evidence.

5. Even though your patience is at an end never say to the person that he or she is hopeless or helpless. If it comes to this it is best to admit, without giving the impression of giving up on the person, that "Sometimes in matters like these stalemates are met. Perhaps, at this point, someone else might have some beneficial advice that will help you."

6. Never hold out the absolute hope that someday they will be entirely free from their problem. Rather, suggest the reasonable hope, and even high probability, that with effort and cooperation they will be able to adjust to the whole problem and experience greater peace.

7. Very frequently, the best policy in searching for a satisfactory solution is to "play it by ear." Through trial and error discover what works best for each individual and capitalize upon

it. In these cases, the best that one can do quite often is to act as a safety valve for the discharge of the person's pent-up guilt feelings.

8. When pathology is clearly in evidence referral obviously is the only course of action. Such a judgment should never be made in haste and its suggestion should never imply a withdrawal of interest on the part of the clergyman in whom the person has placed his trust.

The Future

In our day of permissiveness, when the individual is an ultimate law unto himself, the existence and value of conscience in people's lives is seriously threatened. We certainly do not want our people to be puppets of an establishment or cramped by a despotic system of inner controls, but neither do we want them to sacrifice the value of right order or forfeit their dignity as human persons.

In this context, it is startling to hear the prediction that some 350,000 of our unmarried female population, most of them teenagers, will become pregnant every year during the early seventies, with this number rising to a possible 400,000 a year by the end of the decade. It is equally startling to learn that more than one teenager or young adult contracts a venereal disease every minute in our country and that one boy in every six is referred to a juvenile court.[11] Figures like these are constantly turning up and seem to have become a standard part of our new way of life.

We must at least agree that when properly employed conscience is not a curse but a guarantee of the humanity of man. It is a natural tendency for every man to follow the line of least resistance and to find ways to avoid the need for controls. When this is carried through to completion man very often feels that he has no more fear of worry or guilt, but unfortunately neither does he have any more goals worthy of his striving.

By definition every clergyman is a champion of the humanity of man. As such he cannot permit his people to contradict themselves by falling prey to the belief that man can remain man without a conscience.

For Further Reference

Bier, William C. *Personality and Sexual Problems.* Chapters 2 and 3. New York: Fordham University Press, 1965.

Frankl, Viktor E. *The Doctor and the Soul.* rev. ed. New York: Alfred A. Knopf, 1965.

Hagmaier, George, and Gleason, Robert W. *Counseling the Catholic.* Chapter 7. New York: Sheed & Ward, 1959.

14 Depression

"Cheer up." "Snap out of it." "Why don't you get out and have some fun?" "Laugh a little, will you!"

It's often good advice for people when they are having a fit of the blues. Sometimes, however, it can be the worst advice of all. It can be the proverbial straw that breaks the camel's back. It may even lead to suicide.

A thirty-eight-year-old woman who had attempted suicide revealed in an interview that during her "rough" days she had been given this kind of advice. Her subsequent comments were: "It seemed that after a while that was all I heard from everybody—from my brothers, my friends and those I met at work. I realized that I was anything but the life of the party and that it had been three months since my mother had passed away, but I just couldn't seem to get going. I felt awful and nobody seemed to understand. I tried to cheer up but nothing seemed to work. Even my parish priest, who took care of my mother when she was dying and who was so kind to me, got fed up with my crying and complaining. One day he told me that I was acting like a baby and should grow up; that I was feeling sorry for myself; that I was no different from anybody else in this life and that everybody eventually has to experience death in his family. He was right.

But I got so down that I didn't want to live anymore. So I did what I did."

A quick review of the case revealed that this woman was the sister of two younger and married brothers. She enjoyed a good position with a law firm and supported her widowed mother with whom she lived. Two years before her attempt at suicide she had met a gentleman whom she thought she eventually might marry. She broke off from him, however—a happening she claimed never was really clear to her. Four months later her mother suffered a stroke and died within a day or two. That event triggered such an overwhelming grief that death appeared to be her only source of relief and escape. She eventually attempted suicide but failed. Six electroshock treatments and a relatively brief period of psychotherapy restored her to her former self. Her condition was diagnosed as a severe reactive depression.

Depression is one of the most common forms of mental illness in our society. It is so commonplace that physicians have at times described it as a "disease of general practice" since it is behind so many of the complaints of people. There are depressed people everywhere—in every community, in every neighborhood, in every congregation and, from time to time, in every home.

Although depression is one of man's oldest, most consistent and most obvious foes, it is difficult to define the term precisely because of its extensions. Depression may refer to the physical malaise of the simple headache or to ordinary ennui; it also may include the most complicated psychotic states. Generally speaking, however, there are certain common notes that form the foundation for a working definition. Among these is a retardation of the psychological and physiological functioning of the organism induced by some unhappy circumstance, real or imaginary. Among the depressed there is a consistent sense of loss or abandonment of those physical or psychological factors that provide the support necessary for normal adjustment. This sense of loss and loneliness causes a sadness that goes beyond mere grief or concern over human problems. It is a sadness that induces a persistent affective tone. The patient finds it difficult if not impossible to emerge from this unusual state.

Symptoms

In addition, there are certain indices by which the "depressed" may be recognized. Chief among these are the physiological symptoms of lethargy, listlessness and indolence which are concretely evidenced in the loss of interest in family affairs, recreation and hobbies; in inattention to business and housework and occasionally in the neglect of children. These symptoms may in themselves reflect the mental state of the patient or they may give expression to further indications such as tears or an unusual intonation or modulation of the voice. The patient may reflect his inner mood by his facial expression of dejection, perplexity, hopelessness or fear. His lower eyelids may droop and the skin on his forehead may be furrowed. The corners of his mouth may sag and his eyes may be directed downward. He always finds it difficult to smile and when he does it lacks conviction. An overall "hurt" look predominates.

Such facial expressions most often are accompanied by other complaints such as early morning awakening accompanied by a general feeling of fatigue, loss of weight and appetite, aches, pains or a loss of sexual drive. This complete loss of zest and interest is given consistent expression by such clichés as "What's the use?" or "There's no sense in even trying."[1]

The common psychological symptoms associated with depression are less obvious but no less significant. They include introversion and obsession. This is not the obsession of the personality who constantly seeks to give expression to its many facets. It is an obsession with the individual's refusal to be consoled. It is more commonly a complete withdrawal which manifests itself in a lack of interest and an unwillingness to accept the fact of loss or to determine to make the necessary adjustment.

This withdrawal also frequently involves self-pity and a sense of shame over not having achieved expected standards. More often than not there is a strong sense of guilt over a repressed and, therefore, unconscious hostile drive.

States of Depression

It must not be assumed that the symptoms described are all present or equally present in all cases of depression. Nor should it be thought that depression is necessarily something abnormal or undesirable. There are certainly instances where it is the most natural and expected consequence of loss and any other reaction might be suspect. It is a perfectly healthy response to the "loss" stimulus. Its entire range of expression, from shock through emotional release, depression and physical manifestations to final adjustment, is not only unrelated to poor emotional life, it is a positive indication of normal reaction. Who, for example, does not worry about some problem each day of his life? Who has not suffered misfortune and found himself disheartened and discouraged? Who has not endured the empathy that only true love can bring when he witnesses the suffering of a relative or close friend? Who has not experienced that sense of seemingly irreparable loss which accompanies the death of someone close?

Such loss, grief, guilt and hostility are elements of the integrated personality as it comes to grips with the inevitable, if sometimes completely unfathomable mystery of suffering.[2] But within the framework of the whole person there is always the capacity of ultimately "adjusting" to the demands of reason, to the inevitability of the facts of life or death.

Abnormal depression is quite different. In addition to the symptoms described above it involves excessive inaction in both mental and physical processes. The patient cannot seem to "snap out of it." His grief is not merely uncontrollable; it is in complete control of his every action and reaction. His sense of loss is more than a reasonable reaction to the absence of a psychological and emotional support; it is a refusal to accept the situation of deprivation over which he ultimately must admit he has no control. His sense of guilt is not merely sorrow concerning natural limitation and surrender to the demands of temptation; it is an ever-widening circle which finally makes the original source of guilt confused and obscure.

Psychiatrists distinguish among the various types of depression. In general, they divide the depressions into exogenous or reactive depressions (in which some precipitating factor which stimulates the depression-response is present) and endogenous, whose stimulus is from within the personality itself and whose precipitating factor, if present at all, normally and objectively is in no way capable of producing such reaction.[3] The exogenous depressions include those we have already described as perfectly normal. There are also those, however, whose extent and duration cause them to be classified as neurotic since they are disproportionate to the precipitating cause.[4] Thus, it is perfectly normal for a man to experience depression if he returns from work and finds his house burned and his wife and children hospitalized. On the other hand, if he were one of two hundred men who had been temporarily laid off from a large company and did nothing but withdraw and brood for weeks and months instead of looking for another job, his reaction would be regarded as as unreasonable and abnormal.

In the instance of the endogenous depression, there is an affective psychosis in which the patient is depressed for no apparent reason. Objectively, his sad and despairing reaction and its intensity and duration have no reason. It usually is termed a manic-depressive psychosis. This disorder manifests itself in a number of different forms: (1) the manic-depressive type (manic reaction *or* depressive reaction), in which the patient is predominantly, if not entirely, in the manic or depressed phase as the outward manifestation of his unreasonable reaction; (2) the circular type, in which he alternates from one phase to the other and (3) the mixed type, in which his depression is accompanied by complete agitation. The first form, the manic-depressive type, is by far the most common. Depending upon which phase rules, there are the further designations of manic-depressive reaction, depressed type or manic-depressive reaction, manic type.[5] Some authorities also include the case of involutional melancholia, but this is more properly related to the schizophrenias than to depression properly so-called.

Although it is not our concern here, an illustration of the

manic type of attack may help clarify, by way of contrast, the behavior of the depressed.

Ted is a seventeen-year-old high school senior. In his sophomore year he displayed acute manic symptoms for which he was confined to a private hospital for six weeks. The onset of the disorder occurred with a sudden and intensive application to his schoolwork. In addition to a rapid and dramatic rise in his school grades he also became quite interested in extracurricular activity and acquired a part-time job as a stockboy in a local supermarket. His initiative and drive impressed and he won the praise of his parents and teachers. He began to bring home from the library scientific literature which he read thoroughly and into the early hours of the morning. He became so absorbed in this that he began to neglect his regular school studies. He wrote for applications to numerous engineering colleges in various parts of the country and talked incessantly about one day becoming a great scientist. His parents became worried about this sudden change and overactivity and threatened to confiscate the mass of literature he had acquired. In turn, Ted threatened to quit school and run away. His father sought advice from the family physician and when Ted was faced with the idea of having a checkup he became abusive and started throwing articles of clothing and furniture around his room. He calmed down for about a week only to resume his previous behavior with even more intensity. At the request of his parents, the family physician made a house call. After a brief conversation, Ted broke down and kept repeating "Help me. Help me." Before he arrived at the hospital he again returned to his former behavior.

Irene, on the other hand, is a victim of depression. She is now thirty-nine years old and has been married for twenty years. She was raised in an overly religious atmosphere and after some premarital sexual indulgence, short of intercourse, her husband-to-be threatened to disclose her indiscretion if she did not marry him. The marriage took place and three children were born, two daughters and a son. She reports some incidents of physical abuse during the marriage. About ten years ago she learned of her husband's long-standing infidelity with another married woman.

This caused the breakup of the second home and Irene was intimidated by her husband to the extent of giving false testimony in the divorce trial. The final episode occurred when she learned from her fourteen-year-old daughter that "Daddy had been giving her sex instructions" during Irene's absence from the home. It was revealed that this included sexual abuse not only of her own child but of a few of her daughter's girl friends in the neighborhood.

Since this event occurred one year ago, Irene has suffered a constant depression. She has never recovered from her initial shock. She continues to withdraw and has not resumed any social activities. She still experiences prolonged periods of crying and an overall lack of interest in reconstructing her home life for her children. During intense periods of sadness she reveals thoughts of "not wanting to go on" and "life can never be put together again." All these symptoms continue despite the fact that her husband has recognized his own problem and with professional assistance is well on the way to a reformed and stable life.

Irene's constant depression reaction has gone far beyond the stage of normal grief and developed into at least a neurotic depression. If it continues it will regress into a more serious state.

Sister Mary X, a member of a teaching community of Sisters, developed an unhealthy sadness which became so intense that it seriously disrupted her capacity as a teacher. She eventually had to be removed from the classroom. She was transferred to a variety of tasks in the community and in each instance the same thing occurred. Finally, she was permitted by her superiors to perform only the perfunctory tasks at a retirement convent for elderly and infirm Sisters. Her depression became so severe that hospitalization was the only solution. Prior to her admittance, the depression had led to such classic symptoms as appetite loss, severe psychomotor retardation and some hypochondriacal fears. In her final state, psychotic ideation became manifest in such statements as "I am no longer alive" and "My body is peeling away to nothingness." Investigation into her life pattern revealed evidence of a cyclothymic personality.

In both these cases depression is the dominant note of the

mental illness. In the first case it emerged as a reaction to a series of external circumstances; in the second it was endogenous to a particular individual; that is, it flowed from within the individual herself. In the first case, however, Irene is still very much in contact with reality and capable of living in society. Sister Mary X, on the other hand, has lost contact with reality and cannot function as an integrated personality. There is not merely difference of degree but also in kind. Irene's depression falls into the category of a neurotic-depressive reaction, where the case of Sister Mary X is a psychotic depression.

Both cases are obviously quite severe. Symptoms, however, need not assume such proportions. Cases frequently are not detected because of their mild character or brief duration. In this regard, whenever there is a *recurring* sad mood in the absence of appropriate stimuli, even though it lasts only for a few days or a few hours, a depressive reaction may be suspected. This is especially so when the intermittent periods are marked by fatigue, obsessional preoccupation or unexplainable elation.

Etiology

The causes of the depression reaction are many, varied and often quite obvious. At other times, the stimuli that produce this response are hidden deep in the unconscious. Physical illness, when prolonged or terminal, may lead to a mental state that defies any attempt at normal adjustment. Loss of esteem, love, status or hope for achievement of goals easily may provide a psychological explanation for the development of depression. The loss of property or financial security provides adequate explanation for the depression that often follows.

But these easily identifiable explanations are not always present and the question continues to arise why it is that a person for no obvious reason is in a state of depression. In these instances, particularly when a psychosis is involved, causation must be sought in the complete background and life history of the individual. His depression may be due to faulty identification with parents who represent opposite extremes in the spectrum of depression-stability.

It may be that there is some element of heredity involved, for studies have shown a significant relation between the incidence of depression in children and its presence in their parents.[6]

But the dynamics of this disease may be even more subtle and defy the detection of causation without the aid of depth therapy. For example, the perfectionist will not permit himself to imagine errors or mistakes and so he is never satisfied in the real world of limitation. His natural reaction is to withdraw from such a world or to be depressed at the obvious fact that perfection, if it exists at all, must be found in another world.

The depressed often are those who as children have been rejected by parents or by others from whom they expected acceptance. Loneliness, abandonment and insecurity form the substructure of the stage on which they act out their lives in despair.

A deeper analysis of grief over the loss of a parent frequently reveals that the depression actually may have resulted from the realization of a repudiated or repressed wish for the death of the parent whose life has perhaps prevented personal achievement or fulfillment.

These instances are not as farfetched as might be imagined, but obviously their full understanding must depend upon the technical skill of a highly trained professional. The reason they are mentioned here is to suggest that the clergyman must not be too quick to dispose of a depressed person as one who should be able "to snap out of it." The easy solution may be impossible because of the hidden involvements of causation which must be detected by the long and arduous process of penetrating analysis.

Treatment

The treatment of depression has developed over a period of years and the more obvious methods currently employed involve drugs (antidepressants), psychotherapy and electroshock treatment. Many authorities are of the opinion that these methods should not be employed until it is evident that the depression will not be self-terminating. Frequently, it can be prudently judged that with a reasonable amount of time and with proper supportive influences the patient will come to a realization of his own condition and make a perfectly normal and happy adjustment.

It is in this area of supportive care that the clergyman will be able to offer his best and most effective contribution. But first he must be prepared to recognize the symptoms and prudently inquire into the previous history of the patient. He also must be aware of the sources of referral in the community and when such referral should be made. This will presuppose an assurance of friendship and empathic understanding of the victim's seemingly determined refusal to respond to the efforts of the clergyman to present a view of life filled with meaning and hope. The process of ventilation by which the patient ultimately may express the real needs he has or the real fears he experiences must be encouraged and when the process is begun the clergyman must have sufficient time and rapport so that he will never give the depressed person the image of one who is merely enduring an unpleasant situation. An impression of this type would only cause further rejection and the mood of depression would then have further reason for its existence.

The following recommendations indicate some fundamental rules to be kept in mind in dealing with the depressed person:

1. Be optimistic and reassure the patient that with proper treatment he can and will "overcome."

2. Express confidence in the new medications being used to combat depression. Tell them how people respond dramatically to these medications. Do not mention shock therapy. If the patient is blocked by fear of this kind of treatment assure him that everything can be discussed and worked out favorably with the doctor.

3. If the person resists these suggestions and is negative in regard to a willingness to get well, continue to support him and work toward an acceptance of treatment.

4. Suicidal threats that are judged to be realistic require immediate referral. If the patient is obstinate, consult a psychiatrist as to the next move.

5. Permit the person to ventilate and repeat past stories and events related to his depression provided these are not overly

upsetting. In repeating such accounts these people are in search of a degree of reassurance that they have not yet achieved or are simply seeking the continued reassurance their mental state demands. When either of these needs is satisfied the repetition will be unnecessary and will cease.

6. Never tell the person "Forget it" or "Stop feeling sorry for yourself." Both statements easily may be interpreted as a lack of understanding. If anything of this nature is judged necessary it is better to say "I'll bet your friends say that you're just feeling sorry for yourself. What do you think?"

7. Permit the person to emote (cry) provided this does not interfere with communication.

8. Advice and clichés such as "Life is great," "Have fun" or "Go out and enjoy yourself" should be avoided completely because they hold no meaning for the depressed and only suggest a lack of sympathy and understanding.

9. Be careful not to overemphasize their virtues and talents. They may be so immobilized that they cannot utilize them at this time. This, in itself, can only intensify their depression.

10. Make them aware that you can see (not that you actually do) life and happenings in life as they do (negatively). The realization that someone else can see things as they do will of itself relieve some of the depression. It also will establish the rapport so necessary for communication.

How these guidelines will be utilized by the individual clergyman will be largely a matter of personality and circumstances. But there can be no help or hope for the depressed person until he is reached, until the cause of his depression is faced and he realizes that this life in fact *is* a great opportunity for self-fulfillment in terms of the potential he actually possesses—no more, and surely no less.

To the deeply depressed and downhearted the idea of opportunity is practically always a thing apart and the goal of fulfillment an empty dream. At such a time all the words of all the wise men in the world become as dry straw. Only the words of God seem to help: "Come to me all you who are heavily burdened and I will refresh you." To a world whose horizons are bounded by naturalism and scientism, these words count for nothing. But when the people who inhabit this world come to "the end of the rope" because they *are* "heavily burdened" they are the words that mean everything.

For Further Reference

Arieti, Silvano. "Manic-Depressive Psychosis." In *American Handbook of Psychiatry,* vol. 1, edited by Silvano Arieti. New York: Basic Books, 1959.

Ayd, Frank J. *Recognizing the Depressed Patient.* New York: Grune & Stratton, 1961.

Gutheil, E. A. "Reactive Depressions." In *American Handbook of Psychiatry,* vol. 1.

15 Suicide

Attempted suicide is one of the most concrete cases that develops from the sickness of depression. In such circumstances the clergyman often is asked to intercede. This outward manifestation of depression occurs with dramatic frequency in the United States, where it is now estimated that more than 25,000 people each year–about seventy every day—attempt suicide successfully. It is also estimated that nearly ten times that number fail in the attempt. Louis Dublin, who has made extensive studies of this mystifying phenomenon of man's proclivity to end his own life, has ventured the suggestion that there easily may be two million people in the United States who have a history of at least one suicide attempt. According to official figures, suicide in any given year ranks tenth to twelfth among the causes of death in our nation. These are staggering statistics, but they become even more significant when we consider that there are probably many additional actual suicides that are successfully disguised as accidents or hidden from public notice because of an inaccurate record or knowledge of the facts.

There is no particular group exempt from these statistics, although there are about twice as many cases of attempted suicide among women as among men. That statistic is nearly reversed when the number of *successful* suicide attempts is recorded. Studies show that the number increases in times of financial depression, remains stable during periods of prosperity and is noticeably reduced during times of war.[1] Threats of suicide are more dangerous and more likely to be carried out as the age of the person increases. In recent years, however, there has been a marked increase in the number of suicides among college students, to the point where, on a national basis, suicide is the third largest cause of death in our college population.[2]

Authorities divide all suicidals into two groups. There are the "attempters," or those who employ inadequate means for their projected death, and the "completers," who take every precaution to ensure the fulfillment of their desire to die. Ordinarily, the former group consists primarily of neurotic types and those who generally are classified as "character disorders." The latter are usually of the psychotic family, either temporarily or permanently out of touch with reality. After careful planning, the "completer" employs rather definite and effective means such as jumping from a tall building or inflicting gun wounds on vital organs. For him, death is an end in itself; there is no point of return. Conversely, the planning of the "attempter" gives evidence that his purpose is not actually to take his own life. Rather, he is seeking to hurt someone else or call attention to himself by dramatizing his own hostility. His attempt at suicide is a means to an end, a cry for help or a cry for love.[3]

In those instances when an "attempter" does become a suicide it is invariably due to some flaw in his planning or to circumstances beyond his control. An "attempter," for example, easily might take an overdose of barbiturates but immediately make a phone call for help only to have the wire busy or out of order. In such a case the suicide is an accident rather than the real intention of the patient. He plays a kind of Russian Roulette with death winning the game.

But what motivates the suicidal act? Psychiatric studies indicate that external circumstances are only contributing factors. This principle is illustrated vividly in the following reports of three suicidals. One woman, for example, is reported to have lived her entire married life with a man she despised and whom she knew carried on one affair after another. After his death she told a close friend that she was grateful to God that "at last it's all over—finally I'm free." The day after the funeral she killed herself.

A wealthy retired business executive had faced many financial reverses during his career and had the ability to recoup in each situation. At the age of seventy-two he committed suicide when a minor investment collapsed.

On the other hand, a thirty-four-year-old man attempted suicide while at college when he was "jilted" by his sweetheart. Since then he has been married twice. His first wife ran off with another man and his second wife died of leukemia after five months of marriage. He is reported to be well-adjusted and apparently happy.

The core of motivation, then, does not lie in the external circumstances but in the emotional constitution of the person, which determines the way the external circumstances are interpreted and handled. Even this, however, is quite relative and by no means constant for an individual. As is evident from the cases just cited, the psyche's manner of dealing with the happenings of life can vary from year to year, from day to day.

Dr. Joseph Hirsch of the Albert Einstein College of Medicine has formulated what he terms the L.A.D. syndrome (Loss, Aggression, Depression) as expressive of the intrapsychic condition underlying most suicidal motivation. Although the aggression is not always overt but frequently repressed and inferred, the depression and loss are practically always in evidence. The loss may be related to a person, to self or even to physical values and material possessions. It may stem from death, injury, departure, rejection or desertion. In practically every case this loss generates a depression which may become so severe or aggravated by accompanying factors that a pre-suicidal disposition emerges.

At other times the loss may lead to frustration and hostility. According to Freudian thinking, depression enters this pattern when such outwardly directed hostility grows out of proportion and generates guilt reactions. To solve this situation the self turns this aggression inward against itself. Through the unconscious process of introjection, the suicidal symbolically kills the significant object by taking his own life. In this sense, suicide is a "retroflex murder" in which the executioner becomes the executed.

Some psychoanalysts have emphasized a strong motive of expiation in the suicidal act. Dr. James Knight, for example, explains that when rejection or desertion has occurred the depressed person tends to unleash his resentment on the "lost" but beloved person. This is basically a move to coerce the person to love him. This kind of behavior, however, begets a dominant need for repentance and self-punishment. The person appears to act under the illusion that his supreme sacrifice will secure forgiveness and reunion with the beloved.[4]

Prescinding from these somewhat abstract considerations of the L.A.D. syndrome, we can list some concrete expressions of the syndrome, which when coupled with loss, aggression and especially depression, provide clues to serious suicidal risks:

1. Expressed ambivalence toward life and death

2. A sense of hopelessness and helplessness regarding personal problems

3. An inability to restore order to a confused or chaotic life pattern

4. A cognitive constriction which prevents the person from seeing alternatives

5. A cyclothymic (mood swings) or schizoid (introverted) personality

6. A history of impulsivity or "acting out" impulses

7. A recurring tendency to talk about suicide

8. A resorting to alcohol or drugs under stress

9. An acute illness coupled with loneliness over the real or imagined lack of concern of others

10. A pattern of indulging in dangerous or self-destructive hobbies (motor-car racing, mountain climbing, deep-sea diving)

11. A frequently expressed and great fear of death, which could be a reaction formation to an unconscious longing for death

12. A frequently expressed fear of others killing them, which could be a projection of one's own self-destructive wishes

An attractive, middle-aged woman was referred by a general practitioner to a local mental health clinic. In addition to her physical complaints—all psychosomatic in nature—she was suffering from a debilitating depression and was obsessed with guilt over her husband's recent act of suicide. She had been married to him for nineteen years and was the mother of two teen-age daughters. The trouble started about eight years before the suicide. At that time, her husband, whom she described as "quiet," "unpredictable of mood" and "not a good mixer," became overly moody and depressed to the point of not being able to go to work. By trade he was a roofer and self-employed. These attacks of depression continued and caused a great deal of financial stress. The only thing that kept them from going totally "into the red" was her constant prodding which she said her husband interpreted as nagging. She revealed that "Although he would always eventually snap out of it, he would return to his moody and lazy ways." This pattern continued for years. During this time her husband steadily gained weight until he weighed almost three hundred pounds when he died. She said that in the last few years he was continually telling her to "go out and find a boyfriend." As a result, she rarely went out in the evening except with other ladies to church and neighborhood gatherings. On one occasion when she returned from a PTA meeting he vehemently accused her of infidelity when he discovered a button was open on her blouse. "It seemed that after every one of these episodes he would go into one of his moods and be so down that he couldn't go to work. I didn't mean to nag but I had to keep after him to support the family. I also tried to get him to do something about his appearance. Eventually he began to tell me that some day I would be sorry and would cry. One Sunday morning we had a fight over the same old things. I couldn't stand it anymore, so I told him to go see a doctor or I would go to a lawyer. He got up and told my daughter 'Your mother is going to cry a lot before the day is over.' When it came time for lunch we found him dead in the garage with the car motor on."

The woman also revealed that about two months before the suicide a neighbor had died. She said that after that her husband would say "I wish it had been me. Everybody will be glad when I'm out of the way. Maybe some day I'll do something about it and make everybody happy." She now blames herself for the whole thing and is a potential suicidal herself.

This account illustrates some of the dynamic factors and clues previously cited. Above all, it highlights a very common and serious misconception about potentially suicidal people, that they do not talk about it or send out warnings. The fact is that most of them *will* give some clear indication of their intention. This may be either a direct or an oblique comment. It may be a communication that is related to the patient himself or to someone else whom he claims has been talking about killing himself. It may be contained in his preoccupations with self-injury or injury to others or self-destruction or destruction of others.

This clarification suggests the possibility of other mistaken notions concerning suicide and questions that arise from them.

1. Are all suicidals seriously mentally ill?

Answer: Acts of self-destruction are not invariably the result of mental illness. At times the act is related to religious and cultural factors. At other times the person (primarily the "attempter") is overwhelmed by unhappiness and despair. Among the seriously intentioned (the "completers"), however, reports reveal a high preponderance of diagnosed or diagnosable psychiatric disorders.

2. Is suicide an inherited defect?

Answer: Suicide is an extreme method of problem solving, a distorted defensive response to unresolved conflicts. As such, any recurrence of suicide within a particular family would not be due to genetic transmission but to the process of learning—probably the psychic mechanism of identification.

3. Are all suicidal tendencies long-range?

Answer: The wish to destroy oneself is limited to particular stresses and periods of time. The idea "Once a suicidal, always a suicidal" is not true. Nevertheless, for anyone who plans suicide, psychotherapy is an indispensable measure in the resolution of the deep-seated conflicts that prompted the impulse.

4. Do certain professions have a high suicidal rate?

Answer: Recent comparative studies indicate a greater incidence among higher educated groups. Officers in the armed services, for example, commit suicide more frequently than enlisted personnel. The rate is conspicuously low among clergymen but conspicuously high among physicians, pharmacists, chemists, dentists and lawyers.

5. Do religious factors appear to affect the rate?

Answer: This is difficult to answer. The Catholic religion, for example, is especially stern in her attitude toward suicide. Accordingly, the suicide rate is relatively low in such predominantly Catholic countries as Ireland, Italy and Spain. On the other hand, the rate is high in such Catholic countries as Austria, France and Hungary. The same ambivalance is observed in Protestant countries. Denmark and Sweden have high rates; Norway and Protestant Northern Ireland have low figures. Throughout their history the Jewish people have been remarkably free of suicide. Proportionately, people who have few ties with the community kill themselves more often than do church members.

6. Is the suicide rate distributed equally throughout the United States?

Answer: Relatively recent reports indicate that the highest figures consistently show up on the West Coast, with San Francisco, Los Angeles and Seattle heading the list. New York, Chicago, Pittsburgh, Philadelphia and the larger eastern cities have about the average rate.

7. What do comparative studies reveal about Negroes and whites?

Answer: The figures indicate that suicide among Negroes has been consistently and markedly below that of the white population. It has been equally below that of other nonwhite minorities.

8. Does the choice of method vary with sex?

Answer: A United States government report covering

1950 through 1964 indicates that firearms and explosives accounted for 65 percent of all suicides for males and only 25 percent of those for females. Analgesic and soporific substances were employed by only 6 percent of males as compared with 30 percent of females. Except for poisoning by gases, including motor vehicle exhaust gases, poisoning was used by a greater percentage of women. A greater percentage of females resorted to drowning.

9. Can accident proneness result from an unconscious wish to die?

Answer: Repeated and unaccountable accidents definitely may be a sign of either unconscious self-destruction motivation or unconscious needs for atonement and expiation. Such happenings may be symbolic sacrifical efforts which temporarily quiet a guilty conscience. When such tensions recur, the need to repeat these symbolic acts is revived.

10. Are suicidals also homicidal threats?

Answer: Although it sometimes happens that a suicidal act follows a murder and that psychoanalytical thought holds to the maxim that "Nobody kills himself who did not at some time wish to destroy someone else," it is also true that the very essence of suicide is outwardly directed aggression redirected and turned inward against the self.

11. How does alcoholic and drug abuse relate to suicide?

Answer: Alcoholics attempt and complete suicide at a much higher rate than nonalcoholics. Although the condition itself may not cause suicide its presence must be respected as a strong warning of suicidal risk. The United States government reports no satisfactory data on the relationship of suicide and opiate use. Various threads of evidence suggest that the risk of suicide is greater among illicit drug addicts than for the general population. As for LSD, although suicidal impulses are reported and clinical workers describe attempts, there is to date no substantial data as to the probability of suicidal attempts as a result of dosage or incidence of use. The fundamental difficulty is to distinguish suicidal intents from such drug-induced bizarre behavior as jumping out of windows because "I can fly like a bird."

12. Can improper handling of problems and conflicts increase the possibility of suicide?

Answer: This is possible even in professionally controlled psychotherapy. Special danger exists when a too rapid disclosure of the problem occurs without the patient being sufficiently fortified to sustain its emotional impact. More superficially, any indifferent or casual attitude toward matters that are vitally important to the patient may constitute a serious threat.

Equipped with some knowledge of the facts of the problem and the more common indices of the suicidal personality, the clergyman can make a very positive contribution to the prevention of this all-too-common cause of death. Some of the fundamental rules that should be observed in dealing with a suicide threat are listed here in the hope that they may enable that contribution to bear fruit.

1. Compassion, warm understanding and a total acceptance of the person are essential for an effective relationship. The person who has arrived at the point where he wants to withdraw himself for good from everyone and everything is desperately alone and overwhelmed. A genuine "Let me try to help you" is precisely what his suicidal gesture implores.

2. A sincere and personally interested "Let's have a good talk" may offer the hope of solution. Above all, be a good listener. He has a burden which to you and to anyone else may seem trivial, distorted and completely disproportionate to the solution he has chosen. For him that burden has taken the meaning out of his existence. Listen, then, not just to what he is saying with words, but also to what he is attempting to say through his behavior.

3. In dramatic circumstances *plead for time*. For one who is about to end time for himself there is the experience of control over time. Ask him: "Give me some time to talk to you. When we are finished you can still commit suicide if you wish. Just do *me* this favor and give *me* time."

4. In such emergency situations insist on the possibility of a better approach to the problem. Do not say "There *is* a better

way." This might induce a further sense of inadequacy for not having discovered it. Take the approach "Let's see *if* there is a better way. Let's you and I try to figure it out."

5. Always express empathy for the futility of life's problems from his viewpoint: "I understand why you see the world as bleak. How else could you see it?" Do not agree that it factually is a bleak world, but merely that under these circumstances life has to be overwhelming. Never imply that the person is or has been weak, deficient or incapable of coping with life.

6. Do not promise impossible solutions to his problems. Emphasize his own strengths and resources, which he is ignoring and which with help can bring him through his difficulty.

7. Answer all his questions directly and honestly. All indirect approaches should be put aside. His confused mind and chaotic feelings make it difficult if not impossible for him to define his problem.

8. Always extract a promise not to attempt suicide immediately after his attempt has been discussed and brought under some control. This promise should include the resolution to call for help if the impulse should return.

9. Always allay feelings of moral guilt associated with the suicide attempt. Assure him that God is concerned only for him and his plight and wants to help.

10. Remember that in every depression the danger of suicide is greatest when the person is beginning to "snap out" and "pick up speed." This is triggered by the emergence of new energy and the return to painful reality which instigated the depression with its suicidal potential.

11. When the threat is real always offer the suggestion of psychiatric help and your own continued confidential assistance in order to remedy the situation. In extreme emergencies, notify the family and police. In lesser circumstances, respect the person's confidence. Revelation or its threat may prompt a suicidal act.

12. In every real instance, consult with other professionals with careful regard for the patient's inviolable right of privacy.

Conclusion

For the one who contemplates suicide, the value of being this human person here and now obviously has lost all appeal. The life he received, with no say in the matter, as a gift to the world he now takes into his hands and refuses to give affirmation to. Suicide is by far the most radical act a man can place, striking as it does at the very core of his existence. It is not, then, a matter of surprise to hear that many of those who contemplate putting an end to their lives do not fully recognize that should they die in the attempt they will be permanently finished, forever gone. It is as though the self not merely refuses but finds it impossible to face and comprehend its cessation and departure from the living. This implicit affirmation of life in defense of itself contains hope for both the contemplator and the one who aspires to help.

Every clergyman is ex officio the spokesman of Him who says "I am Who am" and who ultimately affirms every man's right to *be* through his conserving power. The assuring words of the man of God to the one despairing of his life, the suggestion that his life belongs here and now and is a value to be clung to, can give rise to that experience of hope without which survival is impossible.

For Further Reference

Farberow, Norman L., and Shneidman, Edwin S. *The Cry for Help.* New York: McGraw-Hill Book Co., 1961.

Menninger, Karl A. *Man Against Himself.* New York: Harcourt Brace & Co., 1938.

Shneidman, Edwin S., and Farberow, Norman L., eds. *Clues to Suicide.* New York: McGraw-Hill Book Co., 1957.

16 Recovery Needs

There is a great deal of truth in the saying "A man is his own worst enemy." It is somewhat true of all of us from time to time, but it is especially true when it comes to the mentally ill. When a problem occurs, most people are able to deal with it reasonably effectively. They face the problem, come to some satisfying solution and, if necessary, take those precautions necessary to avoid its recurrence. The mentally disturbed person, on the other hand, is usually incapable of doing any of these things. He frequently hinders his recovery by refusing to accept his problem or illness, sometimes even by blinding himself to its very existence and by resisting those therapeutic solutions which alone will terminate his plight. There are dynamic reasons behind such resistive behavior but the critical point is that these negative and highly defensive attitudes constitute for the sick person his greatest obstacles in solving his problem and regaining his equilibrium. Very often it is in these areas of mental illness that the clergyman can make his greatest contribution.

One Giant Step

One of the most difficult adjustments for the mentally ill person to make and one that is absolutely essential to his recovery is the acceptance of the fact that he is ill. When he refuses to do so he sets up a barrier to his recovery in many ways. Initially, such a refusal perpetuates and even intensifies the disorder by permitting its cause and symptoms to breed and flourish. Second, it cuts off the possibility of early therapeutic intervention which is of the essence in combating any kind of illness. Finally, it may impede the effectiveness of therapy if it should persist after therapy has been started.

Such emotionally disturbed persons refuse to admit that they are ill and in need of professional help because they fear the embarrassment or loss of self-esteem that such an admission might entail. Their error is the all too common misconception that mental illness is a personal disgrace, an indication of failure in the business of living or a stigma that the family will never live down. Another person might harbor the fear of being hospitalized or of being subjected to some form of painful or frightening therapy. This fear is equally rooted in ignorance and involves a mistaken notion about the actual therapeutic setting, which is essentially a matter of interpersonal dialogue between the therapist and client, and lack of knowledge of the various modern advances in pharmacology, which not only reduce the distress of symptoms but also render even such convulsive treatments as electroshock therapy painless.

People with such fears usually can be dissuaded from their resistive position by someone they trust who is willing to take the time to sit down with them and explain their misconceptions. These people should never be bluntly told that they are mentally or emotionally sick and should go to see a psychiatrist. They should be advised that they have a problem that is upsetting their peace of mind and that it can be solved if they are willing to follow the correct course of action. They should be assured that talking the matter over with a professional therapist is always the surest course to follow in such situations and that it holds out the highest promise of recovered peace.

It is also encouraging to these people to learn of the friendliness that surrounds the therapeutic relationship and the relief they will experience once the initial meeting with the therapist has taken place. It is always helpful for the person to hear of the clergyman's personal conviction concerning the merits of psychotherapy, of his respect for the professionals who engage in it and of his admiration for the success they achieve in helping people in their distress. It often is helpful to suggest some particular therapist and even to assure the disturbed person that you will initiate the proceedings, if he so wishes, by speaking to the doctor beforehand.

Perhaps the greatest source of consolation and encouragement to people laboring with such fears is to hear the clergyman explicitly express his understanding of their condition and their difficulty in admitting to their need for this kind of assistance. No one likes to admit to personal weakness or to the inability to cope with its consequences. This is especially so when the weakness is viewed as touching upon the very experience of life itself. It is consoling, then, for these people to hear that their emotional condition is not a sign of personal weakness, that everyone from time to time becomes overpowered by the stresses of life and that there is no one who can claim exemption from either the possibility of an emotional breakdown or from the need for support should it occur.

Such obstacles to the admission of emotional illness and the need for therapy are relatively easy to handle by comparison with those other cases in which the individual is so highly defensive or perhaps deluded that he is totally unaware of his sickness and need for help. This frequently happens, for example, with personality and character disorders, with the alcoholic and drug abuser and with the paranoiac who has projected his own illness onto the lives of those about him. It is, however, possible with any of the mental disorders and probably constitutes the general category into which the bulk of our mentally ill population falls.

In these cases the personality disturbance or sickness usually is detected by members of the person's family or by other interested parties. In their concern about what they should do, they often approach the clergyman for his advice. The first thing for the clergyman to do is to obtain an accurate account of specific instances of the suspected behavior. When it is obvious that a definite or even possible pathology is being reported the clergyman can follow one of several courses. He can offer his willingness to intervene himself and talk to the person whose sickness has been reported. If this approach is for some reason judged impractical, he should instruct the inquiring persons about the ways they might go about bringing the disturbed person to an acceptance of his need for help. This approach should consist of an honest but always considerate presentation of the observed facts to the person in question. The clergyman should inform family members and other interested persons that people with mental problems are just waiting and very frequently hoping for someone to reach out to them in this way. The clergyman also should propose those suggestions that were cited previously as advantageous in leading the frightened person to an acceptance of help. Those who make these inquiries should be reminded of the importance of therapy when illness is in evidence and assured of the clergyman's continuing interest and willingness to help should this be needed.

Although less frequent, it sometimes occurs that even the immediate family is blind to the ill person's condition. It may happen that a family member or members, in somewhat the same way as the upset person, is defensive and fails to recognize or refuses to admit that one of their own is mentally ill. These people often rationalize themselves into believing that it is all simply a temporary upset which in the course of time will pass away with a bit of rest, with more recreation and more involvement with persons and things. They sometimes look upon displays of totally unreasonable and bizarre behavior as simply things that this individual is apt to do. It even might happen that under the guise of openness to the situation they themselves come to accept some of the ideas, suspicions and delusions of the disturbed person as possibly real and sound. There is an induced or communicated kind of psychosis called the *folie a deux* in which symptoms and especially paranoid delusions proper to one party are communicated to and introjected by a closely associated second party.[1]

When such circumstances prevail and the clergyman becomes

aware of them through his own observations or through reports from truly interested persons, he should contact a responsible member of the family and tactfully bring the matter to his attention. From that point the modus operandi can be much the same as indicated in the previous considerations. When no such contacts can be made and there is no doubt of the problem's real existence, the clergyman should personally intervene.

The Will to Get Better

Resistance is a psychic phenomenon which can endure long after the ill person has given in and accepted the fact of his illness. Although the person may have placed his trust in a therapist and gained the confidence that he will not be judged or censured by him, he still may resist the degree of self-knowledge and co-operation with his therapist that are necessary to his recovery or at least to the amelioration of his condition. This stage of resistance is a protective move against the anxiety that he fears a fuller degree of self-knowledge would arouse. Such an opposition or aversion to facing certain critical components of his personality and life very frequently results in either the perpetuation of his illness or a postponement of its remission. As such it constitutes a definite but negative disposition toward recovery and may go so far as to prompt the mentally ill person to hold on to his illness in preference to attaining health. To give up the illness will require facing reality or at least some aspect of it that the sick person at this time perceives as an intolerable burden.

Otto Rank, one of Freud's original disciples who left the Freudian group in favor of his own ideas, emphasized the strategic role of the will in the sick person's advance toward self-possession and mental rehabilitation. Rank agreed that analysis may help the sick person to an understanding of his basic emotional situation, but placed special stress on the need for the patient's own personal effort in taking himself in hand and going to work at his own personal reconstruction. He underscored the "will to health" as essential to recovery, not merely because of the tendency in patients to project the burden of recovery onto the therapist but because he also observed in many of his patients the real but negative desire not to get well.[2]

If he is aware of the hidden dynamics beneath such resistance to therapy and recovery, the clergyman can provide the spiritual values to strengthen the spirit of the man and in the long run turn the tide. This is not to say that the ministrations of the clergyman are to be looked upon as a panacea for mental ills or as a substitute for therapy and personal effort. It is simply to say that the ego or spirit of the mentally ill person is just as much in need of spiritual support and as responsive to it as are the physically ill.

Emotionally sick people invariably are hampered by a lack of ego-strength. It is the basis of their many unreasonable repressions and resistive maneuvers. Fear of themselves and their emotions and instincts and of the attitudes of those about them overrides their egos and forces them to run from themselves and from the truths surrounding their existence. An awareness of this intrapsychic condition should be sufficient to stimulate in the mind of the clergyman those spiritual ideas that can reduce fear and build the quality of courage that is necessary for these people to face the truth honestly and humbly.

Without interfering with the therapist's endeavors, the clergyman can contribute to the sick person's will to health by providing those value-ideas that are essential to both the emergence and the maintenance of his desire to get better. The will to get better and to help oneself is meaningless in itself. To be effective, the goal of being well and of merging into the mainstream of life must be grasped as personally desirable and worthwhile. The realistically encouraging words of the clergyman concerning the individual's personal value and his potential for offering something good to the world can serve as a spur to self-improvement and as a springboard to hope for the future. The clergyman always must be keenly aware of the actual emotional condition of the person and respectful of the dynamic intricacies of his ailment. If he can restore some recognition of the truth and hope for the future he will have rendered an invaluable service.

Ups and Downs

The road traveled by the mentally ill is always marked by setbacks and periods of discouragement. Relapses sometimes occur during recovery from a physical ailment and the same is true of mental illness. It is remarkable, really, that the human mind can sustain all the pressures and burdens it does and that it possesses the resiliency to bounce back time and time again. As the primordial center of all consciousness there is no trauma that the mind escapes. Whether the wounds and pains are physical or emotional it is ultimately the self or conscious core of life that sustains and suffers them. Of those, it is the emotional, the mental or spiritual, wounds that affect the mind the most. The physical hurts of life affect the mind only indirectly. The wounds that are strictly mental are immediately experienced by the self and, therefore, profoundly central in their effects. They are the true hurts of life and take the longest to heal. When severe they usually are devastating in their effects.

For this reason recovery from mental illness is rarely sudden or dramatic. For all practical purposes it can be said that there is no such thing as a smooth and rapid progression toward mental rehabilitation. All recovery starts at a low point and reaches out and upward toward the goal of mental health or at least mental peace. There are, however, intermittent lulls or plateaus in the recovery process and also periods of regression. It is during these episodes that the spirit of the sick person suffers deflation and it is at these times that the clergyman can offer invaluable support.

Instances of discouragement in the lives of the mentally ill are numerous and in every case a definite experience of suffering is present. There is, for example, the simple but very real discouragement that comes to the alcoholic who after years of sobriety and constant effort experiences the deflating defeat of slipping back into his former habit. There is the obsessive neurotic who no matter how much he tries cannot stop torturing himself with worries and futile fears that rob him of the peace of mind he longs for. There are those who are disheartened with sexual disturbances—homosexuals, pedophiliacs, the compulsively promiscuous—who hate their condition but nevertheless find themselves constantly failing in spite of professional counseling and personal effort. There are those who, having recovered their health, experience a return of their symptoms and undergo the fear of rehospitalization and the possibility of threatening types of therapy.

Experiences of discouragement and fear in the physically ill usually are met with concern and pity on the part of those who observe them. It requires little thought or effort to sympathize with them in their suffering. The child who is physically handicapped for a lifetime with cerebral palsy, the leukemia victim hoping against hope for recovery and the cancer patient undergoing one surgical operation after another are all given the full measure of our concern and sympathy. The mentally ill, on the other hand, do not always come off so well. We frequently fail them in terms of our support and patience. On occasion, we even treat them as nuisances, as people who should snap out of it and stop feeling sorry for themselves. It is true that mentally ill people often appear to be acting selfishly and that they frequently present difficult problems of adjustment for those about them and those who aspire to help them. They are human, however, and also sick. As such they deserve our patience and the lifting effects of our support.

It is often almost impossible to know precisely what will be lifting in a particular case. Sometimes the simple willingness to take the time to hear someone out is encouragement in itself. Beyond this, and beyond reassuring them of the inevitable "ups and downs" involved in every effort at self-recovery, the clergyman can always help by offering some words of advice on the role and power of habit in all human behavior. This is always beneficial to the emotionally ill since they are beset by the difficult task of uprooting unhealthy behavioral habits and replacing them with others that are less faulty if not necessarily more healthy. Whenever this approach is adopted, the emphasis should be away from the tenacious character of habit with its implied obstinacy to eradication. To dwell on this aspect will only reinforce discouragement and induce the possibility of withdrawal from effort.

The point to stress is that new modes of thinking and emoting are possible. The clergyman should, however, advise the discouraged person that no one ever acquires new habits all at once. Their acquisition requires time and work and the more the self applies itself to the task the more entrenched the new habit becomes. It is always more constructive to channel the individual's attention and efforts toward positive goals and the possibility of their attainment than to concentrate on the negative modes or features of former behavior.

Clergymen sometimes forget and even downgrade the best things they have to offer to men. At an informal conference between a representative group of the clergy and a number of psychiatrists the question "What can we as pastors do when a person who is mentally ill comes to us and is disheartened over his lack of progress or discouraged over the length of time improvement is taking?" was raised. After a number of suggestions one of the doctors simply said "Why not just pray for the person and boost his spirit by telling him you're doing so." The best that a man has to give is often the simplest of his possessions.

The Family of the Sick

To concentrate exclusively on the sick person is to forget the vast number of other people who because of their close association with him are drawn into the many difficulties that can surround a mental illness. Primary among them are the family members of the emotionally ill who also need support and help in sustaining the many strains of such an illness and in understanding its many intricacies. The strictly psychological features of this kind of support and understanding obviously must be reserved to the competency of the professionally trained. There are, however, certain services that the clergyman can and should try to offer.

The clergyman's assistance is surely in order when family members must witness the hospitalization of one of their own.

To those who are not intimately related to the sick person such an occasion may seem somewhat trivial and undeserving of special concern. To the person or persons who love and live with the sick person, however, it can be extremely painful and trying. Perhaps their greatest distress at such a time consists in their personal experience of helplessness in having been unable to bring this loved one to a better solution of his problem and a happier way of life.

The clergyman can bolster the troubled members of the family by assuring them that they have not failed the sick person and that the best they can do for him is simply to stand by him and support him during the period of his hospitalization. This type of assurance is especially necessary when the sick person himself is opposed or unwilling to submit to hospitalization and a family member is called upon to face the heavy burden of commiting him to a mental institution. Once again, the best interests of the sick person must be stressed in order to allay those natural and understandable feelings of guilt that may surround such a decision and occasion its postponement. In such circumstances it is helpful to refer to the current philosophy on hospitalization of the mentally ill, which is basically to keep the time of confinement to a minimum and to get the patient back into the community as soon as possible. It is also reassuring for the family to hear that the modern mental rehabilitative center is decidedly different from that of earlier days. Today practically all of these centers are designed according to a community style of living with respect and concern being extended to each sick person as an individual.

Another concern of these families centers around the behavior of the sick person when he returns home from the hospital and their own deportment when this occurs. Family members frequently do not know what to expect from the sick person. "Will he be dangerous or different?" "Will he exhibit or engage in strange behavior?" These are natural and understandable questions for which the clergyman should have ready and accurate answers.[3]

Journalism thrives on cases in which a patient recently discharged from a mental hospital goes berserk and commits homicide or some other crime of violence. In fact, such occurrences are the rare exception. Patients whose illness involves the possibility of violence are actually less likely to engage in violent or assaultive behavior than their counterparts in society, primarily because of the treatments they have received and the sedating effects of the medication that is always prescribed in such cases.

In much the same way, most patients who return home are less strange and difficult than they were before their departure. Those at home should be assured that although some residual symptoms and some degree of eccentric behavior is to be expected, these too will probably diminish with acceptance of the person, continued therapy and the healing power of time.

Today, a good part of the therapeutic program in mental health centers and hospitals consists in the effort to break down the patient's experience of himself as different and estranged from the rest of people. This is accomplished primarily by building up his self-confidence through acceptance of him as an individual of worth and through the patient's own personal involvement in community activities. If, on his return home, he is made to feel that he is a burden to the family or a source of shame to them, he will naturally be unhappy and tend to isolate himself from the human relations so necessary to his improvement and recovery. If the question of how the family should act toward the patient on his return home arises, a rule of thumb response is that he should be genuinely received and welcomed by all and treated in much the same way as anyone recuperating from an illness. Family members should not be anxious or unreasonable, but expect him to resume his role and function within the family unit and within the community at large. They should permit and encourage him to do as much for himself as he possibly can. It is to be expected that at first he will be uncertain and insecure. Accordingly, he never should be pushed beyond the limits his illness has imposed nor be permitted to place himself in situations in which he surely will fail. Most of all, he never should be threatened with the possibility of a return to the hospital should his behavior fall short of expected standards.

It is largely the behavior, attitudes and reactions of those about the recovering person that will determine his progress toward mental health. When these attitudes reflect a genuine acceptance of the sick person and convey to him an optimism concerning his ability to get better and resume his place among men, the seeds of self-confidence are sown. The individual's vision of himself as a self-contained person in a world of accepting people begins to appear on the screen of consciousness and the day of recovery becomes more than a matter of chance.

Epilogue

But if I speak with the tongues of men and of angels
and have not love, it profits me nothing. . . .
Love is kind. . . . Love always understands.

I Cor. 13:1-7

In the course of these pages we have tried to say many things. Some of them may have struck you as pedantic. Others may have suggested lines of thought that will be productive of effective and significant action. Now, we wish to have a final word. It may be regarded as presumptious, but it is a word we feel conscience-bound to utter.

The word is *love.*

If we as clergymen become "professionals" and nothing more; if we become technicians and are satisfied with that alone, then any efforts we put forth for the "people of God" will be less than we could make them. Our people expect more than technical terms, analysis and diagnosis. They expect that the clergyman is going to be able to penetrate more clearly and with greater precision than the professional who deals only with the natural and the obvious. This "something extra" is a deep affection born of God which is particularly associated in the mind of man with His representative.

Notes

Chapter 1

1. For an excellent treatment of the partnership that can exist between theology, philosophy and psychiatry, see Francis J. Braceland, ed., *Faith, Reason and Modern Psychiatry* (New York: P. J. Kenedy & Sons, 1955).
2. According to the Menninger Foundation, "More people are in hospitals with mental illness at any one time than with all other diseases combined, including cancer, heart disease, tuberculosis and every other killing and crippling disease."
3. New drugs and related therapies are integral to this revolutionary trend toward community mental health programs. As a result of these scientific advances hospitalization is far less necessary than formerly. The focal point of treatment has shifted from state and private hospitals to the community. Walk-in psychiatric clinics, crisis-intervention units, psychiatric units in general hospitals, halfway houses and mental health teaching programs in schools, churches and industries are examples of the community mental health approach.

Chapter 2

1. In order to implement the federal program of community mental health, state and local governments must pour in an additional $30 billion.
2. Statistics on the extent of the national mental health problem are abundant and readily available. Publications of the American Medical Association and the National Association for Mental Health, Inc., are reliable sources.
3. See also J. W. Eaton, "The Assessment of Mental Health," *American Journal of Psychiatry* 108:2 (August 1951): 81-90.
4. For a consideration of the various criteria of normalcy and ab-

normalcy, see James E. Royce, *Personality and Mental Health* (Milwaukee: Bruce Publishing Co., 1955), pp. 49-55, and James C. Coleman, *Abnormal Psychology and Modern Life* (New York: Scott, Foresman & Co., 1956), pp. 10-16.
5. E. Glover, "Medico-Psychological Aspects of Normality," *British Journal of Psychology* 23 (1932): 152-166.
6. John R. Cavanagh and James B. McGoldrick, *Fundamental Psychiatry* (Milwaukee: Bruce Publishing Co., 1958), p. 25.
7. This all-important caution is treated more fully in chapters 5 and 6.
8. For the variety of possible etiological factors involved in a mental illness, see Cavanagh and McGoldrick, *Fundamental Psychiatry,* pp. 51-186.

Chapter 3

1. For a complete summary of the major contemporary theories of personality and a digest and evaluation of each, see Calvin S. Hall and Gardner Lindzey, *Theories of Personality* (New York: John Wiley & Sons, 1957) and Ruth L. Munroe, *Schools of Psychoanalytic Thought* (New York: Holt, Rinehart & Winston, 1955).
2. See Hall and Lindzey, *Theories of Personality,* pp. 29-72, and Otto Fenichel, *The Psychoanalytic Theory of Neurosis* (New York: W. W. Norton & Co., 1945), pp. 33-113.
3. These are instances of the Freudian "preconscious" or "foreconscious." This level of the mind sometimes is referred to as "marginal unconsciousness" or simply as the "subconscious." In a strict Freudian sense, unconscious is not equivalent to subconscious and cannot be known to the subject by his own efforts.

Chapter 4

1. For a study of mental mechanisms see Arthur P. Noyes and Lawrence C. Kolb, *Modern Clinical Psychiatry* (Philadelphia: W. B. Saunders Co., 1958), pp. 40-56, and Fenichel, *Theory of Neurosis,* pp. 141-167.
2. Homeostasis is a technical term originally employed to describe the efforts of the physiological organism to maintain a state of balance or equilibrium among the various organic and functional complexities of the entire system. Physiologically, it also refers to the efforts of the organism to respond to internal and external stresses and to insure the organism's integrity. Its use in psychology is an extension of this basic origin.

Chapter 5

1. For case illustrations of particular disorders, see "neuroses" in Cavanagh and McGoldrick, *Fundamental Psychiatry,* pp. 217-266, and "psychoses," pp. 287-388. For schizophrenia as presented here, see Silvano Arieti, ed., *American Handbook of Psychiatry,* vol. 1 (New York: Basic Books, 1959), pp. 455-84.
2. See Cavanagh and McGoldrick, *Fundamental Psychiatry,* pp. 37-48, and Arthur P. Noyes and E. M. Hayden, *A Textbook of Psychiatry* (New York: Macmillan Co., 1940), pp. 50 ff.

Chapter 6

1. The suggestions in this chapter can be extended beyond the initial interview and to discussions of other than strictly mental problems. For the initial interview as such, see Arieti, *American Handbook of Psychiatry,* vol. 1 (chapter by I. Stevenson), pp. 197-213. For a broader treatment, see Charles A. Curran, *Counseling in Catholic Life and Education* (New York: Macmillan Co., 1952).

Chapter 7

1. *Outlook and Independent* 155 (July 9, 1930): 353-65.
2. Noyes and Kolb, *Modern Clinical Psychiatry,* p. 372.

Chapter 8

1. Definitions extracted from M. Golin, "Robbers of Five Million Brains," *Journal of the American Medical Association* 167, no. 12 (July 19, 1958): 1496-1503.
2. W. L. Keaton, "Understanding Alcoholism" (New York State Department of Mental Hygiene, 1967).
3. Literature and statistics on alcoholism are available from the American Medical Association, 535 N. Dearbon Street, Chicago, Ill. 60610; the General Service Board of Alcoholics Anonymous, 468 Park Avenue South, New York, N. Y. 10016, and the National Council on Alcoholism, Inc., 2 Park Avenue, New York, N. Y. 10016. For alcoholism as a form of "chronic suicide," see Karl Menninger, *Man Against Himself* (New York: Harcourt, Brace & Co., 1938).
4. Roche Laboratories, *Aspects of Alcoholism* (Philadelphia: J. B. Lippincott Co., 1963), pp. 61-63. Reprinted by permission of the publisher.

Chapter 9

1. The Federal Bureau of Narcotics maintains a name file of active opiate addicts. As of December 1965, the list numbered 57,199. Due to the drug explosion this number obviously is much higher today. Cf. United States Task Force Report, *Narcotics and Drug Abuse* (Washington: United States Printing Office, 1967).
2. Odyssey House, a drug rehabilitation center in New York City, under the direction of Dr. Judienne Densen-Gerber, estimated there were 100,000 juvenile heroin addicts in New York City alone in the summer of 1970 (*The New York Times,* January 25, 1970).
3. Donald B. Louria, *Nightmare Drugs* (New York: Pocket Books, 1966), p. 19.
4. John E. Ingersoll, "Drug Menace: How Serious?" Interview in *U. S. News and World Report,* May 25, 1970, pp. 38-42.
5. The drug abuse problem today is far wider than the study of addiction and physical and psychological dependence as such. The latter states are accomplished illnesses and, strictly speaking, they alone fall within the scope of this book. Concentration on them does not, however, imply that they constitute the totality of the current drug crisis in our nation.
6. Louria, *Nightmare Drugs,* pp. 77, 86. "The usual relapse rate among addicts at such centers as the Federal Hospital in Lexington, Kentucky, and Forth Worth, Texas, has been about 92 percent. Even the most advanced experimental centers in the U.S. average a relapse rate of 70 to 75 percent" (E. Ramirez, "Problem of Narcotics Addiction in New York City" [Report of Drug Problem to Mayor of New York, 1966], p. 2).
7. The Expert Committee on Drugs Liable to Produce Addiction of the World Health Organization (United Nations, 1957). Despite the fact that the WHO more or less replaced this global definition in 1963 because of confusion over the term *addiction,* much of the definition remains valid. The WHO chose to stress the term *dependency* rather than *addiction.*
8. This description is currently accepted as applying to the person who is psychologically dependent on drugs. It is reasonably synonymous with what many mean when they speak of "addiction." The more obvious physical dependence occurs mainly as a result of the properties of certain drugs (especially the opiates, and in long-term barbiturate use) and is identifiable with the so-called physical symptoms of withdrawal. A person does not have to be physically dependent in order to be truly dependent psychologically. An example of this would be the individual who is psychologically dependent on marijuana, which most probably will not produce physical dependence.

9. It should be noted that marijuana is now considered a "mild hallucinogen."
10. *The New York Times,* January 9, 1968. © 1968 by The New York Times Company. Reprinted by permission.
11. See Louria, *Nightmare Drugs,* pp. 9-52. Descriptions of these drugs are available from the American Medical Association and all local community narcotics centers.
12. Although the vast majority of those who take the more potent drugs, especially heroin, started with marijuana, the vast majority of those who have used marijuana do not go on to the "hard stuff." Marijuana has been used, at least experimentally, by millions of Americans.
13. Louria, *Nightmare Drugs,* p. 11.
14. Peter Laurie, *Drugs* (Baltimore: Penguin Books, 1967), pp. 97-98.
15. Ibid., pp. 99-100.
16. The U.S. Task Force Report on Drug Abuse, cited above, contains a thorough treatment of the legal aspects of drug abuse.
17. Recent federal legislation makes the simple possession of marijuana by first offenders under twenty-one a misdemeanor punishable by a jail sentence of up to one year. They may, however, be placed on probation at the discretion of a judge. Successful fulfillment of the probation would result in a "non-guilty" finding with an expungement of the public record. In the event of violation of probation, the sentence may be carried out in full, with up to one year in prison and a fine of up to $5,000.

Chapter 10

1. See Judd Marmor, ed., *Sexual Inversion: The Multiple Roots of Homosexuality* (New York: Basic Books, 1965) and Irving Bieber et al., *Homosexuality* (New York: Basic Books, 1962).
2. Marmor, *Sexual Inversion.* (chapter by Irving Bieber), pp. 248 ff.
3. Ibid., p. 4.
4. Ibid., p. 22
5. Ibid., (chapter by E. Hooker), pp. 91 ff.
6. Authorities vary on the question of whether homosexuality is an illness. Freud himself, for example, did not consider the condition, as such, to be a disease but a variation of sexual functioning due to a certain arrest of sexual development. For various views, see Marmor, *Sexual Inversion,* pp. 15-20 and Bieber et al., *Homosexuality,* pp. 3-18.
7. Marmor, *Sexual Inversion,* (chapter by W. H. Perloff), pp. 44 ff.
8. See Benjamin Karpman, *The Sexual Offender and His Offenses* (New York: Julian Press, 1962).

9. For psychological and pastoral considerations of this subject see William C. Bier, ed., *Personality and Sexual Problems* (New York: Fordham University Press, 1964), pp. 204 ff.
10. For a brief statistical survey see James L. McCary, *Human Sexuality* (Princeton: D. Van Nostrand Co., 1967), pp. 212 ff.

Chapter 11

1. There is no universal agreement among authorities that a genuine sexual revolution has taken place in recent years. Some feel that a significant revolution occurred during the twenties and that one now may loom on the horizon. See McCary, *Human Sexuality,* p. 203. Margaret Mead, on the other hand, has referred to the current change as an "evolution" (Interview in *Life,* August 23, 1968, pp. 31 ff).
2. See McCary, *Human Sexuality,* pp. 203-36.
3. See John R. Cavanagh, *Fundamental Marriage Counseling* (Milwaukee: Bruce Publishing Co., 1957), pp. 178-91.
4. Albert Ellis, *The American Sexual Tragedy* (New York: Hillman Periodicals, 1959); *The Folklore of Sex* (New York: Grove Press, 1961).
5. McCary, *Human Sexuality,* p. 9.
6. Arno Karlen, "The Unmarried Marrieds on Campus," *The New York Times Magazine,* January 26, 1969, pp. 29 ff.
7. Based on personal interviews and discussions.
8. See McCary, *Human Sexuality,* pp. 13-14, on Ellis's theories concerning sexual fadism, or Albert Ellis, *Sex without Guilt,* rev. ed (New York: Lyle Stuart, 1966).

Chapter 12

1. Statistics referred to here and elsewhere in this chapter are drawn from a variety of reports and from interviews with prominent specialists.
2. Reference is to those who look upon aggression as an "inborn human instinct."
3. The writings of Margaret Ribble and Lois Murphy are basic sources on early childhood development and those of Rudolf Allers and Alexander Schneiders are recommended on adolescence.
4. Drs. Leonard Berkowitz, Frederic Wertham, Mary Calderone and Kenneth Clarke are among those who have expressed concern about the possible ill effects arising from the violence and sex portrayed in the mass media.
5. Such behavior may indicate psychiatric disturbances known as "explosive personality disorders" and "passive-aggressive disorders."

6. Sheldon S. and Eleanor T. Glueck, *Unravelling Juvenile Delinquency* (Cambridge, Mass.: Harvard University Press, 1951); Eleanor T. Glueck, "Identification of Potential Delinquents at Two or Three Years of Age," *International Journal of Social Psychology,* 6:5-16 (1966).
7. Freud developed this concept of the "death wish" in *Beyond the Pleasure Principle* (1920). For a brief explanation, see Hall and Lindzey, *Theories of Personality,* pp. 39-41, and Munroe, *Schools of Psychoanalytic Thought,* pp. 80-81, 108-109, 623 ff.
8. Idiopathic epilepsy is the diagnosis given when no definite organic pathology can be detected. It is called "symptomatic" epilepsy when seizures are assignable to some organic reason. Some authors consider all epilepsy symptomatic and others believe that it is always idiopathic.
9. Golfing, wood carving and carpentry are examples. Occupational therapy often employs such activities to drain off hostility.
10. See Abraham H. Maslow, *Motivation and Personality* (New York: Harper & Brothers, 1954), pp. 348 ff.
11. Roche Laboratories, *Aspects of Anxiety* (Philadelphia: J. B. Lippincott Co., 1965), pp. 50 ff.
12. The references to neurotic and psychotic symptomatology and personality disorders that follow are based principally on Noyes and Kolb, *Modern Clinical Psychiatry.* These symptoms need not be related exclusively to repressed hostility.
13. E. J. Khantzian, "On Hatred, Violence and Assassinations: A Clinician's View," *Psychiatric Opinion* 5, no. 5 (October 1968): 32-35.
14. See notes 1 and 4.
15. President's Commission, *The Challenge of Crime in a Free Society* (Washington: United States Government Printing Office, 1967), pp. v-xi.

Chapter 13

1. Karl Stern, *The Third Revolution* (New York: Harcourt, Brace & Co., 1954), p. 184.
2. Roche Laboratories, *Aspects of Anxiety,* pp. 73-74.
3. R. G. Sappenfield, *Personality Dynamics* (New York: Alfred A. Knopf, 1954), pp. 182 ff., 401.
4. Arieti, *American Handbook of Psychiatry* (chapter by M. Ostow), pp. 73 ff.
5. Noyes and Kolb, *Modern Clinical Psychiatry,* pp. 460-65.
6. Arieti, *American Handbook of Psychiatry* (chapter by S. Rado), pp. 325 ff. The masochistic symptom of "picking away at the body"

usually occurs in the agitated depression of the so-called involutional melancholia.
7. Ibid., p. 335.
8. For consideration of various authorities on this aspect of guilt, see Bier, *Personality and Sexual Problems,* pp. 36-100.
9. Dereism, "mental activity that deviates from the laws of logic and experience and fails to take the facts of reality into consideration," reaches its fullest development in schizophrenic states (Leland E. Hinsie and Robert J. Campbell, *Psychiatric Dictionary* [New York: Oxford University Press, 1960], p. 203).
10. People in this category very possibly may be referred to a clergyman by a therapist treating the overt symptomatology.
11. Sources of statistics in their order: Joseph Reid, director of the Child Welfare League of America, to a panel at the Academy of Medicine, 1969; G. E. Maxwell, "Why the Rise in Teenage Gonorrhea?" (Chicago: AMA Publications, 1968); President's Commission, *Challenge of Crime in a Free Society,* p.v.

Chapter 14

1. For further description of manifestations of depression, see Noyes and Kolb, *Modern Clinical Psychiatry,* pp. 310-13.
2. Ibid., pp. 315-16.
3. Hinsie and Campbell, *Psychiatric Dictionary,* pp. 201, 265.
4. The description of exogenous depressions as being symptomatic of neurosis and endogenous depression as being signs of a psychosis may be accepted for practical purposes. The 1968 revision of the *Diagnostic and Statistical Manual of Mental Disorders* (Washington: American Psychiatric Association) has, however, presented a different classification of the depressions. According to it, an extremely severe "reactive" depression may be classified as a psychotic state provided the symptomatology meets certain criteria.
5. For full development, see Cavanagh and McGoldrick, *Fundamental Psychiatry,* pp. 367-87.
6. See Noyes and Kolb, *Modern Clinical Psychiatry,* pp. 305-6. A survey of the literature on the subject reveals that hereditary factors are probably more prominent in depressive reactions than in the other psychotic disorders.

Chapter 15

1. Although peaks in the suicide rate have been reached during the depression years, most authorities do not see in this any significant relationship between suicide and economics.

2. Most facts cited here and elsewhere in this chapter are taken from Harry Milt, "The Roots of Suicide," *Trends in Psychiatry* 3, no. 1.
3. Frank J. Ayd, quoted in Milt, "The Roots of Suicide."
4. James Knight, quoted in Milt, "The Roots of Suicide."

Chapter 16

1. Noyes and Kolb, *Modern Clinical Psychiatry,* p. 375.
2. For a brief examination of Rank's therapeutic views, see Munroe, *Schools of Psychoanalytic Thought,* pp. 588 ff. Rank's own position is stated in *Will Therapy and Truth and Reality* (New York: Alfred A. Knopf, 1945).
3. A brief but helpful treatment of this aspect of mental illness is contained in *Helping a Mental Patient at Home* (New York: National Association for Mental Health, 1964).